Illuminating Luke

Michele Tosini (1503–77). *St. Luke.* 1561. Fresco. Paolini, Strozzi Villa. Photo. Heidi J. Hornik with permission from the Ganucci-Cancellieri family.

Illuminating LUKE

The Infancy Narrative in Italian Renaissance Painting

HEIDI J. HORNIK AND MIKEAL C. PARSONS

TRINITY PRESS INTERNATIONAL
A Continuum imprint
HARRISBURG • LONDON • NEW YORK

Trinity Press International, P.O. Box 1321, Harrisburg, PA 17105

Trinity Press International is a member of the Continuum International Publishing Group.

Scripture quotations unless otherwise noted are from the New Revised Standard Version Bible, copyright © 1989 by the Division of Christian Education of the National Council of the Churches of Christ in the U.S.A., and are used by permission.

Cover art: Michele Tosini (1503–77). *St. Luke.* 1561. Fresco. Paolini, Strozzi Villa. Photo: Heidi J. Hornik with permission from the Ganucci-Cancellieri family.

Cover design: Brenda Klinger

Library of Congress Cataloging-in-Publication Data

Hornik, Heidi J., 1962-
    Illuminating Luke : the infancy narrative in Italian Renaissance
  painting / Heidi J. Hornik, Mikeal C. Parsons.
        p.   cm.
    Includes bibliographical references and index.
    ISBN 1-56338-405-1 (pbk.)
    1. Painting, Italian. 2. Painting, Renaissance – Italy. 3. Jesus
Christ – Nativity – Art. 4. Mary, Blessed Virgin, Saint – Art. 5. Bible.
N.T. Luke – Illustrations. 6. Bible. N.T. Luke – Criticism,
interpretation, etc. – History – 20th century.   I. Parsons, Mikeal Carl,
1957-   II. Title.
ND1432.I8H67 2003
755'.53'094509024 – dc21

                                                            2003008784

Printed in Malaysia

03   04   05   06   07   08   10   9   8   7   6   5   4   3   2   1

Contents

List of Illustrations   vii

Foreword   xi

Introduction   1

CHAPTER ONE
Luke the Physician, Painter, and Patron Saint   11

CHAPTER TWO
The *Annunciation* by Leonardo da Vinci (Luke 1:26–38)   29

CHAPTER THREE
The *Visitation* by Jacopo Pontormo (Luke 1:39–56)   59

CHAPTER FOUR
The *Nativity and Adoration of the Shepherds*
by Domenico Ghirlandaio (Luke 2:8–20)   93

CHAPTER FIVE
The *Presentation in the Temple*
by Ambrogio Lorenzetti (Luke 2:22–38)   123

Epilogue   151

Selected Bibliography   153

Index   157

List of Illustrations

Cover/Frontispiece. Michele Tosini (1503–77). *St. Luke*. 1561. Fresco. Paolini, Strozzi Villa.

Figure 1. *Illumination of St. Luke*. Lindisfarne Gospels. Seventh-century manuscript. British Library, London.

Figure 2. *Illumination of St. Luke*. MacDurnan Gospels. Ninth-century manuscript. Lambeth Palace Library, London.

Figure 3. Guercino. *St. Luke Displaying a Painting of the Virgin*. 1652–53. Oil on canvas. Nelson-Atkins Museum of Art, Kansas City, Missouri.

Figure 4. St. Luke. (?) *Portrait of the Virgin and Child*. c. sixth century. Panel. S. Maria Maggiore, Rome.

Figure 5. Rogier van der Weyden. *St. Luke Drawing the Virgin and Child*. c. 1435. Panel. Museum of Fine Arts, Boston.

Figure 6. Vasari. *St. Luke Painting the Virgin*. c. 1565. Fresco. Cappella di S. Luca, SS. Annunziata, Florence.

Figure 7. Figure of St. Luke. Niche of Or San Michele. Florence.

Figure 8. Leonardo da Vinci. *Annunciation*. c. 1473–75. Panel. Galleria degli Uffizi, Florence.

Figure 9. Verrocchio and Leonardo da Vinci. *Baptism of Christ*. 1470. Panel. Galleria degli Uffizi, Florence.

Figure 10. Leonardo da Vinci or Lorenzo di Credi (?). *Annunciation*. 1478–85. Panel. Louvre, Paris.

Figure 11. Leonardo da Vinci. *Study of a Sleeve*. c. 1475. Drawing. Galleria degli Uffizi, Florence.

Figure 12. Leonardo da Vinci. Detail of sepulchral urn. *Annunciation*.

Figure 13. Leonardo da Vinci. Detail of Mary's book. *Annunciation*.

Figure 14. Pontormo. *Visitation*. 1514–16. Fresco. S. Annunziata, Florence.

Figure 15. Mariotto Albertinelli. *Visitation.* 1503. Panel. Galleria degli Uffizi, Florence.

Figure 16. Andrea del Sarto. *Birth of the Virgin.* 1511–14. Fresco. S. Annunziata, Florence.

Figure 17. Fra Bartolomeo. *Mystical Marriage of St. Catherine.* 1512. Panel. Galleria Palatina, Florence.

Figure 18. Copy after Michelangelo. *Battle of Cascina.* 1504–6 (destroyed). Copy by Sangallo. Collection the Earl of Leicester.

Figure 19. Pontormo. *Visitation.* Detail of inscription on the left. Before restoration. Gabinetto Fotografico, Florence.

Figure 20. Pontormo. *Visitation.* Detail of inscription on the right. Before restoration. Gabinetto Fotografico, Florence.

Figure 21. Copy of Pontormo. *Visitation.* 1834.

Figure 22. Domenico Ghirlandaio. *Nativity and Adoration of the Shepherds.* 1483–85. Panel. Sassetti Chapel, S. Trinità, Florence.

Figure 23. Domenico Ghirlandaio. View of Sassetti chapel. Fresco. S. Trinità, Florence.

Figure 24. Domenico Ghirlandaio. *Last Supper.* 1476. Fresco. Badia di Passignano.

Figure 25. Domenico Ghirlandaio and Assistants. *Four Sibyls.* Fresco. Sassetti Chapel, S. Trinità, Florence.

Figure 26. Domenico Ghirlandaio. *Vision of Augustus on the Capitoline Hill.* Fresco. Sassetti Chapel, S. Trinità, Florence.

Figure 27. Domenico Ghirlandaio. *Portraits of Nera Corsi Sassetti and Francesco Sassetti.* Fresco. Sassetti Chapel, S. Trinità, Florence.

Figure 28. Hugo van der Goes. *Adoration of the Shepherds.* 1475. Panel. Galleria degli Uffizi, Florence.

Figure 29. Ambrogio Lorenzetti. *Presentation in the Temple.* c. 1342. Panel. Galleria degli Uffizi, Florence.

Figure 30. Duccio. *Madonna and Child Enthroned.* Reconstruction of original front panel of the *Maestà,* 1308–11. Museo dell'Opera del Duomo, Siena.

Figure 31. Giotto. *Presentation of Christ in the Temple.* 1305. Fresco. Scrovegni Chapel, Padua.

Figure 32. Giovanni di Paolo. *Presentation in the Temple.* 1447–49. Panel. Pinacoteca, Siena.

Figure 33. Ambrogio Lorenzetti. Detail of Moses, *Presentation in the Temple.* Galleria degli Uffizi, Florence.

Figure 34. Ambrogio Lorenzetti. Detail of David, *Presentation in the Temple.* Galleria degli Uffizi, Florence.

Figure 35. Ambrogio Lorenzetti. Detail of Anna, *Presentation in the Temple.* Galleria degli Uffizi, Florence.

Foreword

GIORGIO VASARI, the sixteenth-century biographer, complimented the painting of Michele Tosini by saying that it was executed *con fierezza e senza stento* (with spirit and without effort). The making of this book was executed with much spirit, much effort, and with many *debiti!* An internal grant from Baylor University, combined with a travel grant from the Society of Biblical Literature, allowed us to travel to Florence in the summer of 1999 in order to view each of the four major paintings discussed in this volume, as well as to conduct research at the Kunsthistorisches Institut. Research in Florence continued in the summer of 2001, this time with the support of a Lilly-funded Horizons grant, sponsored by Baylor University's Institute of Faith and Learning and an Albritton Grant for Faculty Research through Baylor's Art Department. There is no substitute for unmediated experience of the paintings under study. We wish to thank the SBL Research and Publications Committee and the Baylor University Research Committee for these monies and the staff of the Kunsthistorisches Institut for their assistance in locating references. We are especially grateful to Baylor University President Emeritus Herbert Reynolds, whose generous Scholarship Enrichment Grant covered copyright permissions and other production costs.

Baylor University provided additional institutional support in the form of sabbaticals, release time, and travel money (with which we were able to visit and consult the Index of Christian Art at Princeton University). Robert Sloan, President, Baylor University, Donald Schmeltekopf, Provost Emeritus, David Lyle Jeffrey, Provost, and Wallace Daniel, Dean of the College of Arts and Sciences, have been especially generous in their support. Michael Beaty, Director of the Institute of Faith and Learning; John McClanahan, Chair of the Art Department; and Randall O'Brien, Chair of the Religion Department, were unswerving in their support. We are especially indebted to The College Sabbatical Committee's recommendation for a full University sabbatical (Hornik) in 1999. Colleagues in the Art and Religion Departments have been unfailing in their encouragement, and we are grateful. We appreciate also Alan Culpepper's invitation to make a presentation on a topic related to *Illuminating Luke* at the 1998 meeting of the National Association of Baptist Professors of Religion (NABPR), a presentation that was enthusiastically received and prompted much fruitful discussion. Alan Culpepper and Louis Alexander Waldman graciously read through an earlier draft of the entire manuscript, and their comments saved us from countless mistakes. Elizabeth Struthers Malbon and Robin Jensen likewise made helpful comments on several chapters. Margaret Miles gave her unqualified encouragement at crucial moments in the process. Continued assistance and support from our dear friends Janet and Fabrizio Gheri in Florence during our research time remains invaluable. Dodi Holland, Leigh Andrews, Stanley Scott, Joyce King, Valentina Lunghi, Francesco Michelazzo, Andy Arterbury, and Chad Hartsock have helped us in so many different ways, and we thank them.

The photographs and permissions were secured through the cooperation of the following individuals and organizations: Art Resource, New York; Badia de Passignano; Bridgeman Art Gallery; British Library, London; Gabinetto Fotografico, Florence; Dianora Ganucci-Cancellieri, Florence; Ministero dei Beni e le Attività Culturali, Florence; Museum of Fine Arts, Boston; Nelson-Atkins Museum of Art, Kansas City, Missouri.

Finally, we are indebted to Henry Carrigan, Amy Wagner, and Trinity Press International, who were willing to see the cross-disciplinary nature of this project as an asset rather than a limitation. Earlier versions of chapters 3 and 5 appeared in *Interpreting Christian Art* (Heidi J. Hornik and Mikeal C. Parsons, eds.; Macon, Ga.: Mercer University Press, 2003) and *Perspectives in Religious Studies* 28 (2001): 31–46, respectively. We express appreciation to Marc Jolley of Mercer Press and Scott Nash, Senior Editor of NABPR publications, for permission to use those materials in this book.

We express gratitude to our parents, Barbara and Joseph Hornik, John Quincy Parsons, and Blanche Parsons. Most of all, we acknowledge the contributions of our first collaborations together, our *due bambini*, Mikeal Joseph (six) and Matthew Quincy (five)! Their inquiries about and interruptions to our work have provided much-needed perspective and relief. In deep gratitude for the joy they constantly bring to our lives, we dedicate this book to them.

HEIDI J. HORNIK AND MIKEAL C. PARSONS
Baylor University, Waco, Texas
June 2003

Introduction

ANY GIVEN YEAR, countless numbers of tourists flood museums and galleries around the globe to catch glimpses of the world's great art. At the Uffizi in Florence, for example, visitors are now advised to make appointments to visit the museum or risk facing lines of over three hours or more during the peak tourist season. These visits generally consist of an hour or two meander through the various rooms and pausing before certain selected pieces of art to listen to a brief statement by a tour guide or a description on an audiotape. Such efforts are laudable, and the experience can be very enriching. Rarely, though, do viewers give enough attention to the original setting and function of the art they are seeing. Many of the world's great works of art depict religious scenes, and the original setting of much of it was in a building of worship. More specifically, much of this art was produced for Christian appropriation within the context of Christian worship in an explicitly Christian architectural space. While experiencing such a work of art as one of several cultural artifacts on the walls of a museum preserving an ancient or antiquated society might prove meaningful, it surely provides only limited access to the art's religious and cultural significance.

This study is an attempt, within a limited scope, to retrieve the religious significance of some of this art, especially for those whose lives are shaped and informed by the Christian tradition. The hope is that such an effort might make a modest contribution to counterbalancing the cultural bombardment of our senses with visual images and their concomitant various messages through the television, Internet, and various forms of mass advertising, with images shaped by and prepared for people who identify with the Christian tradition.

Thus, this project is an interdisciplinary study of the visual representations of subjects unique to the infancy narrative in the Gospel of Luke (chaps. 1 and 2) painted during the Italian Renaissance periods (1300–1520). We have chosen depictions of Luke's infancy narrative in Italian Renaissance paintings, not only because Luke and the Italian Renaissance represent our respective areas of expertise, but because of the particular interests which artists have typically shown in the subjects unique to Luke's Gospel. We pursue the various traditions related to the author of the Third Gospel more fully in the first chapter. However, the early

Figure 1. *Illumination of St. Luke.* Lindisfarne Gospels. Seventh-century manuscript. British Library. Photo. By permission of the British Library, London.

church clearly understood that there was *one* gospel in four versions, the so-called *Tetraevangelium* (the "four-fold Gospel"). Hence, the Gospel titles in the earliest Greek manuscripts were *The Gospel* (implied) "According to Matthew (or Mark or Luke or John)." Nonetheless, the church did distinguish among these four versions of the one gospel, and one of the earliest such attempts was to associate each evangelist with an icono-graphic symbol. Thus, the four gospel writers were early on lined with the "four living creatures" that surround the throne of God in the book of Revelation: "Around the throne, and on each side of the throne, are four living creatures, full of eyes in front and behind: the first living creature like a lion, the second living creature like an ox, the third living creature with a face like a human face, and the fourth living creature like a flying eagle" (4:6–8).

Among the first to make this identification was the church father Ire-naeus (c. 130–202). The ox, he pointed out, "was like a calf, signifying [the Son of God's] sacrificial and sacerdotal order," which he linked to the fatted calf that was sacrificed at the return of the Prodigal Son, a parable particular to Luke's Gospel. The lion symbolized Jesus' royal power, he said, and belonged to John, who "relates His . . . glorious generation from the Father." The human, "an evident description of His Advent as a human being," Irenaeus assigned to Matthew, whose gospel stresses the descent of Jesus from the line of David (in later tradition the human became an angel). The eagle signified "the Spirit hovering with His wings over the Church" and stood for Mark, whose gospel opens with a reference to "the prophetical spirit coming down from on high."[1]

Irenaeus's successors quickly adopted the four living creatures as sym-bols of the evangelists, but wrangled for centuries about the designation scheme, as the table below shows.[2] About Luke, however, most agreed: Luke was associated with the calf or ox (see Figure 1). Jerome applied the ox/calf to Luke "because he began with Zacharias [Zechariah] the priest," who was offering a sacrifice in the temple at the beginning of Luke's Gos-pel, a point that Irenaeus had also raised. Augustine cited the scene in Luke 2:22–24 in which Mary and Joseph presented the infant Jesus at the temple and offered the requisite sacrifice following childbirth (albeit a pair of birds, not a calf).

	Human/Angel	Lion	Ox/Calf	Eagle
Irenaeus	Matthew	John	Luke	Mark
Jerome	Matthew	Mark	Luke	John
Augustine	Mark	Matthew	Luke	John

Though early Christian art reflected these diverse opinions about the identity of the evangelists, Luke appears only with an ox, or later, a bull. The illumination in the MacDurnan Gospels, a ninth-century manu-script from Ireland, shows how closely Luke was identified with the ox

Figure 2. *Illumination of St. Luke.* MacDurnan Gospels.
Ninth-century manuscript. Photo. Lambeth Palace Library,
London, UK/Bridgeman Art Library.

(see Figure 2). Instead of feet, Luke has hooves! By the seventh century
Jerome's iconography had come to dominate the Western visual tradition.

It is true, however, that some early Christian and medieval interpreters,
beginning with Tatian (whose *Diatessaron* was ultimately rejected by the
Catholic Church) and continuing especially with Augustine's influential
Harmony of the Gospels, sought to downplay potential differences between
and among the four Gospels by harmonizing the Gospels into a single
account. This harmonizing tradition continued with the medieval *Glossa
Ordinaria* and later, among Protestants, with Calvin's *Harmony of the Gospels.* So it would be wrong to presume that at the forefront of an artist's or
audience's mind would have stood the question of which particular gospel
served as the basis or inspiration of any particular image. And indeed, with
many works of Christian art, it is difficult to discern any single source, biblical or otherwise. With the rise of modern historical criticism, especially

redaction criticism (which seeks in part to understand a gospel's theology on the basis of material unique to that author), however, the interest in material distinct to each gospel has grown in the last forty years.[3]

Nonetheless, it would be a mistake to think that this interest in what material is found in which gospel is only a recent phenomenon. Again, Irenaeus was quite well aware of the contributions to the Jesus story of each individual evangelist, especially Luke. In *Adversus Haeresis,* Irenaeus writes:

> but if any should reject Luke, on the ground that he did not know the truth, he plainly throws over the gospel of which he claims to be a disciple. For through him we have learned very many quite important parts of the gospel, as the birth of John and the story about Zacharias, and the coming of the angel to Mary, and the cry of Elizabeth, and the coming down of the angels to the shepherds, and the things that were spoken by them, and the testimony of Anna and Simeon concerning the Christ.... And everything of this kind we know through Luke alone....[4]

Thus, our interest in this unique material is not altogether new, and it is certainly appropriate to inquire about how those Renaissance paintings whose subjects are clearly based on stories found in Luke might enrich our understanding of the Third Gospel. The Lukan infancy narrative is a particularly rich fare for visual and theological interpretation.[5]

This book is not primarily an application of a theoretical model; thus methodological considerations, while certainly present, run beneath the text like an underground stream rather than appearing constantly on or near the surface. Nonetheless, our methodology is generally indebted to the vocabulary of German *Rezeptionsgeschichte,* or reception theory, especially as articulated in Wolfgang Iser's notion of the reader actualizing a text.[6]

We are interested in the reception of the biblical text in two moves. First and foremost, we attend to the way in which the artist himself has actualized the text in the production of a visual image. This part of the exercise requires that we examine the work of art in stylistic, historical, and iconographical terms.

Erwin Panofsky, in his seminal essay, "Iconography and Iconology: An Introduction to the Study of Renaissance Art" — first published in 1939 and still available in his *Meaning in the Visual Arts* — also contributes to our methodological stream.[7] Panofsky allowed that "*synthetic intuition* [a sense of the meaning of the whole picture] may be better developed in a talented layman than in an erudite scholar."[8] Yet he warned against pure intuition because a work of art is a symptom of " 'something else' which expresses itself in a countless variety of other symptoms, and we interpret its compositional and iconographical features as more evidence of that 'something else.' "[9] Panofsky called it "intrinsic meaning or content." Intrinsic meaning is "apprehended by ascertaining those underlying principles which reveal the basic attitude of a nation, a period, a class, a religious or philosophical persuasion — unconsciously qualified by one personality [a painter, for instance] and condensed into one work."[10] Intrinsic meaning, therefore, will inform both the "compositional and stylistic methods" and "iconographical significance" of a painting.[11] We are not unaware of the treacherous path down which we trod in order to situate each work of art in its cultural, political, and theological context and to attempt an evaluation of its intrinsic meaning.

John Shearman, an art historian, has focused the problem quite clearly: "It goes without saying, I would have thought, that we cannot step right outside our time, avoiding, as it were, all contamination by contemporary ideologies and intervening histories."[12] Nevertheless, we also agree with Shearman's conclusion:

> ... such inevitable imperfection ought not to be allowed to discourage the exercise of the historical imagination. In the same way it goes without saying that we will not reconstruct entirely correctly, but it is a sign of an unreflexive lack of realism to suppose that because we will not get it entirely right we had better give up and do something else not subject to error.[13]

In this first move of reception history, namely to understand the way the artist has actualized or concretized the biblical text, we have been greatly assisted by another art historian, Paolo Berdini. Berdini understands the interpretation of the text as a "trajectory of visualization," which he labels "visual exegesis." In Berdini's words:

> The painter reads the text and translates his scriptural reading into a problem in representation, to which he offers a solution — the image. In that image the beholder acknowledges, not the text in the abstract, but the painter's reading of the text so that the effect the image has on the beholder is a function of what the painter wants the beholder to experience in the text. This is the trajectory of visualization, and the effect of the text through the image is a form of exegesis. Painting is not the simple visualization of the narrative of the text but an expansion of that text, subject to discursive strategies of various kinds.[14]

These "discursive strategies" we take to be inextricably intertwined with the artist's social, political, and religious contexts as well as the sources and precedents at the artist's disposal in composing the image. Iconography, then, in our work is understood as part of this actualization process of visual exegesis.

While most of our efforts are spent on this first aspect of reception history, our methodology is also explicitly hermeneutical, and herein lies our second move of reception history. We are interested in how this visual exegesis might enrich our understanding of Luke's Gospel and at the same time inform the contemporary faith community's interpretation of Scripture.[15] Several generations of biblical scholars have been trained in the "what it meant/what it means" hermeneutic.[16] In this model, the biblical scholar explicated what a biblical text meant in its original context, and the theologian, building on these insights, discerned what the text now means in contemporary terms.

Unfortunately, this construal has operated from the assumption that we need only understand the context of the first century, in which most New Testament texts were produced, and the twenty-first century, in which these texts are read. In this view, the intervening period (of nearly two thousand years!) is mostly an obstacle to be avoided. The result, in many cases, has been to foster feelings of apathy, ambivalence, or antagonism on the part of the church toward professional biblical studies or vice versa. Between the original communication, "what it meant," and the contemporary interpretive context, "what it means," however, lies a largely neglected element: "what it *has* meant" at critical moments in the church's history. Scholars today, such as Brevard Childs, David Steinmetz, and others, write of the importance of patristic, medieval, and reformation hermeneutics, but they have limited their vision to literary texts.[17] We propose to include examples of visual interpretations as part of the "afterlife" of these stories as they are reconfigured for a different time and place. Of course, we are not the first to examine visual depictions of religious art for its theological content. The efforts of Jaraslov Pelikan and Margaret Miles, for example, to track the development of the Christian tradition through analysis of both verbal *and* visual texts have been rightly praised, but unfortunately seldom followed.[18] One exception is the recent work of John Drury, who examines the religious meaning of various works of art from the National Gallery, London.[19] Our project, while deeply indebted to the approach of Pelikan and Miles, differs from theirs and Drury's in scope and emphasis. We attempt to trace portrayals by individual artists of specific scenes unique to Luke's infancy narrative. This limited scope has enabled us to examine our topic in much more detail, and hopefully has prevented us from making some of the overgeneralizations often associated with such interdisciplinary studies.

Though we allow each text and its visual depiction to determine the particular issues to be pursued, in the subsequent chapters devoted to analysis of particular images and texts we follow a common strategy for each painting. Each of those chapters begins with an overview of the biblical passage and its interpretation, pointing out significant rhetorical features and the overarching theological argument of the text, as well as outlining a brief summary of its subsequent interpretation in the ecclesiastical literature.[20] Next, we contextualize the selected work of art by giving a brief biography of the artist, placing the work within the artist's own *oeuvre,* discussing what is known of the patronage of the specific image, and exploring important social, political, and religious factors which may facilitate our understanding of the painting. A stylistic and iconographic analysis is followed by brief hermeneutical reflections about how this visual interpretation might inform the church's reading of Scripture.

In addition to beginning with a rhetorical overview of the chosen text from Luke, we have placed the chapters in the canonical order of Luke's presentation, rather than in the chronological order of the composition. While we give ample attention to the historical context of each painting, this canonical arrangement allows us to keep the focus on the Gospel of Luke itself and to explore the painting as a visual exegesis of that text.[21]

Notes

1. Irenaeus, *Adversus Haeresis,* III.11.8.

2. This table was adapted from a table by Felix Jus at *http://bellarmine.lmu.edu/faculty/fjust/Evangelists_Symbols.htm,#Rev 4:5–11*. See also Robin M. Jensen, "Of Cherubim & Gospel Symbols," *Biblical Archaeology Review* (July/August 1995).

3. On redaction criticism, see Joachim Rohde, *Rediscovering the Teachings of the Evangelists* (trans. D. M. Barton; Philadelphia: Fortress, 1968); Norman Perrin, *What Is Redaction Criticism?* (Philadelphia: Fortress, 1969).

4. Irenaeus, *Adversus Haeresis,* III.14.3. Irenaeus goes on to list a great many other passages unique to Luke, including the miraculous draught of fish (Luke 5), the bent woman (Luke 7), the man with dropsy (Luke 14), the parable of the banquet (Luke 14), the anointing at Simon's house (Luke 7), the parable of the rich fool (Luke 12), the rich man and Lazarus (Luke 16), the Pharisee and the publican (Luke 18), Zacchaeus (Luke 19), the ten lepers (Luke 19), the parable of the wicked judge (Luke 18), the barren fig tree (Luke 13), and the road to Emmaus (Luke 24).

5. With its focus on uniquely Lukan material, this project is different from other iconographical surveys. For those interested in the history of the iconography of the infancy narrative, see Gertrud Schiller, *Christ's Incarnation — Childhood — Baptism — Temptation — Transfiguration — Works and Miracles* (vol. 1 of *Iconography of Christian Art;* trans. Janet Seligman; Greenwich, Conn.: New York Graphic Society, 1971), 26–126. A good general

introduction to the Nativity in art is the brief work by Jeremy Wood, *The Nativity* (London: Scala Publications, 1992). In addition to Schiller, we have found the work by Helene E. Roberts and Rachel Hall, *Narrative Paintings of the Italian School* (vol. 1 of *Iconographic Index to New Testament Subjects Represented in Photographs and Slides of Paintings in the Visual Collections, Fine Arts Library, Harvard University;* New York: Garland, 1992), indispensable for identifying subjects unique to Luke.

6. See Wolfgang Iser, *The Act of Reading: A Theory of Aesthetic Response* (Baltimore: Johns Hopkins University Press, 1978), esp. 85. On the history of reception theory and especially on the contributions of Robert Jaus and Wolfgang Iser to its theoretical foundations, see Robert C. Holub, *Reception Theory: A Critical Introduction* (London: Metheun, 1984).

7. Erwin Panofsky, "Iconography and Iconology: An Introduction to the Study of Renaissance Art," in *Meaning in the Visual Arts* (Chicago: University of Chicago Press, 1955), 26–54.

8. Ibid., 38.

9. Ibid., 31.

10. Ibid., 30.

11. Ibid.

12. John Shearman, *Only Connect . . . Art and the Spectator in the Italian Renaissance* (Princeton, N.J.: Princeton University Press, 1992), 4.

13. Ibid., 4–5.

14. Paolo Berdini, *The Religious Art of Jacopo Bassano: Painting as Visual Exegesis* (Cambridge: Cambridge University Press, 1997), 35.

15. Clearly here we have moved beyond Berdini's interest.

16. See Krister Stendahl's classic formulation of this method in "Biblical Theology, Contemporary," *Interpreter's Dictionary of the Bible* (ed. George Buttrick, 5 vols.; Nashville: Abingdon Press, 1962), 1:418–32.

17. See Brevard Childs, "The *Sensus Literalis* of Scripture: An Ancient and Modern Problem," in *Beiträge zur Alttestamentlichen Theologie* (ed. Herbert Donner et al.; Göttingen: Vandenhoeck & Ruprecht, 1977), 80–93; David Steinmetz, "The Superiority of Precritical Exegesis," in *A Guide to Contemporary Hermeneutics* (ed. Donald K. McKim; Grand Rapids: Eerdmans, 1986), 65–77.

18. See Jaraslov Pelikan, *Jesus Through the Centuries* (New Haven: Yale University Press, 1985); and Margaret R. Miles, *Image as Insight: Visual Understanding in Western Christianity and Secular Culture* (Boston: Beacon Press, 1985).

19. John Drury, *Painting the Word: Christian Pictures and Their Meaning* (New Haven: Yale University Press, 1999).

20. In the brief history of interpretation of the text, we are following the lead, for example, of commentators like François Bovon (*Das Evangelium Nach Lukas. 2. Teilband Lk 9:51–14.35* [Evangelisch-Katholischer Kommentar zum Neuen Testament; Zürich: Benziger Verlag, 1996]) and Ulrich Luz (*Matthew: A Commentary* [trans. Wilhelm Linss; Minneapolis: Augsburg, 1989]), both of whom write of the "Wirkungsgeschichte" of the text, which may be roughly translated the "history of influence."

21. Because of our focus on the Gospel of Luke itself, we have chosen to use the New Revised Standard Version for the translation provided at the beginning of each chapter and for references to our modern understanding of the text. Where we deal with the specific, historical understanding of the text for the artist and/or his audience, we have consulted the Latin text of the Vulgate.

Figure 3. Guercino. *St. Luke Displaying a Painting of the Virgin.* 1652–53. Oil on canvas. Nelson-Atkins Museum of Art, Kansas City, Missouri. Photo. E. G. Schempf. With permission of The Nelson-Atkins Museum of Art, Kansas City, Missouri (Purchase) F83-55.

Chapter One

Luke the Physician, Painter, and Patron Saint

T HE CHOICE OF St. Luke's Gospel for the subject of this study is appropriate because of the traditions that not only associate him with the profession of medicine, but also claim that he was himself a painter. Moreover, later traditions made him the patron saint of the artists' guild in Florence. We explore these various traditions below.

Luke the Beloved Physician

Most students of the Bible are familiar with the traditions associating the author of the Third Gospel with "Luke, the beloved physician" and companion of Paul (see Col 4:14; 2 Tim 4:11).[1] Though much of the tradition of the early church regarding the authorship of Luke and Acts has been collected elsewhere, for convenience in reevaluating the evidence, the more important witnesses from the first four centuries will be considered.[2]

The Gospel title, *euangelion kata Loukan* ("The Gospel according to Luke"), is found at the end of P75.[3] This fragmentary manuscript dates only to about 175–225, or 100 to 125 years after the Gospel is thought to have been written. Joseph Fitzmyer has noted, "In general, such ms. titles date from the end of the second century, when the attribution of the four canonical Gospels to their traditional authors was already a common heritage."[4] This title, though not original to the Gospel, probably reflects the oldest tradition linking an author named Luke to the writing of the Third Gospel.

In the prologue to the Gospel, the author seems to identify himself as a second-generation Christian relying on others' eyewitness testimony. He cannot therefore be counted among the apostles. Furthermore, throughout the book of Acts, when describing Paul's activities the narrator occasionally shifts from the third- to the first-person plural "we" (Acts 16:10, 20:5–15, 21:1–18, 27:1–28:16).

On the basis of the so-called "we" passages in Acts, Irenaeus clearly identifies Luke as a companion of Paul: "But that this Luke was inseparable from Paul and was his fellow-worker in the gospel he himself makes clear, not boasting of it, but compelled to do so by truth itself."[5]

Refuting especially the followers of Marcion and Valentinus, Irenaeus argues on the basis of the common authorship of Luke and Acts that the veracity of the two works must stand or fall together. For Irenaeus, the book of Acts is the glue which holds together the two major portions of the New Testament, the "Gospel" and the "Apostle," as they were called by early Christian writers.

That the book of Acts is not the only potential source of information from which Irenaeus and others drew is clear. Irenaeus continued:

> That he [Luke] was not only a follower, but also a fellow-worker of the apostles, especially of Paul, Paul himself made clear in his letters saying, "Demas forsook me and went away to Thessalonica, Crescens to Galatia, Titus to Dalmatia; only Luke is with me." By this he shows that he was always joined to him, and was inseparable from him. And again in that letter which is to the Colossians he says, "Luke, the beloved physician, saluteth you." Now if this Luke, who always preached with Paul and was called by him "beloved," and preached the gospel with him, and was entrusted with handing on the gospel to us, learned from him nothing else, as has been shown from his words, — how do they, who were never associated with Paul, boast that they have learned hidden and unspeakable mysteries?[6]

The Muratorian canon is an early list of documents accepted as sacred authorities in some early Christian communities. If a second-century date is accepted for the Muratorian canon,[7] then a second witness to the common authorship of Luke and Acts is found:

> The third book of the Gospel, according to Luke, Luke that physician, who after the ascension of Christ, when Paul had taken him with him as companion of his journey, composed in his own name on the basis of report.... But the Acts of all the apostles were written down in one volume. Luke compiled for "most excellent Theophilus" what things were done in detail in his presence, as he plainly shows by omitting both the death of Peter and also the departure of Paul from the city, when he departed for Spain (Lines 2–5; 34–39).

Likewise, a second-century extratextual prologue to the Gospel, the so-called "anti-Marcionite Prologue," reads:

> Luke was a Syrian of Antioch, by profession a physician, the disciple of the apostles, and later a follower of Paul until his martyrdom.

He served the Lord without distraction, without a wife, and without children. He died at the age of eighty-four in Boetia, full of the Holy Spirit.[8]

From the fourth century, we may consider the testimony of Eusebius and the Monarchian prologue.[9]

By the time of the *Ecclesiastical History* (c. 312–24 C.E.), Eusebius was able to consolidate the traditions about Luke:

> Luke, being by birth one of the people of Antioch, by profession a physician, having been with Paul a good deal, and having associated intimately with the rest of the apostles, has left us examples of the art of curing souls that he obtained from them in two divinely inspired books — the Gospel, which he testifies that he wrote out even as they delivered to him who from the beginning were eyewitness and ministers of the word, all of whom [or all of which facts?] he says he had followed even from the beginning, and the Acts of the Apostles, which he composed, receiving his information with his own eyes, no longer by hearsay.[10]

The date of a later extratextual prologue to the Gospel, known as the Monarchian Prologue, is difficult to establish (330–50? C.E.), but many assume that the traditions about Luke date back to the fourth century.[11] The text, in part, reads:

> Luke, a Syrian of Antioch by nation, by profession a physician, a disciple of the Apostles, later followed Paul until his confession, serving God without blame. For he never had wife or children, and died at the age of seventy-four in Bithynia, full of the Holy Ghost. When Gospels had already been written, by Matthew in Judaea and by Mark in Italy, at the instigation of the Holy Spirit he wrote this Gospel in the parts of Achaia, and he also signified in the commencement that others had previously been written.... To this Luke ministerial power was deservedly given of also writing the Acts of the Apostles....[12]

Picking up on the reference in Col 4:14, all of these sources not only identify the author of Luke and Acts as Luke, but they all also identify him as a "physician." This point was elaborated in the literature of the early and medieval church where Luke is credited with expertise, as Eusebius says, with the "art of curing souls." The comments by Jacobus de Voragine (1229–98) in *The Golden Legend* are typical of later embellishments of this same point:

Second, just as Luke's gospel is permeated with truth, it is also filled with much usefulness. Its author was a physician, to signify that he prescribed a very healthful medicine for us. There are three kinds of medicine: some cures, some preserves, some improves. In his gospel Luke shows us that the heavenly physician has prescribed these three medicines for us. The medicine that cures diseases is penance, which cures every spiritual sickness.... The medicine that improves, i.e., that increases good health, consists in the observances of counsels, for the counsels make people better and more perfect.... The preservative medicine is that which saves us from falling, and this consists in avoiding the occasion in sinning and the company of sinners.[13]

In summary, a number of assertions about the author of Luke and Acts emerge from the tradition preserved by the early church — the Third Gospel and Acts were composed by the same person, Luke, a companion of Paul and a native of Antioch.[14] Not the least important among these traditions is the assertion that Luke was a physician, a point that continues to be elaborated, embellished, and spiritualized in subsequent Christian contemplation.[15]

Luke the Painter and Patron Saint

Readers may be less familiar with two long-standing traditions regarding the identity of the writer, namely, that "Luke" was an artist and also that he was the patron saint of the artists' guild. We take up each of these traditions in turn.

Images Attributed to Luke

Eunice Howe has conveniently catalogued the various images of the Virgin Mary attributed to Luke.[16] A sixth-century story, attributed to Theodorus Lector (c. 530) depicts Luke as the painter of an icon of the Virgin Mary: "Eudocia [wife of Emperor Theodosios II — *reg* 408–50] sent to Pulcheria [her sister-in-law, who held it at Constantinople] from Jerusalem an image of the Mother of God painted by the apostle Luke."[17] Eunice Howe has commented: "This icon came to be accepted as a portrait from life made by St. Luke, and the designation *Hodegetria* ('she who points the way') for icons of this sort may have derived from the name of the building in which it was housed, the monastery of the Hodegon."[18] Though some hold that this icon was destroyed during the Turkish conquest of Constantinople in 1453, others maintain that this image and others by Luke were transported

Figure 4. St. Luke. (?) *Portrait of the Virgin and Child.* c. sixth century. Panel. S. Maria Maggiore, Rome. Photo. Copyright Alinari/Art Resource, NY.

to the West during the Crusades and became objects of veneration within the growing Marian cult.

In addition to the *Hodegetria,* now accepted as one of the earliest images representing the Virgin and Child, other Byzantine icons attributed to Luke include the Virgin *Glykophiloussa,* where the Christ Child presses his face to the Virgin's; the Virgin *Galactotrophousa,* which depicts the Virgin suckling the child; the Virgin *Kyriotissa,* where the Virgin stands and holds the child to her chest; and the Virgin *Haghiosoritissa,* where the Virgin stands in profile with raised arms.[19]

In some cases, the traditions of Luke as physician and painter coalesced in a most remarkable way around the image of the Virgin and Child in S. Maria Maggiore.[20] Jacobus de Voragine reports that St. Gregory the Great (c. 540–604) carried St. Luke's portrait of the Virgin through the city streets in an effort to stop the plague (Figure 4):

The plague was still ravaging Rome, and Gregory ordered the procession to continue to make the circuit of the city, the marchers
chanting the litanies. An image of the blessed Mary ever Virgin was
carried in the procession. It is said that this image is still in the church
of Saint Mary Major in Rome, that it was painted by Saint Luke, who
was not only a physician but a distinguished painter, and that it was a
perfect likeness of the Virgin. And lo and behold! The poisonous un-
cleanness of the air yielded to the image as if fleeing from it and being
unable to withstand its presence: the passage of the picture brought
about a wonderful serenity and purity in the air. . . . Then the pope
saw an angel of the Lord standing atop the castle of Crescentius,
wiping a bloody sword and sheathing it. Gregory understood that
that put an end to the plague, as, indeed, it happened. Thereafter
the castle was called the Castle of the Holy Angel.[21]

Luke's work of art becomes itself a vehicle of healing. The number of
icons traditionally attributed to Luke number literally in the hundreds,
testimony to the deep ways in which this tradition has taken root in the
imagination of Christians across the centuries.

Images of Luke Painting the Virgin/
Luke, Patron Saint of Artists

During the Renaissance, the image of Luke painting the Virgin became
a popular subject in the regions north and south of the Swiss Alps.
One of the earliest Renaissance examples is *St. Luke Portraying the Virgin* (Figure 5), c. 1435–40, by the Flemish artist Rogier van der Weyden
(c. 1399/1400–64), which offers an intimate portrait of Luke and the Virgin and Child in a contemporaneous Flemish household. The panel, today
located in the Museum of Fine Arts, Boston, is an example of the instruc-
tional power of art.[22] The painting is steeped with Christian symbolism.
The Virgin sits in front of the bench, not on it, showing the Christian
virtue of humility. The armrest of the bench shows the figures of Adam
and Eve reminding the viewers that Christ and Mary represent the New
Adam and the New Eve, who have returned for their salvation.[23] Luke,
as evangelist, records the life of the Virgin and Christ and, as the first
Christian artist, preserves the likeness of the Virgin and Child. The ox,
the iconographic symbol of Luke, is seen here standing on the floor of the
artist's study on the right side of the painting.[24]

Artists take pride in their holy lineage to Luke, gospel writer and artist.
This picture was probably painted for the guild of St. Luke and was intended to hang above an altar maintained by artists in a local church.[25]

Figure 5. Rogier van der Weyden. *St. Luke Drawing the Virgin and Child.* c. 1435. Panel. Museum of Fine Arts, Boston. Photo. Courtesy, Museum of Fine Arts, Boston. Gift of Mr. and Mrs. Henry Lee Higginson. Photograph. © 2003 Museum of Fine Arts, Boston. All rights reserved.

Artists often painted their own portrait in the face of St. Luke, further establishing the sense of pride and association the artists have with this evangelist. Rogier van der Weyden's likeness is known from other contemporary portrayals, and thus we know the artist appears as the face of St. Luke.[26]

Giorgio Vasari (1511–74), Italian artist, architect, and biographer of artists, also portrayed himself as the figure of St. Luke in his fresco version of *St. Luke Painting the Virgin,* c. 1565 (Figure 6). Like the van der Weyden

Figure 6. Vasari. *St. Luke Painting the Virgin*. c. 1565. Fresco. Cappella di S. Luca, SS. Annunziata, Florence. Photo. With permission from the Ministero dei Beni e le Attività Culturali.

piece, this painting hung over the altar of the artists' chapel, in this case, the Cappella di S. Luca in the Florentine church of SS. Annunziata. The chapel was maintained by the *Accademia del Disegno,* founded in 1562 to train and support artists.[27]

In Vasari's painting, one sees that the symbols of the artist — the box of paints, palette, and mahlstick — share the frontal space of the composition with the symbol of Luke, the ox. The message we receive from both the Vasari painting and *Saint Luke Displaying a Painting of the Virgin,* 1652–53 (Figure 3, p. 10), by the Italian Baroque painter Guercino (1591–1666), is that St. Luke is a divinely inspired artist and that all artists share in this inspiration because of their association with their patron saint.[28] The

Guercino, located in the Nelson-Atkins Museum of Art, Kansas City, Missouri, shows the artist still holding the palette and brushes while he invites the viewer to study the finished portrait still on its easel next to an angel.[29] A sculpture of an ox, a quill pen, and inkpot sit upon a book resting on a table to the right of St. Luke. These objects, combined with the palette and brushes, continue the traditional symbolism of Luke as gospel writer, evangelist, and artist.

Florentine painters also belonged to the Guild of Doctors and Pharmacists not only because they ground their colors as pharmacists ground materials for medicines, but also because painters and doctors enjoyed the protection of the same patron saint, St. Luke. Luke's place as patron saint of the guild of Florentine painters, pharmacists, and physicians was secured by the placement of his statue in a niche of Or San Michele (Figure 7).

The origins of the legend about Luke the painter and patron saint are not clear. In her 1933 Hamburg dissertation, Dorothee Klein attempted to trace the origins and evolution of Luke the physician into Luke the painter.[30] Klein makes the fascinating suggestion that the motif of the painting evangelist had a long prehistory. The image of the reading philosopher in the classical period became, in the Augustan period, that of a writer, which served as a model for the writing evangelist. Later a painting board was substituted for the codex, transforming the figure into the painter saint. What Klein fails to account for is why it is Luke and not one of the other evangelists around whom this legend grows. Two possibilities commend themselves.

First, note that all the paintings attributed to Luke are paintings of Mary, and in fact, countless Byzantine images of the Madonna have been attributed to Luke. Augustine had commented that no one knew what the Virgin looked like,[31] but at some point there arose the need to have a *"vera ikon"* (a true image) of the Madonna. Logically, the image had to have been painted by someone who lived in Mary's time. Who better than Luke, who writes more about Mary and the infancy of Christ than all the other canonical gospel writers combined, fits the bill? Thus, the desire for an "authentic" likeness of the Madonna may have spurred the transformation of Luke into a painter.[32]

Second, in addition to Luke's presumed knowledge of Mary, his literary artistry as a writer may also have contributed to his depiction as a painter. Luke's literary prowess has certainly been recognized among modern biblical scholars. As long ago as 1896, Alfred Plummer both acknowledged the traditions of Luke as painter and suggested that this legend may owe its origin to Luke's literary skills: "And the legend has a strong element of truth.

Figure 7. Figure of St. Luke. Niche of Or San Michele. Florence. Photo. Heidi J. Hornik, with permission from the Ministero dei Beni e le Attività Culturali.

It points to the great influence which Luke has had upon Christian art, of which in a real sense he may be called the founder."[33] B. H. Streeter referred to Luke as the "consummate literary artist."[34] Ernst Haenchen recognized that Luke was not only a historian and a theologian but also an accomplished writer.[35] Haenchen attributes to Luke the "gift of enlivening bare facts."[36] Slightly modifying Haenchen's rubric, Mark Allen Powell speaks of Luke as "Historian, Theologian, and Artist."[37] This swell of interest in the literary aspects of the Third Gospel and Acts, acknowledged by Powell's chapter title, has only increased the references to Luke's literary artistry.[38]

Observations about Luke's literary prowess are not a modern phenomenon and, in fact, may provide a partial answer to the question about the origins of the traditions of Luke the painter.

Jerome comments several times on the quality of Luke's writing style. In his *Commentary on Isaiah,* he asserts that Luke's "language in the Gospel, as well as in the Acts of the Apostles, that is, in both volumes is more elegant, and smacks of secular eloquence."[39] Elsewhere he notes that Luke "was the most learned in the Greek language among all the evangelists."[40] In light of these passages, when Jerome claims that Luke is the anonymous believer who "wrote the Gospel, of which the same Paul says, 'We have sent together with him the brother whose praise is in the gospel through all the churches,'"[41] that praise must also include Luke's literary ability to write elegantly in Greek.

John Chrysostom, in the first of a series of sermons on Acts that he preached in 401 as the newly appointed bishop of Constantinople, inquired concerning the reason for Luke's two volumes: "And why did he not make one book of it, to send one man Theophilus, but has divided it into two subjects? For clearness, and to give the brother a pause for rest. Besides the two treatises are distinct in their subject matter."[42] This view of Luke's literary prowess continued right through the medieval and Renaissance periods. In the thirteenth century, Jacobus de Voragine remarks that "Luke was well ordered in relation to his appointed task, that of writing his gospel. This is shown by the fact that his gospel is permeated with much truth, filled with much usefulness *adorned with much charm,* and confirmed by many authorities" (our emphasis).[43] Later, he expands this third point that Luke's writing is "adorned with much charm":

> His style and manner of speaking are indeed charming and decorous. If someone wants what he says or writes to have grace and charm, then, as Augustine says, it must be pleasing, clear, and touching. If his words are to please, they should be eloquent; to be clear, they

should be easy to follow; to touch hearers, they should be fervent. Luke had these three qualities in his writing and in his preaching.[44]

Clarity is combined with vividness as virtues celebrated in the ancient rhetorical handbook tradition. Quintilian says: "It is a great gift to be able to set forth the facts on which we are speaking clearly and vividly. For oratory fails of its full effect . . . if its appeal is merely to the hearing . . . and not displayed in their living truth to the eyes of the mind."[45] Later Quintilian lauds those rhetors who were able to represent facts "in such vivid language that they appeal to the eye rather than the ear."[46] Likewise, the anonymous author of *Ad Herennium* defines vividness in terms of clarity: "Vivid description is the name for the figure which contains a clear, lucid, and impressive exposition of the consequences of an act."[47] Also noteworthy is the fact that the handbooks at times make comparisons between styles of oratory and styles of painting. Quintilian writes: "The question of the 'kind of style' to be adopted remains to be discussed. This was described in my original division of my subject . . . for I promised that I would speak of the art, the artist, and the work. But since oratory is the work of both rhetoric and of the orator, and since it has many forms, as I shall show, the art and the artist are involved in the consideration of all these forms."[48]

These comments on vividness, clarity, and style were not limited to orators. Not only do the rhetorical handbooks draw examples from a wide variety of literature, but the authors of the so-called *Progymnasmata* (rhetorical exercises for schoolboys) celebrated the rhetorical skills of both the accomplished speaker and writer. The first-century C.E. author Aelius Theon argued:

> So then, these subjects I have set forth not because I think that they are all suitable to every beginner, but in order that we might see that practice in the exercises is absolutely necessary, not only for those who intend to be orators, but also if someone wants to be a poet or prose-writer, or if he wants to acquire facility in some other form of writing. For these exercises are, so to speak, the foundation stones of every form of writing.[49]

Theon devotes an entire chapter to a discussion of *ekphrasis,* which he defines as "an informative account which brings vividly into view what is being set forth."[50] Theon also combines clarity and vividness when he asserts that the "desirable qualities of a description are these; above all, clarity and vividness, in order that what is being reported is virtually visible."[51] Theon also compares the training of the novice orator with that of the aspiring artist: "Just as it is of no advantage for those who want to be painters to look at the works of Apelles, Protogenes, and Antiphilus unless they themselves also attempt to paint, so also for those who are going to be orators."[52]

While many modern commentators have intuited the connection between Luke's artistry with words and the legend of Luke the painter, we suggest on the basis of the evidence cited above that, using the language of the rhetorical tradition to describe Luke's writing as "elegant," "learned," and especially "clear," early interpreters were acknowledging Luke's rhetorical skills as a writer. Because those skills were often compared to the skills necessary to produce visual art (painting, sculpture) and since "clarity" was so often linked to "vividness" (i.e., appealing to the eye and not the ear), it was a simple move to characterize Luke the rhetorical artist as the painting evangelist. Thus, while we cannot know who is the first to make this connection, we can at least understand the rhetorical situation that allowed it to develop.[53]

Conclusion

The author of the Third Gospel is first recognized as a physician whose writing is holy medicine to heal the soul. Later, Luke is acknowledged as a painter, probably based on the wide recognition of his rhetorical prowess as a literary artist who paints with words. Finally, in medieval times, he becomes the patron saint of the painters' guilds. He also held notoriety as the patron of one of the first of the *Compagnia di San Luca* in Florence. Although these stories of Luke as physician, painter, and patron of the arts are most probably all apocryphal, the fact remains that the author of the Third Gospel lived and wrote in a first-century Mediterranean world filled with visual images — wall paintings in peristyle houses, monumental art in the city forum, as well as panel paintings that we know about only from written sources. At least in the sense that word and image informed one another, Luke's world was much closer to the time of the Renaissance than to our own. The visual image can enrich our understanding of the written text by drawing attention to details of the story often neglected in the literary interpretations. It is to such images that we now turn our attention.

Notes

1. For the different approaches to the identity of Luke taken in biblical studies and art history, it is instructive to consider the entries under "Luke" in the two major multivolume dictionaries in each field. In the *Anchor Bible Dictionary* entry on "Luke (Person)," *Anchor Bible Dictionary* (ed. David Noel Freedman; 5 vols.; New York: Doubleday, 1992), IV:397–403, the authors (Eckhard Plümacher and I. Howard Marshall) assess Luke's accomplishments as both a historian (IV:398–402) and as a theologian (IV:402–3). On the other hand, the entire article on "Luke" by Eunice Howe in the *Dictionary of Art* (ed. Jane Turner; 34 vols.; New York: Grove's Dictionaries, 1996), 19:787–89, is devoted to the traditions concerning Luke as a painter of icons and as patron saint of artists.

2. Most of the texts on which the tradition depends may be found in Kurt Aland, *Synopsis Quattuor Evangeliorum* (Stuttgart: Württembergische Bibelanstalt, 1976), 531–48. Henry Cadbury also conveniently collected much of the primary data from the early church in "The Tradition," *The Beginnings of Christianity* (vol. 2; Grand Rapids: Baker, 1979, reprt), 207–64 (hereafter cited as *Beginnings*). See also in the same volume, "The Case for the Tradition," by C. W. Emmet, 265–97; "The Case Against the Tradition," by H. Windisch, 298–348; and "Subsidiary Points," by H. J. Cadbury and the editors, 349–59. Unless otherwise noted, the texts and translations are taken from Cadbury's collection in *Beginnings*, 2:209–45. The Greek and Latin texts in *Beginnings* have been compared with Aland's *Synopsis Quattuor Evangeliorum* (hereafter *SQE*).

3. See Victor Martin and Rudolf Kasser, eds., *Papyrus Bodmer XIV* (Cologny-Geneve: Bibliotheque Bodmer, 1961), 61.

4. Joseph Fitzmyer, *The Gospel According to Luke: Introduction, Translation, and Notes*, Anchor Bible 28 (Garden City, N.Y.: Doubleday, 1981), 36.

5. Irenaeus, *Adversus Haeresis*, III.14.1.

6. Ibid.

7. But see the arguments against this dating by Thomas A. C. Sundberg, "Canon Muratori: A Fourth-Century List," *Harvard Theological Review* 66 (1973): 1–41. This view has not gained wide acceptance and, in fact, has been rather harshly criticized. See Joseph Fitzmyer, *Luke the Theologian: Some Aspects of His Teaching* (New York: Paulist, 1989).

8. Translation from Fitzmyer, *The Gospel According to Luke*, 1:38.

9. We shall deal with the witness of Jerome under the section on Luke the painter. For traditions about Luke the physician later than the fourth century, see *Beginnings*, 2:246–64.

10. Eusebius, *Ecclesiastical History*, III.4.

11. A fourth-century date is argued by Dom Chapman, *Early History of the Vulgate Gospels* (cited by Cadbury, *Beginnings*, 2:243).

12. The text may be found in *SQE*, 539.

13. Jacobus de Voragine, *The Golden Legend: Readings on the Saints* (trans. William Granger Ryan; Princeton, N.J.: Princeton University Press, 1993), 2:251–52.

14. With the exception of those works noted below, most commentaries on Luke and Acts omit any reference to the traditions about Luke as a painter, even those which devote large sections to discussions of authorship.

15. This embellishment continued into modern times, especially in the work of William K. Hobart (*The Medical Language of St. Luke: A Proof from Internal Evidence*

that "The Gospel according to Luke" and "The Acts of the Apostles" Were Written by the Same Person, and that the Writer was a Medical Man [1882; reprint, Grand Rapids: Baker, 1954]). Hobart searched the healing stories in Luke for what he believed were medical terms, such as "crippled," "pregnant," or "abscess," or ordinary words used in a "medical" sense. Henry Cadbury, in The Style and Literary Method of Luke (Cambridge, Mass.: Harvard University Press, 1920), however, dismantled this argument by demonstrating that the terms on Hobart's lists occur in the Septuagint, Josephus, Plutarch, and Lucian — all nonmedical writers. Cadbury (50) concluded, "The style of Luke bears no more evidence of medical training and interest than does the language of other writers who were not physicians." In a subsequent tongue-in-cheek lexical note ("Luke and the Horse-Doctors," Journal of Biblical Literature 52 [1933]: 55–65), Cadbury also demonstrated that Luke's vocabulary shows a remarkable similarity with the corpus of writing of ancient veterinarians! His refutation was so effective that he virtually eliminated this special pleading to a so-called medical vocabulary. His students used to jest that Cadbury earned his doctorate by taking Luke's away. Still, we should note that Cadbury is careful to say that his own work did not prove that the author of the Third Gospel was not a physician, only that this point could not be proved on internal grounds.

16. See Howe, "Luke," 787–89.

17. Cited in the fourteenth-century writer Nicephoros Callistes Xanthopulos; for the text, see Migne, Patrologiae cursus completus: Series Graeca (Paris: Migne, 1857–66), vol. 86, col. 165; hereafter Migne, PG.

18. Howe, "Luke," 787.

19. Ibid., 788.

20. On the history of this painting, see Henrietta Irving Bolton, The Madonna of St. Luke: The Story of a Portrait (New York: G. P. Putnam's Sons, 1895).

21. Jacobus de Voragine, The Golden Legend, 1:174.

22. Craig Harbison, The Mirror of the Artist: Northern Renaissance Art in Its Historical Context (New York: Harry N. Abrams, 1995), 10.

23. For literature on Mary as the "second Eve," see the notes in the next chapter on Leonardo's Annunciation. On the specific image of a nursing Madonna as a second Eve figure, see especially Beth Williamson, "The Virgin Lactans as Second Eve: Image of the Salvatrix," Studies in Iconography 19 (1998): 105–38.

24. On the symbol of the ox for Luke, see the Introduction.

25. Harbison, The Mirror of the Artist, 10.

26. Ibid.

27. The classic work on the Italian academies remains Michele Maylender, Storia delle Accademie d'Italia (5 vols.; Bologna: L. Capelli, 1926–30). For a discussion of the Accademia del Disegno in Florence, see two works by Karen-edis Barzman, The Florentine Academy and the Early Modern State: The Discipline of Disegno (Cambridge: Cambridge University Press, 2000); "The Florentine Accademia del Disegno: Liberal Education and the Renaissance Artist," Leids Kunsthistorisch Jaarboek 5–6 (1986–87): 14–32; Nikolaus Pevsner, Academies of Art: Past and Present (Cambridge: Cambridge University Press, 1940); Mary Ann Jack Ward, "The Accademia del Disegno in Sixteenth-Century Florence: A Study of the Artists' Institution," Ph.D. dissertation, University of Chicago, 1972; T. Reynolds, "The Accademia del Disegno in Florence: Its Formation and Early Years," Ph.D. dissertation, Columbia University, 1974; Sergio Rossi, Accademia del Disegno in Dalle botteghe alle academie: Realtà sociale e teorie artistiche a Firenze dal XIV al XVI secolo (Milan: Feltrinelli, 1980); Zygmunt Wazbinski, L'Accademia

Medicea del Disegno a Firenze nel Cinquecento: Idea e istituzione (Florence: Leo S. Olschki, 1987); Karen-edis Barzman, "Academies, Theory, Critics (1527–1770)" in *The Oxford Illustrated History of Western Art* (ed. Martin Kemp; Oxford: Oxford University Press, 2000).

28. Marilyn Stokstad, *Art History* (New York: Harry N. Abrams, 1995), 2.22.

29. See *Nelson-Atkins Museum of Art: A Handbook of the Collection* (New York: Hudson Hills Press, 1993).

30. Dorothee Klein, *St. Lukas als Maler der Maria: Ikonographie der Lukas-Madonna* (Berlin: Oskar Schloss Verlag, 1933). For more recent analyses of these traditions, see Michele Bacci, *Il pennello dell'Evangelista: Storia delle immagini sacre attribuite a san Luca* (Pisa: Gisem, 1998) and Gisela Kraut, *Luka Malt die Madonna: Zeugnisse zum künstlerischen Selbstverständis in der Malerei* (Mainz: Wernersche Verlagsgesellschaft, 1986), as well as the relevant sections in Georg-W. Költsch, *Maler Modell: Der Maler und sein Modell* (Cologne: Dumont, 2000) and Hermann Ulrich Asemissen and Gunter Schweikhart, *Malerei als Thema der Malerei* (Berlin: Akademie Verlag, 2000).

31. Augustine, *The Trinity*, 8.5.7.

32. We are grateful to Louis Alexander Waldman for this suggestion.

33. Alfred Plummer, *The Gospel According to St. Luke,* International Critical Commentary 28 (New York: Charles Scribner's Sons, 1896), xxii. Plummer's sensitive comments about the connections between Luke's literary artistry and the painting tradition have largely been ignored by subsequent scholarship.

34. B. H. Streeter, *The Four Gospels* (London: Macmillan, 1924), 548.

35. See, e.g., Ernst Haenchen, *The Acts of the Apostles: A Commentary* (trans. Bernard Noble et al.; Philadelphia: Westminster, 1971), 90n. 1.

36. Ibid., 104.

37. Mark Allen Powell, *What Are They Saying about Luke?* (New York: Paulist Press, 1989), 5–15. Powell (10) has also briefly commented on the relationship between these references to Luke the "literary artist" and the traditions of Luke the painter: "At some point in church history, a legend arose that Luke was a skilled painter.... This is not, however, what scholars mean when they say that Luke is an artist. The reference, rather, is to his literary art, his skill in composing a narrative." Powell may have too quickly dismissed the possible links between Luke the consummate literary writer and Luke the "skilled painter."

38. In one of the first literary-critical treatments of Luke, Robert Tannehill (*The Narrative Unity of Luke-Acts* [vol. 1; Philadelphia: Fortress, 1986], 1) called Luke "an author of literary skill and rich imagination." Gerhard Krodel (*Acts* [Minneapolis: Augsburg Press, 1986], 15) calls Luke "a great storyteller" who "could sketch vivid scenes." See also J.-N. Aletti, *L'art de raconter Jésus Christ: L'écriture narrative de l'évangile de Luc* (Paris: Seuil, 1989); Charles H. Talbert (*Literary Patterns, Theological Themes, and the Genre of Luke-Acts* [Philadelphia: Fortress, 1974], 1–5) chronicles efforts to understand the literary genius of Luke.

39. Jerome, *Commentary on Isaiah,* iii.6; for the text, see J.-P. Migne, *Patrologiae cursus completus: Series Latina* (Paris, 1866–), vol. 24, col. 98; hereafter Migne, *PL.*

40. Jerome, *Epistual ad Damasum,* xx.4; for the text, see Migne, *PL,* vol. 24.

41. Jerome, *De viris illustribus,* vii; for the text, see Migne, *PL,* vol. 24.

42. John Chrysostom, Homily I, *Acts of the Apostles,* I.7.

43. Voragine, *The Golden Legend,* 2:252.

44. Ibid.

45. Quintilian, *Institutio Oratoria* (trans. H. E. Butler; New York: G. P. Putnam's Sons, 1922), VIII.iii.62.

46. Ibid., IX.ii.40.

47. [Cicero], *Ad Herennium* (trans. Harry Caplan; Cambridge, Mass.: Harvard University Press, 1964), IV.xxxix.51.

48. Quintilian, XII.x.2. In XII.x.3–6. Quintilian discusses a number of specific painters and sculptors and follows that by a discussion of oratory style.

49. Aelius Theon, *Progymnasmata* (trans. James R. Butts; Ann Arbor: University Microfilms International, 1986), 2:138–42.

50. Ibid., 7:1–2.

51. Ibid., 7:53–55.

52. Ibid., 1:85–89.

53. For renewed interest in the person of Luke the Evangelist as artist and iconographer, see Giordana Canova Mariana, ed., *Luca Evangelista: Parole e Immagine tra Oriente e Occidente* (Padua: Il Poligrafi casa editrice, 2001).

Figure 8. Leonardo da Vinci. *Annunciation.* c. 1473–75. Panel. Galleria degli Uffizi, Florence. Photo. With permission from the Ministero dei Beni e le Attività Culturali.

Chapter Two

The *Annunciation*
by Leonardo da Vinci

(Luke 1:26–38)

THE IMPORTANCE OF the Annunciation to medieval and Renaissance Florentines is best reflected in the fact that until 1750 the beginning of their new year corresponded directly to the event's feast day, March 25. The annual celebrations on this date, exactly nine months before the traditional celebration of the birth of Christ, included elaborate theatrical and artistic productions. In and around Florence, the popularity of the painted Annunciation theme was immense. It seems that every great Tuscan artist painted at least one version of the Annunciation, including one of Florence's most famous sons and master of the High Renaissance style of painting, Leonardo da Vinci. When Leonardo was in his early twenties he was commissioned to paint the *Annunciation,* probably by the monks for the monastery of Monte Oliveto, outside Florence (Figure 8).[1] It is currently located in the Uffizi Gallery, Florence, and is the object of our discussion in this chapter.[2]

Overview of the Biblical Text

[26]In the sixth month the angel Gabriel was sent by God to a town in Galilee called Nazareth, [27]to a virgin engaged to a man whose name was Joseph, of the house of David. The virgin's name was Mary. [28]And he came to her and said, "Greetings, favored one! The Lord is with you." [29]But she was much perplexed by his words and pondered what sort of greeting this might be. [30]The angel said to her, "Do not be afraid, Mary, for you have found favor with God. [31]And now, you will conceive in your womb and bear a son, and you will name him Jesus. [32]He will be great, and will be called the Son of the Most High, and the Lord God will give to him the throne of his ancestor David. [33]He will reign over the house of Jacob forever, and of his kingdom there will be no end." [34]Mary said to the angel, "How can this be, since I am a virgin?" [35]The angel said to her, "The Holy Spirit will

come upon you, and the power of the Most High will overshadow you; therefore the child to be born will be holy; he will be called Son of God. [36]And now, your relative Elizabeth in her old age has also conceived a son; and this is the sixth month for her who was said to be barren. [37]For nothing will be impossible with God." [38]Then Mary said, "Here am I, the servant of the Lord; let it be with me according to your word." Then the angel departed from her.

Both Luke and Matthew connect their stories of Jesus' birth to the story of Israel. Matthew uses a quotation formula, "All this took place to fulfill what had been spoken by the Lord through the prophet" (cf. Matt 1:22–23; 2:15; 2:17–18; 2:23). Luke is more subtle in his echoes of the Old Testament. His technique is more like an X-ray of a painting that allows a reader to see one set of figures through another. So, for example, the barren couple, Zechariah and Elizabeth, recall the barren couple, Abraham and Sarah, from Israel's ancestral period. The annunciation of Jesus' birth to Mary also shares important elements with Old Testament commissioning stories, and the authorial audience was sure to hear these verbal echoes.[3]

Commissioning stories, or stories where a messenger of God delivers a message to one of God's people, are found throughout the Old Testament and contain a number of elements that remain fairly stable. Among Hebrew storytellers evidently there was a traditional way of telling a commissioning story. The Old Testament commission contained five essential elements: (1) the appearance of an angel, (2) the explicit or implicit expression of fear or resistance on the part of the recipient, (3) the message of commissioning, (4) an objection expressed on the part of the one receiving the commission, and (5) the giving of a sign to confirm the authenticity of the message.[4] We can illustrate these elements by referring to several Old Testament commissioning stories.

In Exod 3, we find the commission of Moses. This story contains all the elements of an annunciation story:

1. *Appearance of angel:* "There [Horeb] the angel of the Lord appeared to him [Moses] in a flame of fire out of a bush" (Exod 3:2).

2. *Reaction:* "And Moses hid his face, for he was afraid to look at God" (3:6).

3. *Angel's message:* "The Lord said, 'I have observed the misery of my people who are in Egypt. . . . So come, I will send you to Pharaoh to bring my people, the Israelites, out of Egypt'" (3:7–10).

4. *Objection to message:* "But Moses said to God, 'Who am I that I should go to Pharaoh, and bring the Israelites out of Egypt?'" (3:11).

5. *Giving of sign:* "He [God] said, 'I will be with you; and this shall be the sign for you that it is I who sent you: when you have brought the people out of Egypt, you shall worship God on this mountain'" (3:12).

Likewise in the story of the call of Gideon in Judg 6.

1. *Appearance of angel:* "Now the angel of the Lord came and sat under the oak at Ophrah"; "The angel of the Lord appeared to him and said to him, 'The Lord is with you, you mighty warrior'" (Judg 6:11, 12).

2. *Reaction:* "Gideon answered him, 'But sir, if the Lord is with us, why then has all this happened to us?'" (6:13).

3. *Angel's message:* "Then the Lord turned to him and said, 'Go in this might of yours and deliver Israel from the hand of Midian; I hereby commission you'" (6:14).

4. *Objection to message:* "He responded, 'But sir, how can I deliver Israel? My clan is the weakest in Manasseh, and I am the least in my family'" (6:15).

5. *Giving of sign:* "Then he [Gideon] said to him, 'If now I have found favor with you, then show me a sign that it is you who speak with me'" (6:17). The angel then causes sacrificial meat and cakes, which Gideon offers, to be consumed with fire (6:18–21).

The audience familiar with these stories and others like them would recognize all of these elements in the annunciation to Mary.

1. *Appearance of angel:* "In the sixth month the angel Gabriel was sent by God to a town in Galilee called Nazareth. . . . And he came to her [Mary] and said, 'Greetings, favored one! The Lord is with you!'" (1:26–28).

2. *Reaction:* "But she was much perplexed by his words and pondered what sort of greeting this might be" (1:29).

3. *Angel's message:* "Do not be afraid, Mary, for you have found favor with God. And now, you will conceive in your womb and bear a son, and you will name him Jesus. He will be great, and will be called the Son of the Most High, and the Lord God . . ." (1:30–33).

4. *Objection to message:* "Mary said to the angel, 'How can this be, since I am a virgin?'" (1:34).

5. *Giving of sign:* "And now, your relative Elizabeth in her old age has also conceived a son; and this is the sixth month for her who was said to be barren" (1:36).

The form of this story so closely follows that of the commissioning stories that the first auditors must have heard these echoes. What is the rhetorical effect? First the connection of the Annunciation to its Old Testament pattern helps explain the rather enigmatic note that Mary pondered what kind of greeting this could be.[5] The phrase, "the Lord is with you," is found in an angel's message elsewhere only in the Old Testament in the Gideon story, "The Lord is with you, you mighty warrior" (Judg 6:12). Mary also knows her Scriptures, and perhaps knows that this same greeting given to Gideon is followed by a commission. Her puzzled pause over these words encourages the audience to do the same. The commissioning pattern also encourages the audience to expect that, like Moses and Gideon, Mary too will be given a task to do. What is surprising is the specific assignment: she will become pregnant with "the Son of the Most High." Her objection, like Gideon and Moses, is expected. Moses says, "Who am I?" (Exod 3:11). Gideon complains he is from the smallest tribe and is the least in his own family (Judg 6:15). Mary objects: "How can this be, since I am a virgin?" In each case, of course, the angel gives a sign to confirm the authenticity of the commission. For Mary, the convincing sign is that her relative Elizabeth, barren all those years, is now in her sixth month of pregnancy.

Not only does this story announcing Jesus' birth share elements in common with Old Testament commissioning stories, the pattern is found repeated in the Lukan birth narrative. In the passage just prior to this one is the annunciation of the birth of John the Baptist (1:11–20). This text, too, contains the elements of a commissioning story: (1) Appearance of angel (1:11), (2) reaction (1:12), (3) angel's message (1:13–17), (4) objection to message (1:18), and (5) giving of sign (1:20).

The obvious similarities between these two stories underscore their connection as commissioning stories.[6] Zechariah is commissioned to be father of John the Baptist, forerunner of the Messiah, and Mary is commissioned to be mother of the Son of the Most High. But the redundancy of elements also highlights the differences between the two accounts. The account of Jesus' birth is parallel to John's birth, but Jesus' birth is superior in every way. John is to be born to aged parents who desperately want a child; Jesus is to be born to a young girl to whom the news comes as a total surprise. John is to be conceived by sexual intercourse; Jesus is to be conceived by the Holy Spirit overshadowing Mary, a virgin. Both will be great before the Lord, but John is "to make ready a people prepared for the Lord"; Jesus will be called "the Son of the Most High" and "will reign over the house of Jacob forever." This theme of Jesus' annunciation, conception, birth, and commission as parallel but superior to John continues throughout the rest of the birth narrative (cf. 1:57–66, 80 with 2:15–27, 34–40).

God has chosen two of his people, an old priest and a young virgin, to carry out his task. For Zechariah, the commission is to father John, who will go before the Lord, making the people ready. For Mary, the assignment is to give birth to Jesus, to whom will be given the throne of his ancestor David.

Subsequent History of Interpretation

It did not take long before the story of the Annunciation captured the imagination of early Christians. In the apocryphal *Protevangelium of James* (second century?), Mary has been included in a group of "pure virgins" to make a new veil for the temple, and it falls to Mary to weave with the "pure purple" and "scarlet" thread (10:1). In the midst of this task, she encourages Gabriel:

> And she [Mary] took the pitcher and went forth to draw water, and behold, a voice said: *"Hail, thou art highly favored, [the Lord is with thee, blessed art thou] among women."* And she looked around on the right and on the left to see whence this voice came. And trembling she went to her house and put down the pitcher and took the purple and sat down on her seat and drew out (the thread). And Behold, an angel of the Lord (suddenly) stood before her and said: *"Do not fear, Mary; for you have found grace before the Lord of all things and shall conceive of his Word."* When she heard this she doubted in herself and said: "Shall I conceive of the Lord, the living God, [and bear] as every woman bears? *And the angel of the Lord said:* "Not so, Mary; for a *power* of the Lord *shall overshadow you; Wherefore also that holy thing which is born of you shall be called the Son of the Highest. And you shall call his name Jesus; for he shall save his people from their sins."* And Mary said, *"Behold, (I am) the handmaid of the Lord before him: be it to me according to your word"* (11.1–3).[7]

In subsequent interpretation, the Annunciation is a pivotal point, marking as it does a new start for humanity.[8] From early on in Christian interpretation, the Annunciation was seen as the moment when Mary, the "second Eve," reversed the havoc wrought by the first Eve (in much the same way that Christ, the "second Adam," provided a solution to the sin of the first Adam). Irenaeus (taking his cue from Paul's typology of Adam and Christ in Rom 5) framed his interpretation of the Annunciation in this way: "as the former [Eve] was led astray by an angel's discourse to fly from God after transgressing his word, so the latter [Mary] by an angel's discourse had the Gospel preached unto her that she might bear

God, in obedience to his Word. And if the former was disobedient to God,
yet the other was persuaded to obey God, that the Virgin Mary might become an advocate for the virgin Eve" (*Adv. omens haer.* 5.19.1; also Justin
Martyr, *Dialogue with Trypho*). In his widely popular thirteenth-century
work, Jacobus de Voragine continues and expands this comparison of the
Annunciation scene with the Fall:

> It was fitting that the Annunciation should precede the Incarnation
> . . . the order of reparation should correspond to the order of trans-
> gression or deviation. Therefore since the devil tempted the woman
> to lead her to doubt, through doubt to consent, and through con-
> sent to sinning, so the angel brought the message to the Virgin by
> the announcement to prompt her to believing, through believing to
> consent, and through consent to the conceiving of the Son of God.[9]

Further, the *Ave Maria,* a prayer immensely popular since the eleventh
century, is based on the Vulgate rendering of Gabriel's greeting: "Ave
gratia plena; Dominus tecum; benedicta tu in mulieribus" (Hail, [Mary]
highly favored one [traditional, full of grace]; the Lord is with you; blessed
are you among women).

Such focus on Mary's role in the Annunciation is not surprising. But
other details were amplified as well. For example, the presence of Gabriel
is lauded. St. Ambrose referred to Gabriel as the herald of the Holy Spirit
(*De Spirito Sancto,* 1), and St. Bernard of Clairvaux pointed out that the
meaning of Gabriel's name ("God's fortitude") was "in harmony with his
message" since the power of God announced the advent of Christ (*Hom.*
1). Likewise Voragine, in *The Golden Legend,* claimed that the Incarnation
made reparation not only for human transgression but also for "the fall of
the angels"; hence, it was appropriate for the harbinger of the Incarnation to be the angel, Gabriel, who was, in effect, proclaiming the coming
of the Savior not only for humankind but for the angels as well.[10] *The
Golden Legend* and pseudo-Bonventure's *Meditations on the Life of Christ*
were both important literary sources for Renaissance renditions of the
Annunciation.

The Artist and the Painting

The Florentine painter Leonardo da Vinci (1452–1519) is considered to
be the father of the High Renaissance style. Although the scholarship on
Leonardo is vast, discussions of the *Annunciation* (Figure 8) are limited.[11]

Leonardo da Vinci

Leonardo was born in Anchiano, near the Tuscan town of Vinci, on April 15, 1452, as the illegitimate first child of Ser Piero da Vinci and Caterina. Ser Piero's family members were property owners and notaries in Vinci. Leonardo's mother would later marry a resident of Vinci, and his father married four times after the birth of Leonardo. Tax documents reveal that Leonardo was raised in the house of his paternal grandfather, and he was quite close to his uncle Francesco da Vinci.[12] His father was a notary with a successful legal practice and was based in Florence beginning in 1469. This corresponds to Leonardo's matriculation in the painters' Compagnia di S. Luca in Florence in 1472. The beginning date of his training with Verrocchio (1435–88) is uncertain. That workshop provided Leonardo with experience in a wide range of materials and techniques: bronze, stone and terracotta sculptures; painting; and decorative work in metals and stones.

The first dated work (August 1, 1473) by Leonardo is a pen-and-ink drawing of a *Tuscan Landscape*.[13] The documentation between this work and his Milanese period, which began c. 1482, is very sparse and thus a problem for establishing the early portion of the artist's *oeuvre*.[14] This is precisely the period in which the *Annunciation* is believed to have been painted. Leonardo worked in Milan c. 1482–99 and painted some of his most famous works, including the *Virgin of the Rocks* (London, National Gallery) and the *Last Supper* (S. Maria delle Grazie, Milan). He was also frequently employed by the Sforza court in Milan during these years. Leonardo returned to Florence in 1500 and remained until mid-1508. There are numerous unfinished works from this period, but what is probably the most famous picture in the world, the *Mona Lisa* (Paris, Louvre), was also produced at this time.[15]

Leonardo returned to Milan in 1508 and worked initially for the French rulers of the city under the direction of the governor, Charles II d'Amboise, Comte de Chaumont.[16] The *Virgin of the Rocks* was finished, and he executed the *St. John the Baptist* (Paris, Louvre). A large number of Leonardo's anatomical drawings are dated to this period. In October 1513 Leonardo visited Florence on his way to Rome and was hosted by Giuliano de'Medici.[17] Leonardo assisted Giuliano in the military projects which he was working on for the Medici Pope, Leo X. Leonardo had frequently worked on various military fortifications and instrument designs throughout his career. The new French king, François I, attracted Leonardo to his homeland, where he is recorded as "First painter and engineer" to the King.[18] Leonardo took some of his most famous works with him to France

(*Mona Lisa, St. John the Baptist, Leda and the Swan,* and the *Virgin and Child with St. Anne*).[19] Leonardo died in Amboise, near Tours, on May 2, 1519, leaving most of his works, literary and artistic, to his assistant, Francesco Melzi, from Lombardy.[20]

We know much about Leonardo from thousands of pages of drawings and writings today known as his notebooks. Leonardo was left-handed and wrote from right to left, for his convenience. Leonardo's *Treatise on Painting* (compiled after his death by his pupil Francesco Melzi) extolled painting as a necessary element of the liberal arts. For Leonardo, painting was more important than poetry or music, because those depended on the ear, and the eye is the superior organ.[21]

His advancements in the manipulation of light and shade, color technique, and perspective are just a few of his many contributions to the study of painting. Leonardo set standards in figure drawing and draftsmanship still revered today and studied by studio artists around the world. Hartt may best summarize his thoughts:

> Leonardo was able to make innovations in both art and science by virtue of his conviction that the two were intimately interrelated. He did not consider them interchangeable, for science was to him an investigation of nature and art an expression of beauty. In both artistic and scientific activities he rejected authority and explored the natural world independently and without traditional prejudices or the restrictions put on investigations by religious beliefs. In an era in which the revived authority of antiquity competed with that of Christianity, he had little respect for either source. Final authority to Leonardo emanated from a single source: the human eye. No text, no matter what its pretensions to divine revelation or philosophic authority, could block the evidence of sight or impede the process of induction based on sight.[22]

Leonardo excelled as an architect, designer, theorist, engineer, and scientist.

The Patron, the Commission, and the Date

The *Annunciation* is usually dated between 1473 and 1478.[23] It entered the Uffizi collection in 1867 and was exhibited as a work by Leonardo. Before that the painting was owned by the monks of S. Bartolomeo at Monte Oliveto, outside Florence. There are no documents regarding the commission. The *Annunciation* has been the subject of various connoisseurship issues regarding attribution and dating because no early historian or biographer, including Vasari, mentions this work.[24] Although the dating is still discussed in the literature, scholars at least agree with an attribution of the composition's design, landscape, and figure of Gabriel to Leonardo. These issues of connoisseurship and the role of the workshop tradition are discussed fully in the stylistic analysis below.

According to Jack Wasserman, the monks apparently believed the painting was by Leonardo's younger contemporary, Domenico Ghirlandaio.[25] Wasserman finds the painting to have been executed in the studio of Verrocchio shortly after Leonardo's matriculation into the confraternity of St. Luke in 1472. Ghirlandaio was probably also in the studio at that time, 1473–75.

Stylistic and Iconographic Analysis

Artistic Sources and Technique

Since it is generally agreed that this early work by Leonardo was painted while he was in the studio or *bottega* of Andrea del Verrocchio, the master's style must be examined to understand the sources known to Leonardo. Verrocchio, the nickname of Andrea di Michele Cioni, means "true eye." This nickname was taken from a Florentine family who were early patrons of the artist.[26]

An example of Verrocchio's style that also shows its similarities to and differences from the style of Leonardo can be found in the joint work, *Baptism of Christ* (Figure 9), c. 1470, Uffizi Gallery, Florence. Verrocchio's composition style was simple, direct, and balanced. He placed the figure of Christ in the center foreground of the painting. John the Baptist is positioned to the right of Christ in the act of baptizing. Two angels kneel on the other side of Christ to balance the figure of John. The hands of God are open, freeing the spirit in the form of a dove, as John pours the water over Christ's head. Verrocchio emphasized the emotion and spirituality of the scene. Christ looks downward past his praying hands. John, emaciated from his prior time in the wilderness, moves toward Christ and is intensely focused on his task. The palm tree of eternal life on the left and the bluff on the right move the viewer's eyes backward into a correctly perspected composition. The hazy landscape in the background is a point of interest expanded upon in the works of Leonardo.

The hand of Leonardo is found in the leftmost kneeling angel whose face and hair have a softness not present in the other figures. The curves of the angel's face are in contrast to the hard edges of the faces of the other angel, Christ, and John. The method of expressing drama and emotion used by Verrocchio in painted and sculpted works influences the art of Leonardo.

Figure 9. Verrocchio and Leonardo da Vinci. *Baptism of Christ*. 1470.
Panel. Galleria degli Uffizi, Florence. Photo. With permission from
the Ministero dei Beni e le Attività Culturali.

Specific sources for the Annunciation theme in Florence, as mentioned
above, are vast. Leonardo was certainly familiar with the Italian Trecento
paintings of the Annunciation by Giotto, Duccio, Simone Martini, and the
Lorenzetti brothers.[27] Among the numerous Florentine paintings available
to Leonardo are the works of Fra Angelico (c. 1400?–1455) and Alesso
Baldovinetti (1425–99).[28] Sculptural models, such as those by Donatello
(c. 1386/90–1466) and Ghiberti (1381?–1455) would be studied by members of Verrocchio's *bottega*.[29] Stylistically, Leonardo's Gabriel and Mary
reflect the feminine type of figures found especially in the paintings of Botticelli (1445–1510).[30] It should also be noted that another, slightly later
scene of the *Annunciation* (Figure 10), today in the Louvre, Paris, is often
attributed to Leonardo da Vinci.[31]

The medium of the painting was believed to be oil on panel until
the 1998 monograph by Carlo Vecce, who identifies it as oil and tempera on panel.[32] Several contemporary drawings have been associated

and compared with this work.[33] These, like Leonardo's other two thousand surviving drawings confirm the importance he placed on the use of preparatory drawings.

The drapery, solid and sculptural, reveals Leonardo's method as recorded by Vasari: after soaking a piece of soft linen in gesso Leonardo would arrange it over a small figure and allow it to harden. He would then move this model into a satisfactory illumination and draw it with a brush on linen canvas before starting the final picture.[34]

Leonardo also uses *sfumato* and *chiaroscuro* in his paintings.[35] These painting methods give a realistic and three-dimensional quality to otherwise flat, two-dimensional panels. Leonardo received basic training in the technique of artist's perspective while in Verrocchio's *bottega*.[36] The *Annunciation* shows the beginning of Leonardo's technique of perspective that he will advance in his later works. The use of perspective in the *Annunciation* is addressed more thoroughly later in the chapter.

Product of the Workshop Tradition

There are several hands at work in this composition of the *Annunciation,* which is typical of the Renaissance workshop. By this time, Leonardo was a skilled assistant of Verrocchio and probably entrusted with the overall design of the composition. He executed some of the more difficult areas, such as the landscape and perhaps the voluminous drapery. He may also have assisted in the heads of the figures. Other artists were typically called upon to execute the application of paint based on a drawing by the master, in this case Leonardo.[37] Wasserman uses this as an explanation for why the paint has been applied thickly and crudely in some areas.[38] Although we do not agree with all of Wasserman's assertions regarding the specific areas painted or not painted by Leonardo, there is significant merit to his claim

Figure 10. Leonardo da Vinci or Lorenzo di Credi (?). *Annunciation.* 1478–85. Panel. Louvre, Paris. Copyright Erich Lessing/Art Resource, NY.

that the panel is a product of the workshop tradition. This may also explain the prior attribution to Domenico Ghirlandaio, who was in the workshop at this time and may have assisted Leonardo with this painting.[39]

Light and Color

The earthtones further unite the natural with the supernatural, foreground with the background, and vertical with the horizontal elements of the painting. John Shearman observes that, "In this picture, immature and inconsistent as it is in so many other ways, there are already two revolutionary principles of the greatest importance: every form is modeled independently of colour, and every coloured object is invested with a common range of tone."[40] This "tonal unity" results in a single, homogeneously colored figure as opposed to a traditional Quattrocento color-modeled figure which appears fragmented. It also unites light, color, and form in a more accurate rendering of their scientific and naturalistic behavior.[41] One of Leonardo's most significant contributions to painting occurs in the *Annunciation* and is explained by Shearman:

> Now, colour is a function of light; it appears and disappears according to the lighting condition, and its specific qualities at a given point are governed by the fall of the light upon it, and not by the properties of the pigment. In other words light is perceived as an exterior force, outside the object and governing the relative visibility of the properties of the object; the colour of the form is now, in the Albertian sense, one of its permanent qualities, rather than temporary or accidental ones.[42]

Perspective

The workshop of Verrocchio provided Leonardo with an excellent training in perspective based on the treatises of Leon Battista Alberti and Piero della Francesca.[43] The *Annunciation* once again reveals the work of a young artist painting in the way that he was trained and thus in the way expected. For example, the tiles on the floor are patterned in a diagonal orientation. Kemp recognizes this as a lateral point system and states that both the sculptors Donatello and Ghiberti used this method.[44] The Albertian system of perspective depends on a central axis leading to a vanishing point. Orthogonals, formed by continuing the lines of architectural elements, converge on this vanishing or focal point. The central axis in the *Annunciation* is located along the rearmost line of the balustrade. The orthogonals found by extending the lines of the lectern, the edges of the bricks, and the diagonally disposed tiles converge along the balustrade and form a vanishing point. Kemp identifies lines incised in the gesso priming of the square top of Mary's lectern.[45] Perhaps this is best explained in Leonardo's earliest written definition of perspective:

> Perspective is a rational demonstration by which experience confirms that the images of all things are transmitted to the eye by pyramidal lines. Those bodies of equal size will make greater or lesser angles in their pyramids according to the different distances between the one and the other. By a pyramid of lines I mean those which depart from the superficial edges of bodies and converge over a distance to be drawn together in a single point. A point is said to be that which cannot be divided into any parts, and such a point, located in the eye, received all the points of the pyramids.[46]

Perspective helps the mind's eye "read" a painting as having depth. As Leonardo's painting technique matures, his compositions become more perspectivally complex.

Iconography

The Annunciation is one of the most frequently depicted scenes in all the Bible, and until recently, many have thought that Leonardo contributed little by way of innovative interpretation of the scene. In fact, as late as 1982, Paul Caudile was able to write: "The iconography of Leonardo da Vinci's early masterpiece, the Uffizi *Annunciation,* has been accepted as being so traditional that a close analysis of its composition and meaning has never been undertaken."[47] In order to understand the significance of Leonardo's painting, it is necessary first to situate it within the larger context of Annunciation scenes.[48] Here we are not limited to sources and precedents that Leonardo may have used or been aware of. Rather, we are interested in the repertoire of Annunciation scenes, as well as contemporary interpretations of the text, which the audience may have brought to a viewing of Leonardo's work. Our strategy is similar to the one employed in interpreting the text of Luke itself. In the case of Luke 1:26–38, we demonstrated how knowing the pattern of the Old Testament commissioning story (e.g., Exod 3, Judg 6) sheds light on the Annunciation scene, in terms of how the Annunciation both repeats the Old Testament pattern and deviates from it. We also pointed out that Luke's use of this pattern several more times in the infancy narrative could shed light on its function in the Annunciation scene. So, too, understanding how Leonardo's depiction both repeats and deviates from the received visual tradition of Annunciations will illuminate our understanding of its reception by the authorial audience. Leonardo may also have painted another

Annunciation scene (Figure 10), and we may gain further insight by a comparison of the two. We will take up the iconography of the landscape setting, the figure of the angel Gabriel, and the figure of Mary in the Uffizi *Annunciation*.[49]

Landscape

The landscape is unquestionably by Leonardo. Even at this young age, his perception of painted atmosphere is apparent. Later on, Leonardo would comment on one's actual perception of horizons in the natural world: "In the successively more distant object, observe . . . first the contours are less clear, and then the parts of the composition, and finally the whole is less clear both in form and in color."[50]

Leonardo furthermore thought that artistic depictions of the natural world, including horizons, ought to correlate with the reality of that world. In the context of commenting about horizons, he wrote, "It is true that there should be some mountains, behind one another, at the sides, with color diminishing by degrees, as is required by the rule for the diminution of colors seen at great distances."[51] Hence, in our painting, the mist which hangs between the middle and far-off mountains is believable and creates a setting for the painting. Wasserman suggests that it creates the mood of dusk.[52] Luba Freedman has argued this "blurred horizon" is essential to comprehending the painting's meaning:

> Leonardo's obscuring of the horizon in the Annunciation perplexes the viewer: Leonardo's painting, of course, features a garden neighboring on a harbor, which is surrounded in turn by distant mountains. The indistinct outlines of the background, however, force the viewer's gaze to repeatedly shift between the foreground figures and the background view, just the type of active perception that Leonardo wished to arouse. The viewer has to confront the complexity of the background, which thus ceases to function as a mere foil for the foreground figures. The horizon's obscurity then assists Leonardo in rendering St. Luke's narration of the Annunciation as a mystery, and in demanding the same intense attention on the part of the viewer of the scene as would be required of a reader of the Gospel or a listener to a sermon on the subject.[53]

The horizon also serves to give an aesthetic and compositional unity of setting in the painting, a unity that was, as we shall see, a rare accomplishment in the history of Annunciation scenes.

David Robb points out that until the fourteenth century the setting of the Annunciation in visual art was "of relatively subordinate significance"

[handwritten margin note: Graduation of Annunciation Painting]

and was "not treated in a realistic fashion."[54] Beginning in the fourteenth century, "two general types can be distinguished, both of which continue through the fifteenth century. The first is that employed in Italy, where the setting usually contains some implication of an exterior, being either a portico or entirely in the open. The second is the ecclesiastical interior type, . . . which was employed almost exclusively in France during the fifteenth century, exceptions usually being of the Italian exterior type."[55] In either setting, whether exterior or interior, Gabriel and Mary typically occupied discrete spaces, separated by a wall or column or some other architectural means.[56]

Giotto, in one of the first representations of the subject to suggest a specific setting (*Annunciation,* Arena Chapel, Padua, 1305), depicts an open portico in which Gabriel and Mary are placed in separate bays. The impact of Giotto on subsequent Italian depictions is profound: "Reminiscences of this arrangement (a column separating the two figures, e.g.) are almost never absent from Italian representations of the Annunciation, even as late as the end of the fifteenth century, and are often found as a traditional element in examples which are much more realistic in other respects."[57] Until the work by Jacopo del Casentino (1320), even those depictions that placed Gabriel and Mary in an interior space tended to separate the two figures by some architectural means, usually a pillar of some sort.[58]

Compositionally, Leonardo's *Annunciation* follows the Italian tradition of setting the Annunciation outdoors, but "he goes so far as to eliminate the portico altogether in his *Annunciations* in the Uffizi and the Louvre."[59] Further, while the Uffizi *Annunciation* can be divided into two equal parts giving both Mary and Gabriel their own space, clearly the landscape renders Leonardo's composition symmetrical, organized, and harmonious. The landscape serves to connect these parts by a set of horizontal, parallel lines formed by the parapet and ground behind the figures. The landscape of three cypress trees behind Gabriel is vertically balanced by the single cypress and quoins of the *pietra serena* architecture behind Mary. Whether the garden of grass and flowers in which Gabriel kneels reflects botanical accuracy is hotly debated,[60] but it does seem to be in keeping with the spirit of the spring season with which the feast day of the Annunciation (March 25) was traditionally associated.[61] The flowers most certainly would have recalled for Leonardo's audience an association with Nazareth, given their widespread association at the time with that village. Noteworthy, for example, is the *Summa Theologica* of the archbishop of Florence, Antonino Pierozzi, whose work would have been available by the 1460s and who explicitly identifies Nazareth with a richly flowering field.[62] The landscape behind Gabriel, devoid of people or human-made

[handwritten margin note: A Key]

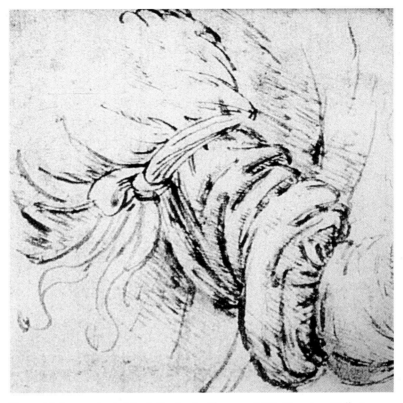

Figure 11. Leonardo da Vinci. *Study of a Sleeve.* c. 1475. Drawing. Galleria degli Uffizi, Florence. Photo. With permission from the Ministero dei Beni e le Attività Culturali.

objects, may allude to the Garden of Eden and subtly suggest that Mary is the "New Eve,"[63] commissioned here to give birth to the New Adam who will come to reverse the sinful actions of the first Adam.[64]

This aesthetic unification highlights the very moment of exchange between Gabriel and Mary, as do the presence of a port city with ships and towers in the distance. Perhaps even more important are K. R. Eissler's observations: "It is remarkable — as I think has not been sufficiently considered — that no human beings at all appear in those landscapes.... All this conveys the impression of a strict separation of the world of man from nature."[65] The lack of human presence in the landscape draws the audience's attention to the main figures in the foreground, Gabriel and Mary.

Gabriel

The figure of the angel is often cited as support for a secure attribution to Leonardo. A comparison with the angel in the *Baptism of Christ*

(Figure 9) reveals a beauty and softness conveyed through the handling of light and volume in both figures.[66] There is a contemporary drawing of a sleeve by Leonardo (Figure 11) which is quite similar to Gabriel's sleeve.[67] The drapery style of Gabriel is voluminous and elegant. Gabriel wears an off-white undergarment. The neckline contains a gold band below the raised collar. The thick, red mantle has fallen off his raised arm and is folded back to reveal a green interior lining. The weight of the mantle drapes over Gabriel's bent right leg. Light reflected off of the upper half of this kneeling leg accentuates the deep folds and texture of the drapery.

In both of Leonardo's *Annunciations* (Figures 8 and 10), Gabriel kneels before Mary and raises his right arm toward her. This particular posture was one of several that the angel assumed in Annunciation scenes. In some depictions, Gabriel is depicted as a "flying" or "floating" angel (cf. Giovanni da Milano's Prato altarpiece, 1364). The "flying angel," according to Robb, "appears to have developed from the walking angel of the Italo-Byzantine scheme, which itself derives from the classic Nike, the act of flying being suggested by the levitation of the walking figure."[68] The standing or walking angel is also common in medieval annunciation scenes (cf. Rome S. Maria in Trastevere). More rarely depicted is the so-called "diving angel." The "diving angel" is most often used in subjects related to the Annunciation and not usually in the Annunciation itself (an exception is Taddeo Gaddi's *Annunciation* in the Baroncelli Chapel in S. Croce). And, of course, the kneeling angel, as we have here, is a common posture in the history of Annunciation depictions.[69]

The significance of depicting the angel kneeling as opposed to standing and especially floating or diving is that it suggests that the encounter between Gabriel and Mary has begun. Appropriately, Gabriel's hand is in the traditional blessing gesture of extending the first two fingers. He kneels in reverence before the mother of his Lord. The long-stemmed lily he holds is symbolic both of the purity of the Virgin and also of the good news of new life that he has been sent to announce. Leonardo has captured the very moment of the Annunciation, not just some moment prior to it or after it. As such, the viewer is led to recall the greeting extended by Gabriel to Mary: "Greetings, thou art highly favored! the Lord is with you! Blessed are you among women!" (*Ave gratia plena Dominus tecum benedicta tu in mulieribus*).[70]

The Lectern and the Bible

In Leonardo's Uffizi *Annunciation*, Gabriel interrupts Mary as she is reading. There is a lectern with elaborate sculptural detail placed between

Mary and Gabriel (Figure 12). Functionally, the lectern serves to hold Mary's Bible, but as Caudile rightly observes, "the overall design of the tomb as interpreted by Leonardo in so central a Christian mystery as the Incarnation requires by the sheer prominence of its location in the Uffizi composition a sacred Christian meaning."[71] Caudile's observations about the lectern are particularly illuminating:

> The lion hocks are frequently found in images associated with Mary at the Annunciation . . . and are used as supports in small portable altar tables. The lion as a symbol of majesty is well-known, and it may also serve as a symbol for the Incarnation. The stylized acanthus leaves stemming from the lion hocks are attributes of Mary, while the garland of pears symbolizes Mary's sweetness in the eyes

Figure 12. Leonardo da Vinci. Detail of sepulchral urn. *Annunciation.* Photo. With permission from the Ministero dei Beni e le Attività Culturali.

of God....The scallop shell at the top of the lectern's base is an object which refers to heaven when found as a part of a ceiling in an architectural setting. If it has any symbolic meaning at all in the Uffizi image, it refers to the heavenly sphere....[72]

The lectern had not always been part of the Annunciation iconography. A number of Byzantine examples of the Annunciation evidently draw on details from the apocryphal gospels. Some place her by a well at the time of Gabriel's arrival, a detail mentioned in *Pseudo-Matthew* 9 (written down in the eighth or ninth century). Others depict Mary holding a spindle, evidently inspired by *Protevangelium of James* 11[73] and *Pseudo-Matthew* 9, which state that the Virgin was engaged in spinning thread for the veil of the temple when Gabriel appeared.[74] By the fourteenth century, the spindle had been almost universally replaced by the book and lectern. This lectern has been variously identified as a sepulchral urn, a sarcophagus, or a Roman altar. Too large, however, to be an urn and too square to be a sarcophagus, the lectern is best understood as an altar, thus contributing to the understanding of Mary's priestly role in humanity's salvation.[75] This interpretation of Mary as priestess had already been suggested in the writings of Antonino Pierozzi, archbishop of Florence. Furthermore, the port and ships in the landscape reflect Mary's title of "Star of the Sea" (underscored in the medieval hymn, *Ave Maris Stella*) and "Port of the Shipwrecked," another allusion to her important intercessory role in redemption.[76]

What of the book which lay open and fluttering on this altar? Presumably, the blowing of the pages is a clue that Garbriel has just flown in! It is impossible to make out the words on the page where Mary has stopped (Figure 13), but we are helped by texts like pseudo-Bonaventure's *Meditations on the Life of Christ*, which suggests that Mary may have been reading Isaiah's prophecy of the virginal birth at the moment Gabriel appeared.[77] Thus, it is reasonable to expect that the authorial audience, knowing traditions like that of pseudo-Bonaventure, would have imagined that Mary had marked the place in Isaiah which reads, "A virgin shall conceive and bear a son" (cf. Isa 7:14, KJV, and Matt 1:25). The many images of Mary where this text is legible support this point.

Mary

Iconographically, Mary is the central figure in the painting. The fingers of her left hand mark the page from which she had been reading as the book blows closed.[78] Her left hand is raised although her upper body remains in a vertical posture. Leonardo uses the traditionally colored drapery for Mary.

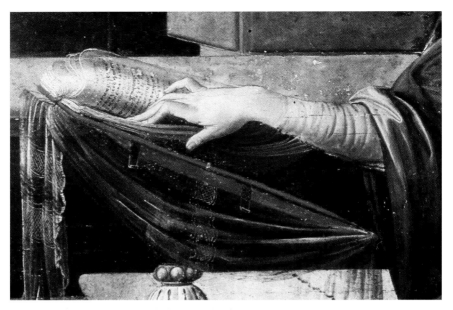

Figure 13. Leonardo da Vinci. Detail of Mary's book. *Annunciation.* Photo. With permission from the Ministero dei Beni e le Attività Culturali.

The pink gown with bodice reveals a slender figure without overly accentuating the breasts. The application of paint on Mary's face is thick and opaque, which is not typical of Leonardo. This may be evidence of another hand working on the composition. This will be further discussed below.

As with Gabriel, artists positioned Mary in a variety of postures. In some early Eastern representations, Mary is depicted standing when Gabriel arrives (cf. Homilies of Gregory Nazianzenus, Paris, B.N. ms. Gr. 510). In other medieval depictions, she is found kneeling.[79] And, of course, any number of artists depict Mary seated, as does Leonardo here. By portraying her in a seated position, Leonardo is able to allude to Mary's impending pregnancy. The royal blue mantle, with yellow lining, draped over her lap subtly emphasizes the separation of her thighs and knees, a typical birthing metaphor.

Michael Baxandall has shed additional and considerable light on the way in which visual depictions of the Annunciation in general, and Mary's reaction in particular, may have been understood in fifteenth-century Italy.[80] He cites a sermon by Fra Roberto Caracciolo da Lecce on the Annunciation as being typical of the theological categories through which visual depictions like that of Leonardo may have been viewed by the original audience. Fra Roberto distinguished three mysteries of the Annunciation: the angelic mission, the angelic salutation, and the angelic colloquy. The last mystery is of particular interest to our understanding the significance of Mary's gesture. Fra Roberto attributed five successive spiritual states to Mary:

> The third mystery of the Annunciation is called Angelic Colloquy; it comprises five laudable Conditions of the Blessed Virgin:
>
> 1. *Conturbatio* — Disquiet
> 2. *Cogitatio* — Reflection
> 3. *Interrogatio* — Inquiry
> 4. *Humiliatio* — Submission
> 5. *Meritatio* — Merit
>
> The first laudable condition is called *Conturbatio*; as St. Luke writes, when the Virgin heard the Angel's salutation — *"Hail, thou art highly favored, the Lord is with thee; blessed art thou among women"* — *she was troubled.* This disquiet, as Nicholas of Lyra writes, came not from incredulity but from wonder, since she was used to seeing angels and marvelled not at the fact of the Angel's apparition so much as at the lofty and grand salutation, in which the Angel made plain for her such great and marvellous things, and at which she in her humility was astonished. . . .
>
> Her second laudable condition is called *Cogitatio: she cast in her mind what manner of salutation this should be.* This shows the prudence of the most Holy Virgin. So then *the angel said unto her, Fear not, Mary: for thou has found favour with God. And, behold, thou shalt conceive in thy womb, and bring forth a son, and shalt call his name JESUS.* . . .
>
> The third laudable condition is called *Interrogatio. Then said Mary unto the angel, How shall this be, seeing I know not a man?* That is to say, . . . "seeing I have the firm resolve, inspired by God and confirmed by my own will, never to know a man?" Francis Mayron says of this "One could say the glorious Virgin desired to be a virgin more than to conceive the Son of God without virginity, since virginity is laudable, while to conceive a son is only honourable, being not a virtue but the reward for virtue; and the virtue is more desirable than its reward, since virtue subsumes merit whereas reward does not." For that reason this modest, pure, chaste, maidenly lover of virginity inquired how a virgin could conceive.
>
> The fourth laudable condition is called *Humiliatio.* What tongue could ever describe, indeed, what mind could contemplate the movement and style with which she set on the ground her holy knees? Lowering her head she spoke: *Behold the handmaid of the Lord.* She

did not say "Lady"; she did not say "Queen." Oh profound humility! Oh extraordinary gentleness! "Behold," she said, "the slave and servant of my Lord." And then, lifting her eyes to heaven, and bringing up her hands with her arms in the form of a cross, she ended as God, the Angels, and the Holy Fathers desired: *Be it unto me according to thy word. . . .*

The fifth laudable condition is called *Meritatio. . . .* When she had said these words, the Angel departed from her. And the bounteous Virgin at once had Christ, God incarnate, in her womb, according with that wonderful condition I spoke of in my ninth sermon. So we can justly suppose that in the moment when the Virgin Mary conceived Christ her soul rose to such lofty and sublime contemplation of the action and sweetness of divine things that, in the presence of the beatific vision, she passed beyond the experience of every other created being. And the bodily sensations of the Child being present in her womb rose again with indescribable sweetness. Probably, in her profound humility, she raised her eyes to heaven and then lowered them towards her womb with many tears, saying something like, "Who am I, that have conceived God incarnate. . . ."[81]

We are, of course, not suggesting that Leonardo or his audience heard this particular sermon of Fra Roberto — it was after all published some twenty years after the Uffizi *Annunciation* was completed. We do, however, wish to argue that Fra Roberto's sermon, far from a unique or idiosyncratic interpretation of the Annunciation, rather represented the conventional thinking about this text in fifteenth-century Italy. Further, as Baxandall has observed: "Most fifteenth-century Annunciations are identifiably Annunciations of Disquiet, or of Submission, or — theses being less clearly distinguished from each other — of Reflection and/or Inquiry. The preachers coached the public in the painters' repertory, and the painters responded within the current emotional categorization of the event."[82] Baxandall then goes on to cite examples from Florentine Annunciations, painted between 1440 and 1460, of each of the Laudable Conditions: (1) Disquiet — Filippo Lippi, Florence, S. Lorenzo, Panel; (2) Reflection — Master of the Barberini Panels, Washington, National Gallery of Art, Kress Collection, Panel; (3) Inquiry — Alesso Baldovinetti, Florence, Uffizi, Panel; (4) Submission — Fra Angelico, Florence, Museo di S. Marco, Fresco.[83] Baxandall notes that the fifth condition, merit, "belongs with representations of the Virgin on her own." Baxandall further comments that "though we, unprompted by Fra Roberto, respond to a general sense of excitement or thoughtfulness or humility in a picture of the scene, the more explicit categories of the fifteenth century can sharpen our perceptions of the differences. They remind us, for instance, that Fra Angelico in his many Annunciations never really breaks away from the type of *Humiliatio;* while Botticelli has a dangerous affinity with *Conturbatio. . . .*"[84]

Leonardo's *Annunciation* belongs to the category of *Conturbatio,* though clearly he is not given to excesses of emotional display.[85] In fact, the portrayal of Mary here corresponds with Leonardo's own observations about tendencies toward the violent mode in other artistic renderings of the Annunciation:

> . . . some days ago I saw the picture of an angel who, in making the Annunciation, seemed to be trying to chase Mary out of her room, with movements showing the sort of attack one might make on some hated enemy; and Mary, as if desperate, seemed to be trying to throw herself out of the window. Do not fall into errors like these.[86]

Mary's upraised left hand should not, therefore, be taken as a sign of surprise.[87] The gesture, rather, seems to be one more of affirmation or welcome than disquiet (and thus is similar to the gesture of Venus welcoming Spring in Botticelli's famous *Primavera,* c. 1482, Uffizi, Florence).[88] Interpreting fifteenth-century visual depictions of the Annunciation within the fifteenth-century categories of emotional experience sheds considerable light on the probable impact of the painting on the authorial audience, and ultimately, on the contemporary audience as well. Thus, despite the dangers of emotional excess, of the various conditions available to him, Leonardo chooses to render the moment of Gabriel's greeting, *"Ave gratia plena Dominus tecum,"* and the affirming welcome of Mary's response. Of what hermeneutical value to the contemporary faith community is this quattrocento visual interpretation?

Conclusion

The words Gabriel speaks to Mary, *Dominus tecum,* were slightly revised (changing the "you" from singular to plural) and became the beginning of the liturgy for Holy Communion where the presider said, *"Dominus vobiscum."* Unfortunately, in most English translations, these words are rendered, "The Lord be with you!" to which the congregation responds, "And also with you." Both the Latin and Greek are missing the verb, and as W. C. van Unnik has pointed out, in such cases it is customary to supply "is."[89] This shift has profound theological implications. Whereas the translation "the Lord be with you" suggests nothing more than a mere wish or pious hope, the phrase *Dominus vobiscum*, "the Lord IS with you," "announces the indispensable prerequisite that God's Spirit is given to people to enable them to do the work of God."[90] This very greeting "troubled" Mary, not because it was delivered by an angel, as Fra Roberto reminds us, "since she was used to seeing angels and marvelled not at the fact of the Angel's apparition" but rather "from wonder... at the lofty and grand salutation, in which the Angel made plain for her such great and marvellous things, and at which she in her humility was astonished." Leonardo's *Annunciation* serves also as a visual reminder of the humble astonishment that we, no less than Mary, should experience when we hear those powerful words: *Dominus vobiscum*. The Lord IS with you!

Notes

1. Although most scholars state the painting was commissioned for this monastery, no archival documentation has been located. Several recent monographs list the monastery only as the beginning of the known provenance. This is discussed in more detail later in the chapter.

2. The *Annunciation* is 38 ¾ x 85 ½″. The painting underwent restoration from 1999 to 2001, which will certainly result in important scientific and art historical scholarship in the near future.

3. Charles Talbert (*Reading Luke: A Literary and Theological Commentary on the Third Gospel* [New York: Crossroad, 1982], 18) sees theophanies as the stereotypical pattern on which the Annunciation is based and concludes that "in such a form the emphasis is not on the parent(s), but on the child as the fulfillment of the divine promise." See also Raymond E. Brown, *The Birth of the Messiah: A Commentary on the Infancy Narratives in the Gospels of Matthew and Luke* (Garden City, N.Y.: Doubleday, 1977), 156–59, 296–97.

4. We have slightly modified Raymond Brown's proposal in *An Introduction to the New Testament* (New York: Doubleday, 1997), 230–31. For yet another still slightly different analysis, see Benjamin Hubbard, "Commissioning Stories in Luke-Acts: A Study of Their Antecedents, Form and Content," *Semeia* 8 (1977): 103–26. For an application of Hubbard's study to the Lukan infancy narrative, see Robert Tannehill, *Luke* (Nashville: Abingdon Press, 1996), 43–44. Further, literary critic Robert Alter has pointed to the importance of the form of these stories, which he calls "type scenes," though he examines only "annunciation" stories; cf. Robert Alter, "How Conventions Help Us Read," *Prooftexts* 3 (1983): 115–30. Although our texts are annunciation stories, Luke uses the convention in several "non-annunciation" contexts in which the notion of commission seems to be the unifying theme.

5. R. Alan Culpepper ("Luke," *The New Interpreter's Bible* [vol. 9; Nashville: Abingdon, 1995], 51) also explores the connection of Mary's being troubled with the story in the apocryphal book of Tobit, that "tells of a jealous angel who appeared on a bride's wedding night each time she married and killed her bridegroom."

6. For more on the parallels between the births of John the Baptist and Jesus, see Mark Coleridge, *The Birth of the Lukan Narrative: Narrative as Christology in Luke 1–2* (Journal for the Study of the New Testament Supplement Series 88; Sheffield: Sheffield Academic Press, 1993), 51–74.

7. The translation is taken from Wilhelm Schneemelcher, ed., *New Testament Apocrypha* (trans. R. McL. Wilson; vol. 1; Philadelphia: Westminster, 1963), 380. The italicized words, found in Schneemelcher, indicate a verbatim quote of the canonical text.

8. See Phillip Rogers, "Annunciation," in *A Dictionary of Biblical Tradition in English Literature* (ed. David Lyle Jeffrey; Grand Rapids: Eerdmans, 1992), 43–44. For a full history of interpretation of the annunciation story in patristic to medieval sources, see Maria Elizabeth Gössmann, *Die Verkündigung an Maria: im Dogmatischen Verständnis des Mittelalters* (Munich: Max Hueber, 1957).

9. Jacobus de Voragine, *The Golden Legend: Readings on the Saints* (trans. William Granger Ryan; Princeton, N.J.: Princeton University Press, 1993), 1:196.

10. Ibid.

11. The most frequently cited monographs in English include: Ludwig Heydenreich, *Leonardo da Vinci* (London: Allen and Unwin, 1954); Cecil Gould, *Leonardo: The Artist and the Non-artist* (London: Wiedenfeld and Nicolson, 1975); Carlo Pedretti, *Leonardo da Vinci: A Study in Chronology and Style* (Berkeley and Los Angeles: University of California Press, 1973); Jack Wasserman, *Leonardo* (New York: Harry N. Abrams, 1975); Martin Kemp, *Leonardo da Vinci: The Marvellous Works of Nature and Man* (Cambridge, Mass.: Harvard University Press, 1981). David Arasse, *Léonard de Vinci: Le rythme du monde* (Paris: Haxan, 1997); Rafaelle Monti, *Leonardo da Vinci: dalla Adorazione dei Magi alla Annunciazione* (Livorno: Sillabe, 1998); Carlo Vecce, *Leonardo* (Roma: Salerno Editrice, 1998); Alessandro Vezzosi, *Leonardo da Vinci: The Mind of the Renaissance* (New York: Harry N. Abrams, 1997). Mauro Guerrini is currently preparing a compilation of Leonardo bibliography.

12. Martin Kemp, "Leonardo da Vinci," in *Dictionary of Art* (ed. Jane Turner; 34 vols.; New York: Grove's Dictionaries, 1996), 19:180.

13. Ibid., 181.

14. Ibid. According to Kemp there are two documented commissions during this Florentine period. The first commission is in January 1478 for an altarpiece in the chapel of S. Bernardo in the Palazzo della Signoria. The second recorded commission from this period was in March 1481 for an altarpiece, believed to be the unfinished *Adoration of the Magi* (Florence, Uffizi), in S. Donato a Scoperto.

15. For a discussion of the dating and identification of the sitter, see Kemp, *Dictionary*, 184.

16. Ibid., 185.

17. Ibid.

18. Ibid., 186. This title was recorded by the secretary to Cardinal Louis of Aragon, Ambrogio de'Beatis, on the occasion of the Cardinal's visit to the King on October 10, 1517.

19. Ibid.

20. Ibid., 187.

21. See Frederick Hartt, *History of Italian Renaissance Art* (4th ed.; revised by David G. Wilkins; New York: Harry N. Abrams, 1994), 432.

22. Ibid., 430.

23. Kemp (*Dictionary*, 187) dates the painting to c. 1473. Wasserman (*Leonardo*, 54) dates it between 1473 and 1475. Pedretti (*Leonardo da Vinci*, 30) gives it the date of about 1478–80. Hartt (*History of Italian Renaissance*, 437) uses "late 1470s" for its date. Vecce (*Leonardo*, 46–47) considers it Leonardo's first work after entering St. Luke's confraternity in 1472.

24. Bruno Santi, *Leonardo da Vinci* (Florence: Scala, 1975), 10.

25. Wasserman, *Leonardo*, 54. For a discussion of Domenico Ghirlandaio, see chapter 4.

26. Hartt, *History of Italian Renaissance Art*, 323.

27. Giotto (c. 1277–1337), *Annunciation*, commissioned by Enrico Scrovegni, Arena Chapel, Padua, after 1305, fresco; Duccio (active 1278–1318), *Annunciation*, from the *Maestà*, commissioned by the Opera del Duomo, Siena, 1308–11, panel; Simone Martini (active 1315–44), *Annunciation with Two Saints*, commissioned by the Opera del Duomo for the cathedral of Siena, 1333, panel; Pietro Lorenzetti (c. 1290–1348?), *Madonna and Child with Saints, Annunciation and Assumption*, commissioned by Bishop Guido for the Pieve di Sta. Maria, Arezzo, 1320, panel.

28. Fra Angelico, *Annunciation*, in monk's cell, Monastery of S. Marco, Florence, 1438–45, fresco; Alesso Baldovinetti, *Annunciation*, commissioned by the Salvestrini Fathers for S. Giorgio alla Costa, Florence, 1460, panel.

29. The works of these two artists become significant in the study of perspective discussed later in this text. See also Martin Kemp, *The Science of Art: Optical Themes in Western Art from Brunelleschi to Seurat* (New Haven and London: Yale University Press, 1990), 44.

30. See Vecce, *Leonardo*, 46–47.

31. Ibid. This panel was part of the predella of the *Madonna di Piazza* altarpiece in the Duomo, Pistoia. It was commissioned to Verrocchio, but may have been executed by Lorenzo di Credi between 1478 and 1485. The Louvre maintains the attribution to Lorenzo di Credi.

32. Ibid., 387 n. 62. It is certainly possible that Leonardo experimented with the blending of tempera and oil, but it should also be recognized that several areas, such as the face and right hand of Mary, have been extensively overpainted. See Wasserman, *Leonardo*, 58. Again, the results of the current restoration may produce more scientifically conclusive results.

33. Wasserman (*Leonardo*, 54–57) discusses two contemporary drawings: fig. 38, *Study of a Sleeve*, Christ Church, Oxford; fig. 12, *Study of Hands*, Royal Library, Windsor Castle. Hartt, *History of Italian Renaissance Art*, 437, dates a *Study of Drapery*, fig. 454, National Gallery, Rome, to the 1470s.

34. The observations in this paragraph can be found in Hartt, *History of Italian Renaissance Art*, 437. See also K. R. Eissler, *Leonardo da Vinci: Psychoanalytic Notes on the Enigma* (New York: International Universities Press, 1961), 302–3.

35. Hartt, *History of Italian Renaissance Art*, 667. Hartt defines *sfumato:* "Italian term for smoky, used for the method developed by Leonardo da Vinci of modelling figures by virtually imperceptible gradations from light to dark." Hartt (*History of Italian Renaissance Art*, 663) defines *chiaroscuro:* "In painting, the contrast of light and shade — from the Italian *chiaro* (light) and *oscuro* (dark) — to enhance modeling."

36. Kemp, *The Science of Art*, 44.

37. Jacque Mensil in, "Botticelli, les Pollaiuolo et Verrocchio," *Rivista d'Arte* II–III (1905): 37, has difficulty deciphering the hand of Verrocchio from that of Leonardo in the *Annunciation*. More recently, see Arasse, *Léonard de Vinci*, 297.

38. Wasserman, *Leonardo*, 58.

39. For additional discussion of the attribution issue, see Marco Rosci, *The Hidden Leonardo* (Milan: Arnoldo Mondadori, 1976), 28–30.

40. John Shearman, "Leonardo's Colour and Chiaroscuro," *Zeitschrift für Kunstgeschichte* 25 (1962): 16–17.

41. Ibid., 18. More recently, see Arasse, *Léonard de Vinci*, 296–97.

42. Ibid. Shearman refers to Leon Battista Alberti, who wrote a treatise on painting (Latin, 1435; Italian, 1436) frequently consulted by contemporary artists. See L. B. Alberti, *Della Pittura* (ed. Luigi Mallé; Florence: Sansoni, 1950), 56.

43. Kemp, *The Science of Art*, 44.

44. Ibid. See also Kemp, figs. 72, 73, for perspective diagrams. See also Kim H. Veltman and Kenneth D. Keele, *Studies on Leonardo da Vinci I. Linear Perspective and the Visual Dimensions of Science and Art* (Munich: Deutscher Kunstverlag, 1986), pls. 2.1, 2.2.

45. Kemp, *The Science of Art*, 44. More recently, see Arasse, *Léonard de Vinci*, 293–94.

46. Cited by Kemp, *The Science of Art*, 45n. 88.

47. Paul J. Caudile, "Observations on the Iconography of Leonardo da Vinci's Uffizi 'Annunciation,'" *Studies in Iconography* 7–8 (1981–82): 189. In fact, Caudile offers just such a close analysis, and we are indebted throughout this section to his insights, though we think the moment depicted extends beyond the *"Ave gratia plena"* to include the rest of Gabriel's greeting, *"Dominus tecum."* The importance of this point will be seen later.

48. For a history of Annunciation scenes in art, see David M. Robb, "The Iconography of the Annunciation in the Fourteenth and Fifteenth Centuries," *Art Bulletin* 18 (1936): 480–526. Also see Helen Rosenau, "A Study in the Iconography of the Incarnation," *Burlington Magazine* 85 (1944): 176–79.

49. Caudile ("Observations on the Iconography of Leonardo da Vinci's Uffizi 'Annunciation,'" 191), who had the opportunity to examine radiographs of the painting, observes that the open window above Mary's head was originally barred. He then makes this fascinating observation: "A barred window, the fenestra cancellata, is a symbol of Mary's purity and may be found in some Florentine and Sienese images. It is linked symbolically with the Incarnation, since the window is seen as the window of heaven and the bars as the mortal ladder by which Christ assumed human flesh. The reason for Leonardo's alteration of the symbol in the final version of his painting can only be conjectured. However, the moment of the event, the *"'Ave gratia plena,'* might have made the inclusion of this symbol of the Incarnation less meaningful than in an Annunciation representing the moment of the *'Ecce ancilla domini.'* An open window, which may symbolize Mary as the window of heaven thus emphasizing her role rather than the deed, would be more in keeping with the overall iconography of the Uffizi image."

50. Leonard da Vinci, *Treatise on Painting* (ed. A. P. McMahon; Princeton, N.J.: Princeton University Press, 1956), 1:93.

51. Ibid., 1:331.

52. Wasserman, *Leonardo*, 58.

53. Luba Freedman, "The 'Blurred' Horizon in Leonardo's Paintings," *Gazette des Beaux Arts* 129 (1997): 188.

54. Robb, "The Iconography of the Annunciation in the Fourteenth and Fifteenth Centuries," 485.

55. Ibid., 500. In some cases, a mixture of exterior/interior is presented, with Mary standing in the doorway of her abode to receive approaching Gabriel. In these scenes, the threshold of the doorway serves to delineate and define the separate spaces assigned to Mary and Gabriel.

56. See also John Spencer, "Spatial Imagery of the Annunciation in Fifteenth Century Florence," *Art Bulletin* 37 (1955): 273–80.

57. Robb, "The Iconography of the Annunciation in the Fourteenth and Fifteenth Centuries," 486.

58. Ibid., 488. The artist Casentino replaces the column with a lectern, "thus acknowledging the traditional dichotomy but making it less emphatic."

59. Ibid., 519. Caudile ("Observations on the Iconography of Leonardo da Vinci's Uffizi 'Annunciation,'" 191) thinks that some interpreters (including Robb) have overestimated the innovativeness of Leonardo's setting.

60. Hartt (*History of Italian Renaissance,* 437), for example, argues for the botanical accuracy in the Uffizi *Annunciation,* while Caudile ("Observations on the Iconography of Leonardo da Vinci's Uffizi 'Annunciation,'" 193–94) argues that "upon close examination, however, the plants and trees in the Uffizi work prove to be fantasy images." For a discussion of botanical accuracy at this time in Florence, see Mirella Levi d'Anconca, *Botticelli's 'Primavera', a botanical interpretation including astrology, alchemy and the Medici* (Florence: L. S. Olschki, 1983).

61. Caudile, "Observations on the Iconography of Leonardo da Vinci's Uffizi 'Annunciation,'" 193.

62. See Antonino Pierozzi, *Summa,* tit. 15, cap. 9, c. 971; cited by Caudile, 201. See also note 81 below on the sermon on the Annunciation by Fra Roberto. At one point he makes this connection between Nazareth and flowers.

63. Caudile, "Observations on the Iconography of Leonardo da Vinci's Uffizi 'Annunciation,'" 192. On the theme of Mary as the new Eve, see Jaraslov Pelikan, *Mary Through the Centuries* (New Haven: Yale University Press, 1996).

64. Caudile, "Observation on the 'Iconography of Leonardo da Vinci's Uffizi 'Annunciation,'" 192.

65. Eissler, *Leonardo da Vinci,* 307.

66. Wasserman, *Leonardo,* 56. Wasserman states that the baptism angel is far superior to the Annunciation angel: "The head of the later angel (Uffizi) fails to evolve as a three-dimensional volume in space; it is flat and rather disjointed, for all the gentle modeling of surfaces. Furthermore the hair is strangely stiff and dry without the silken curls and sparkling light we see in the *Baptism* angel."

67. Ibid.

68. Robb, "The Iconography of the Annunciation in the Fourteenth and Fifteenth Centuries," 487.

69. Gabriel here, as in most renditions, enters the scene from the viewer's left. A minority of depictions, however, have Gabriel enter, as it were, on stage right. On those images and their significance, see Don Denny, *The Annunciation from the Right from Early Christian Times to the Sixteenth Century* (New York: Garland, 1977).

70. We might note at this point that the figure of the Christ Child is one element missing from Leonardo's *Annunciation,* but present in some fourteenth- and fifteenth-century Annunciations. For a discussion of possible explanations, see the appendix in Robb's article, 523–26.

71. Caudile, "Observations on the Iconography of Leonardo da Vinci's Uffizi 'Annunciation,'" 191.

72. Ibid., 191–92.

73. See our earlier comments on this text under Subsequent History of Interpretation.

74. Robb, "The Iconography of the Annunciation in the Fourteenth and Fifteenth Centuries," 481.

75. Caudile, "Observations on the Iconography of Leonardo da Vinci's Uffizi 'Annunciation,'" 191–92. On Mary's role as priestess, see below.

76. See ibid., 192–93, who cites Antonino (*Summa,* Tit. 15, cap. 13, cc. 999–1001) in support of this interpretation.

77. *Meditations on the Life of Christ* (trans. Isa Ragusa; ed. Isa Ragusa and Rosalie B. Green; Princeton, N.J.: Princeton University Press, 1961), chapter 3.

78. According to Wasserman, *Leonardo,* 58, "The fingers … were later lengthened to give them a slender elegance that is reminiscent of a drawing of hands by Leonardo at Windsor Castle."

79. See E. Baldwin Smith, *Early Christian Iconography* (Princeton, N.J.: Princeton University Press, 1918), 11–13 for examples.

80. Michael Baxandall, *Painting and Experience in Fifteenth-Century Italy: A Primer in the Social History of Pictorial Style* (2d ed.; Oxford: Oxford University Press, 1988), 49–56. Caudile ("Observations on the Iconography of Leonardo da Vinci's Uffizi 'Annunciation,'" 189–90) cites several other writers, ancient and modern, who suggest from three to seven discrete moments in the Annunciation scene. All of them agree that Gabriel's greeting would have constituted the first moment, and, as we shall see, Leonardo's depiction belongs to this first moment, no matter how the scenes are counted.

81. Robertus Caracciolus, *Sermones de laudibus sanctorum* (Naples 1489), cxlic r.–clii r; translation given by Baxandall, *Painting and Experience in Fifteenth-Century Italy,* 51, 55.

82. Baxandall, *Painting and Experience in Fifteenth-Century Italy,* 55.

83. Ibid.

84. Ibid.

85. See also Caudile, "Observations on the Iconography of Leonardo da Vinci's Uffizi 'Annunciation,'" 190.

86. Leonardo da Vinci, *Treatise on Painting* (ed. Amos Philip McMahon; Princeton, N.J.: Princeton University Press, 1956), I.58 and II.33 r; cited by Baxandall, *Painting and Experience in Fifteenth-Century Italy,* 56.

87. In this light, even Frederick Hartt's suggestion (*History of Italian Renaissance,* 436) that Mary lifts her hand "in a gesture of somewhat patrician surprise" is somewhat misleading.

88. See Baxandall, *Painting and Experience in Fifteenth-Century Italy.* This interpretation seems preferable to Caudile ("Observations on the Iconography of Leonardo's Uffizi 'Annunciation,'" 190) who appeals to arcane monastic sign language to explain the significance of the uplifted hand.

89. W. C. van Unnik, "*Dominus Vobiscum:* The Background of a Liturgical Formula," in *New Testament Essays: Studies in Memory of T. W. Manson* (ed. Angus Higgins; Manchester, England: Manchester University Press, 1959), 270–305.

90. Marc Kolden, "'Dominus Vobiscum': Luke 1:26–31," *Currents in Theology and Missions* 21 (1994): 456.

Figure 14. Pontormo. *Visitation.* 1514–16. Fresco. S. Annunziata, Florence. Photo. With permission from the Ministero dei Beni e le Attività Culturali.

Chapter Three

The *Visitation*
by Jacopo Pontormo
(Luke 1:39–56)

Our study of the birth and childhood of Christ in the previous chapter began with a discussion of the Annunciation as told in Luke 1:26–38 and as painted by Leonardo da Vinci in 1470. The Visitation is sequentially the next narrative written by Luke (1:39–56). The sequence of the biblical text is mirrored by the artistic sequence, perhaps better described as a legacy, through the master-pupil relationship of Leonardo da Vinci and Jacopo Pontormo. According to Giorgio Vasari, Pontormo (1494–1556) probably received his first artistic training with Leonardo in 1508[1] and was probably very familiar with his master's *Annunciation.*[2] Pontormo's *Visitation,* 1514–16 (Figure 14), located *in situ* at the Chiostrino dei Voti or atrium of SS. Annunziata, Florence,[3] also moves the discussion forward historically from the fifteenth to the sixteenth century and stylistically from the Early Renaissance to a period contentionally referred to by art historians as the High Renaissance.

Overview of the Biblical Text
and Its Subsequent Interpretation

[39]In those days Mary set out and went with haste to a Judean town in the hill country, [40]where she entered the house of Zechariah and greeted Elizabeth. [41]When Elizabeth heard Mary's greeting, the child leaped in her womb. And Elizabeth was filled with the Holy Spirit [42]and exclaimed with a loud cry, "Blessed are you among women, and blessed is the fruit of your womb. [43]And why has this happened to me, that the mother of my Lord comes to me? [44]For as soon as I heard the sound of your greeting, the child in my womb leaped for joy. [45]And blessed is she who believed that there would be a fulfillment of what was spoken to her by the Lord."

In visual depictions, Luke 1:39–45 is a discrete scene, "The Visitation," distinguishable from Luke 1:46–56, which is often depicted and entitled in visual renderings, "The Madonna of the Magnificat."[4] In the rhetorical flow of the Third Gospel, Luke 1:39–45 is part of a larger unit, 1:39–56, which itself functions as a kind of bridge between the annunciations of John and Jesus (1:5–38) and the births and early lives of John and Jesus (1:57–2:52).[5] Luke 1:39–56 is composed of a narrative introduction (39–41), two hymns (42–45, 46–55) and a narrative conclusion (56).[6] Just as Mary is the object of attention in 1:26–38, so also is she the focus of this passage.[7] The unit begins and ends by narrating Mary's arrival in and departure from the hill country (cf. 1:39, 56). Mary serves as the subject of all the verbs in vv. 39–40 — Mary "set out," "went with haste," "entered the house of Zechariah," and "greeted Elizabeth." Even when the subject changes to Elizabeth in v. 41, Mary remains the focal point. The sound of Mary's greeting causes the babe in Elizabeth's womb to "leap," and Elizabeth is filled with the Holy Spirit. Mary is the subject of Elizabeth's speech (42–45), and then Mary is the speaker of the hymn in 1:46–55.[8] Visual depictions notwithstanding, in 1:41 the scene moves into "aural mode," and there is no mention in the text of any physical contact between the two women, nor is any mention made of Zechariah (both important iconographical details in Pontormo's painting). It is Mary's greeting that triggers the subsequent action of the narrative.[9] The importance of this greeting is seen in the detail of the leaping babe in v. 41. Elizabeth's quickening recalls other examples of "prenatal signs" in the Jewish Scriptures — Jacob and Esau's embryonic struggle causes Rebekah to lament, "If it is to be this way, why do I live?" (Gen 25:22; cf. Gen 38:27–30).[10] The significance of Mary's greeting is seen also in Elizabeth's mention of her greeting in v. 44. Still, the narrator says nothing about its content.

The first hymn by Elizabeth celebrates Mary as the "ideal believer."[11] The absence of Mary's name from the canticle suggests that Mark Coleridge is correct in arguing that it is "not Mary in her own right who appears in the speech, but Mary in relation to God's plan."[12] Elizabeth's speech contains four oracles.[13] The first declares that both Mary and her unborn child are "blessed" (1:42; cf. 11:27). The second oracle is in the form of a question ("Why…") but contains in it a reference to the "mother of my Lord," a thoroughly Christian confession (1:43). The third oracle gives Elizabeth's interpretation for why her babe moved in the womb: "the child in my womb leaped for joy" (1:44 — "joy" is an important motif in the Lukan infancy narrative, cf. 1:14; 2:10). The last oracle is a beatitude on Mary and her faith and underscores her depiction as the ideal disciple.

If Elizabeth praises Mary in the first speech, Mary praises God in the second.[14] This second hymn, the Magnificat, "clarifies the links between what
God has done for one individual and what he will do for the structures of
society at large."[15] In this light, the canticle divides into two strophes: the
first is Mary's declaration of what God has done for her (1:47–50); the
second is concerned with God's activity in the larger society (1:51–55).[16]
As such, the Magnificat is not a direct response to Elizabeth's hymn of
praise, but rather a theological reflection of the work of God throughout
the Lukan infancy narrative to this point.[17] There are important links between the two parts: Mary speaks of her own "lowliness" (v. 48) and later
talks of what God has done for the "lowly" in general (v. 52). In the first
strophe, God is the "Mighty One" (v. 49); in the second, God brings down
the "powerful" (v. 52). In both parts, God shows both his strength (49,
51) and his mercy (50, 54). The most powerful language about the social
reversal that God effects is found in a chiastic pattern in vv. 52–53:

> A   God brought down the *powerful;*
>
> B   God lifted up the *lowly;*
>
> B[1]   God filled the *hungry;*
>
> A[1]   God sent the *rich* away empty.

These themes are repeated in Jesus' "messianic woes" recorded in Luke
6:20–26. Mary's speech ends with reference to the "remembrance of his
mercy" in relationship to "Abraham and his descendants" (1:55).[18] The
Abrahamic covenant is mentioned also in Zechariah's prophecy (1:73–
75) and in Peter's temple sermon in Acts 3:25 (cf. also 3:8, 19:9, 7:2–
17).[19] The end of Mary's speech is rarely given much consideration in the
biblical commentaries, but in light of the prominence Pontormo gives to
the connection between Abraham and the unborn Christ, we shall return
to this theme in the discussion of the iconography of the *Visitation.* The
scene concludes, as we noted, with Mary returning to her home.

In terms of the reception history of the story, the Visitation scene was
popular in the visual arts, being depicted as part of a Nativity cycle as
early as the sixth century, and finally claiming an independent position
in pictorial history in the Late Middle Ages.[20] In subsequent Christian
literature and liturgy, however, the Visitation and its characters did not
fare quite so well. Apart from Mary, whose popularity did, of course, continue to increase with the development of the cult of the Virgin, neither
the scene itself nor Elizabeth, the other major character, received much
attention among the ecclesiastical commentators. *The Golden Legend* and

pseudo-Bonaventure's *Meditations on the Life of Christ,* both well known for their embellishments of the biblical narrative, add little to the Visitation scene or to the development of the character of Elizabeth.[21] Augustine's reference to Elizabeth's role as primarily that of the mother of John the Baptist was fairly typical of the church fathers.[22] That is not to say that Elizabeth was neglected altogether. We are told the name of Elizabeth's mother (Hismeria according to *The Golden Legend;* Sobe according to St. Hippolytus) and that she — Elizabeth's mother — was the sister of Anna, Mary's mother (thus explaining the blood relationship mentioned briefly in Luke).[23] And according to the *Protevangelium of James* (22:3), Elizabeth protected John from the slaughter of the innocents by fleeing to the desert, where a rock opened up to conceal them until danger had passed. In another medieval document, we are told that when John the Baptist was seven and a half years old, Elizabeth died on the same day as did her nemesis Herod, and Mary and Jesus came to comfort John the Baptist and to assist in Elizabeth's burial.[24]

Likewise the Visitation scene itself has not been totally neglected. In 1263, Bonaventure introduced the feast of the Visitation into the Franciscan calendar, and from 1389 it was celebrated as one of the Marian feasts in the entire Roman Catholic Church.[25] Analyses of the Visitation, however, have mushroomed in the latter half of the twentieth century as feminist scholars have observed the importance of the scene of two women, meeting in a private home but discussing matters profoundly public, political, and theological.[26] Likewise, advocates of liberation theology have noted the profound political and social implications of Mary's Magnificat.[27] Any interpretive reflection on this text, or its visual depictions, would need to take into account our contemporary context of interpretation.

The Artist and the Painting

Jacopo Pontormo

Jacopo Carucci was born on May 26, 1494, in Pontormo and died in Florence on December 31, 1556, at the age of sixty-two.[28] Pontormo, as he was known to his contemporaries, was a skilled painter and draftsman and the leading artist in mid-sixteenth-century Florentine mannerism. As we noted, Pontormo's training probably began with Leonardo da Vinci, then continued in the workshop of Mariotto Albertinelli (1474–1515)[29] and finally was completed with Piero di Cosimo.[30] Pontormo became the assistant to Andrea del Sarto around 1512.[31]

The first independent works are a group of frescoes reflective of the High Renaissance classicism of Andrea and Fra Bartolomeo.[32] Pontormo's collaboration with the Medici began in 1515 with Pope Leo X's visit to Florence.[33] He was commissioned to paint a lunette fresco of St. Veronica and the vault frescoes of God the Father and Putti with the Arms of Leo X in Santa Maria Novella.[34] The dramatic rhetoric and classical amplitude of form of the High Renaissance is also found in the *Visitation*, 1514–15, a part of the cycle of the Life of the Virgin in SS. Annunziata, Florence.[35]

The *Visitation*, therefore, is an early work but its importance in Pontormo's *oeuvre* is best understood by discussing not only what he did before it but also what came after it. Around 1517, Pontormo experimented with spatial relationships, increased the visible signs of emotion in the figures, and destabilized the compositional forms. His incorporation of these aspects of the new style of the day, mannerism, into his paintings is first apparent in the *Virgin and Child with Saints*, 1518, in San Michele Visdomini, Florence, and the *Joseph in Egypt*, 1518, commissioned for the Borgherini family and today located in the National Gallery, London.[36]

The mature works are usually dated 1520–30 and include his masterpieces of *Vertumnus and Pomona*, painted in the Gran Salone of the Medici villa at Poggio a Caiano (1520–21), the fresco series of the Passion at the Certosa del Galluzzo (1523–26), and the *Lamentation* altar panel and fresco decoration for the Capponi Chapel in S. Felicità, Florence (1525–28).[37] The artificial elegance and emotionality of the figures, the spatial uncertainty, and the vibrant color palette used in the *Lamentation* define a mannerist composition. Also painted during this period of mannerism is the *Visitation* from S. Michele in Carmignano dated to the late 1520s.[38] Pontormo also devised a typical Florentine mannerist portrait type that is pursued and then abandoned by other mannerists such as his pupil in the 1520s, Agnolo Bronzino (1503–72), Francesco Salviati (1510–63), and Giorgio Vasari.[39] The late works, 1530–56, are heavily influenced by Michelangelo. He painted frescoes in two Medici villas at Careggi (1535–36) and Castello (1537–43) and in the choir of S. Lorenzo, Florence.[40]

Pontormo was an advocate of the concept of Florentine *disegno* and participated in the *paragone* (debate) on the primacy of painting or sculpture in 1546.[41] Much is known about the eccentric and often depressed character of Pontormo through his own diary.[42]

The Commission and the Servites

The Servites or the Ordine dei Servi di Maria were founded in 1234 by seven Florentines. The Church of SS. Annunziata was built in 1250 and reconstructed by Michelozzo between 1444 and 1481. Andrea di Cosimo Feltrini, an artist held in high esteem for his own limited field of pure decoration (much of which might be considered menial tasks such as painting candles), occupied a position of general factotum at the Annunziata even before the election of the Medici pope.[43] Shearman cites documentation that Pontormo, most likely hired by Feltrini, received payment on January 31, 1513, for painting candles for the church.[44]

The decoration of several areas, including the façade and the Chiostrino dei Voti, which began in c. 1460 (with Baldovinetti), and continued in 1509 (with Andrea), climaxed with the celebration of the election of Cardinal Giovanni de'Medici to the papacy (Leo X) on March 11, 1513. In the summer following that election, Andrea del Sarto, Franciabigio (1482/83–1525), and Rosso Fiorentino were all working in the Chiostrino dei Voti.[45]

Vasari tells a story about Pontormo's selection to work in the Annunziata.[46] Feltrini had been assigned to paint a new stone coat of arms for the pope to be placed over the principal arch of the façade that required gilding, grotesques, and the figures of *Faith* and *Charity*.[47] Feeling inadequate for the allegorical figures, he called on Pontormo.[48] According to Vasari, after hiding himself in Sant'Agostino alla Porta a Faenza and producing a series of drawings for the coat of arms, Pontormo showed them to a "stupefied" master, Andrea del Sarto. From that point forward, Pontormo was no longer allowed to frequent the master's *bottega*.[49] Although this may be one of Vasari's famous tales, it does indicate the solitary and whimsical character of Pontormo.[50] Pontormo finished the coat of arms, received payment, and then almost immediately destroyed it.[51] He replaced it with a now nearly destroyed *Faith and Charity,* which contained two putti. Vasari thoroughly enjoyed this fresco (he discusses it for two pages),[52] especially the putti, which were famous throughout the sixteenth century.[53]

The frescoes in the Chiostrino dei Voti, six dedicated to scenes from the life of the Virgin and six to the life of St. Filippo Benizzi, were not completed by the time of Pope Leo X's arrival on November 15, 1515.[54] The entrance to the atrium is in the center of the structure. The door to the nave is opposite it. The frescoes from the life of the Virgin beginning from the right side of the atrium door in a counterclockwise direction continuing to the church entrance are: *Assumption, Visitation, Marriage, Birth of the Virgin, and Adoration of the Magi.* The *Nativity of Christ* is located on the other side of the nave entrance and had been painted earlier, 1460–62, by Alesso Baldovinetti. Fra Mariano dal Canto alle Macine[55] commissioned Franciabigio to execute the *Marriage of the Virgin,* which was completed by September 1513,[56] and Andrea del Sarto to paint the

Figure 15. Mariotto Albertinelli. *Visitation*. 1503. Panel. Galleria degli Uffizi, Florence. Photo. With permission from the Ministero dei Beni e le Attività Culturali.

Birth of the Virgin in 1513–14.[57] Fra Jacopo de'Rossi preferred the talents of the younger artists, Rosso Fiorentino and Pontormo, probably because Andrea was reluctant to work cheap anymore![58] Rosso Fiorentino began to paint the *Assumption of the Virgin* toward the end of 1513.[59] Pontormo was paid by the Servites from December 1514 to June 1516 to conclude the cycle.[60] It has been suggested that, instead of for the pope's arrival, the painting was completed by January 17, 1516, for the new consecration of SS. Annunziata.[61]

Stylistic and Iconographic Analysis of the Painting

Artistic Sources and Composition

The stylistic sources are clearly his masters, Andrea del Sarto and Mariotto Albertinelli. Albertinelli's *Visitation* (Figure 15) of 1503 indicates a loving rapport between the two women that Pontormo maintains in his composition of the same subject over ten years later. Pontormo's training with Albertinelli, sometime around 1506 at the age of twelve, would

Figure 16. Andrea del Sarto. *Birth of the Virgin.* 1511–14. Fresco.
S. Annunziata, Florence. Photo. With permission from the Ministero
dei Beni e le Attività Culturali.

have been in the classical Renaissance style.[62] Andrea's *Birth of the Virgin*
(Figure 16), painted in the same cloister in 1513–14, is a compositional
source.[63] Pontormo's variation in gesture and the female facial types is
similar to Andrea's painting. Andrea's monumental figures are fewer and
positioned well within the fresco's space while Pontormo's figures seem
crowded and their positioning recalls another master of the classical High
Renaissance, Fra Bartolomeo. The *Mystical Marriage of St. Catherine,* 1512
(Figure 17), today located in the Accademia of Florence, represents a
stepped composition with a cylindrical niche placed behind the central
scene. Pontormo did not copy the static quality of the Fra Bartolomeo figures, but instead the younger artist turns to Michelangelo's cartoon of the
Battle of Cascina (Figure 18).[64] Raphael's frescoes in the first two of the
Vatican Stanze are nearly contemporary and may justify the hypothesis of
a first journey to Rome in 1515.[65] The influence of Raphael can be found
in the soft colors, natural movements, and certainly with the placement

Figure 17. Fra Bartolomeo. *Mystical Marriage of St. Catherine.* 1512. Panel. Galleria Palatina, Florence. Photo. With permission from the Ministero dei Beni e le Attività Culturali.

of the figures in front of an illusionistic architectural setting open to the front and made of marble.[66]

Heinrich Wölfflin was among the first to write about the classicism of this work.[67] He notes the triangular area of the central figures and the semi-cylindrical architectonic frame behind them, the verticals of the side figures, and then the circular movement back to the center of the composition.[68] Mary and Elizabeth are centered and "staged" in this event.[69] Mary's gown is pinkish-orange, and she wears a pale blue mantle, worn almost as a long coat over the right side of her body, and then gently draped over her left arm as it extends to the kneeling figure of Elizabeth. Elizabeth is aged and grasps Mary's right hand with hers. Elizabeth's left hand falls to her lap to assist her balance as she falls to her knees after the realization that Mary is carrying the Lord Jesus. Elizabeth's head is

Figure 18. Copy after Michelangelo. *Battle of Cascina*. 1504–6 (destroyed). Copy by Sangallo. Collection the Earl of Leicester. Copyright Foto Marburg/Art Resource, NY.

covered as is Mary's, and both Elizabeth's gown and Mary's head covering consist of a radiant yellowish-orange-colored drapery, which moves the spectator through the painting. This color, brightest in the picture, appears in the gown of the male figure holding the book on the right side of the composition, the upper half of the gown of the seated female figure on the steps, and finally in the gown of the female figure directly behind this seated woman.

There is a strong diagonal that also brings the audience from Mary to Elizabeth and continues to the seated boy on the steps.[70] The foot of the boy, who seems to be focused on a brown indeterminate object, is placed directly below the male figure holding the book whose drapery catches the eye and moves the viewer back into the center. Once at the top of the Virgin's head, which is covered in the same colored drapery, the viewer may follow the curve of her back around to the standing woman holding a child whose left arm has just a sleeve visible of this orange drapery, to the standing figure of the woman with the orange gown and rose mantle, and finally down to the seated woman on the left side of the steps whose legs guide the spectator back into the center.

Iconography

The sacrifice of Isaac depicted above the architecture suggests a parallel between the faith of Abraham and that of the Virgin Mary, united by the common sacrifice of their sons. The first public recognition of the moment of incarnation occurs when Elizabeth identifies Mary as the mother of her

Lord. We begin our study of the iconography of this painting by returning for a moment to the figures on the left of Mary, whose compositional function we have just described. In fact, when these figures are treated at all, it is almost always in terms of their composition and style.

Inattentive Figures

A recent study by Robert Gaston suggests that these "minor" figures may play a more important role in the meaning of the painting than is generally acknowledged.[71] Drawing on the work of Vasari and other Renaissance observers of art, Gaston concludes, "In most narrative pictures a high degree of inattentiveness to the principal personages was regarded as appropriate."[72] Gaston explores the various functions of these figures in visual art who are seemingly inattentive to the main action of the protagonists.[73]

Some figures, whose gaze takes them to another minor character or some unfocused spot in the narrative "have more to do with the artist's ability to create such an impression of naturalness in his groups, and in their interaction that the beholder is, in a sense, induced to 'forget about' the inattentive figures."[74] Nonetheless, these figures contribute to the

> very naturalness of his [the artist's] depiction. The courtiers' behaviour seems inappropriate only to someone who does not share the painter's knowledge that courtiers were permitted to chat among themselves while their lords executed the affairs of state. Their inattentive behaviour is decorous within special limits.[75]

This is an apt description of the four female figures (and child) who stand to Mary's left; they contribute to the "naturalness of the depiction," yet are ignored in most iconographic analyses.

Second, Gaston observes that some figures "look out at the viewer and 'invite his attention.'"[76] The result is that "the beholder is flooded with attention, which induces dis-ease if his expectation is to be merely the observer of interaction by others."[77] Both the woman seated on the steps and the prophet holding the open book look out to the audience and invite their participation in this scene.

Finally, Gaston points out that many figures neither gaze at another "minor" character on the canvass nor stare out at the viewer, but rather "remain deeply absorbed." He adds: "One might conclude that they are thus highly attentive to the *means* by which the heavenly vision can be attained by the beholder of the painting. Such a picture requires the beholder to divide his attention between the saints who show the way of attentive prayer and contemplation, and the Madonna and Child [and here with Pontormo, Elizabeth and John] who represent the object of that

Figure 19. Pontormo. *Visitation*. Detail of inscription on the left. Before restoration. Gabinetto Fotografico, Florence. Photo. With permission from the Ministero dei Beni e le Attività Culturali.

process."[78] The curious nude figure on the right, as we have observed, is shown here deeply absorbed by something other than the action taking place behind him. We explore his possible identity later, but here we point out that the child seems to function as one of these inattentive figures who models the means — contemplation — by which one can attain the vision offered here, namely a fuller understanding of the sacrificial dimensions of the Visitation scene.[79]

Flanking Inscriptions

Three inscriptions offer potential assistance in the interpretation of this moment of recognition, though interpreters have often despaired of deciphering their meaning.[80] Nonetheless, Timothy Verdon has ventured the guess that the Latin of all three inscriptions "is of Renaissance origin, vaguely imitating classical Latin but intended to 'explain the composite image.'"[81] Jack Wasserman has also recently explored the iconography of this painting, paying close attention to these inscriptions.[82] The flanking inscriptions most probably contain phrases that refer to the sacrifice of Isaac, which is depicted between the two putti.

The putto on the left holds a tablet with an inscription. The first problem is to decipher what the letters are. Working from a photograph of the fresco taken on September 9, 1958, before the painting was removed and restored (Figure 19) and also drawing on Frederick Mortimer Clapp's reconstruction of the inscription, Wasserman has reconstructed those letters NUM/DEE/EVM.[83] Based on a fifteenth-century inscription from a monument in the church at Domjulien, France, that reads VNVM CREDE DEVM NE IVRAS VAN,[84] Wasserman suggests that the left inscription can be amended to read [V]NVM [CRE]DE [D]EVM, which he translates, "Believe in one God." Wasserman further comments: "In this case, we must assume . . . that the final 'E' in DEE must have been a 'D' originally which is to say, the first letter of the succeeding word DEVM. This assumption is easily made, because incomplete words, and letters of words distributed on separate lines, occur frequently in Renaissance inscriptions."[85]

This reconstruction is certainly plausible and made all the more attractive by the existence of a chronologically close (though geographically distant) antecedent. We wish, however, to offer an alternative interpretation for this inscription. Following a lead by Timothy Verdon, we suggest that the original inscription read NUM/DEB/EUM and should be reconstructed as NUM[INI] DEB[ET] EVM: "He [Abraham] owes him [Isaac] to God." That is, Abraham, who owes his son to God, the son originally given to him in fulfillment of the ancestral promise, is now giving him back (cf. Gen 12). This reconstruction does not require amending the inscription to place the beginning of the third word at the end of the second line. Though undoubtedly this occurs in other Renaissance inscriptions, it does not occur with any of the other five words in *this* one. This reconstruction also makes more sense in the immediate context.[86]

Inscription	Wasserman	Hornik & Parsons
NVM	[V]NVM	NVM[INI]
DEE or DED or DEB	[CRE]DE[D]	DEB[IT]
EVM	EVM	EVM
	"Believe in One God"	"S/He owes him to God"

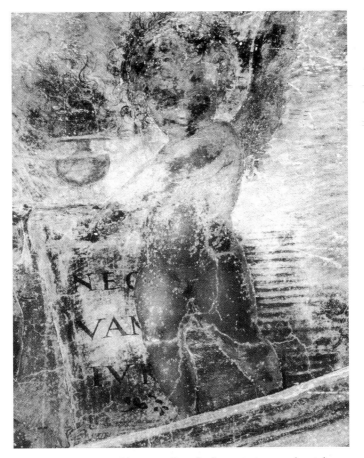

Figure 20. Pontormo. *Visitation*. Detail of inscription on the right. Before restoration. Gabinetto Fotografico, Florence. Photo. With permission from the Ministero dei Beni e le Attività Culturali.

NEC/VAN/IVR is inscribed on the putto's tablet on the right (Figure 20). Here we are in agreement with Wasserman, who reconstructs NEC/VAN/IVR as NEC VAN[E] IUR[AT]: "Nor does he swear (or promise) in vain."[87] This inscription has two possible meanings. The sense could be that Abraham does not swear in vain to obey God, or God did not promise in vain to grant Abraham a glorious descendence.[88] Both meanings should probably be kept in mind. In fact, Gen 12–25 is moved along by a series of threats to God's promise to make of Abraham a mighty nation, and no threat was more severe than the near death of Isaac at the hands of Abraham himself.[89] The inscription echoes the Vulgate translation of the words spoken by Zechariah at John the Baptist's birth: "salutem ex inimicis nostris et de manu omnium qui oderunt nos ad faciendam misericordiam

cum patribus nostris et memorari testamenti sui sancti iusiurandum quod
iuravit ad Abraham patrem nostrum" (Luke 1:72–73, emphasis ours).[90]
Here in Pontormo's interpretation, then, God's promise to Abraham (to
give him offspring through which the nations would be blessed), on the
one hand, is preserved when God's angel stays Abraham's hand from sac-
rificing Isaac. On the other hand, the promise is brought to full fruition in
the birth of Christ himself, anticipated in the main scene of the Visitation.
Thus, "he [God] did not swear in vain [to bless Abraham with offspring,]
and — behold — Christ now enters the scene."[91]

Isaac and Christ

Reflection on the relevant New Testament passages makes the connection between Isaac and Christ even clearer. Isaac is mentioned explicitly
by name forty-one times in the New Testament, though references to
Abraham's seed, covenant, promise — references in which Isaac is embedded — would dramatically increase allusions to him and the ancestral
promise which he represented to the Jews, including Christian Jews. For
example, in Rom 8:32, Paul alludes to the Gen 22 scene when he claims,
"He [God] who did not withhold his own Son, but gave him up for all
of us, will he not with him also give us everything else?" The function
of the occurrences vary from giving a place to Isaac in Jesus' genealogy
(Matt 1:2; Luke 3:34; cf. Acts 7:8), listing in reports by Paul of Isaac as
the fulfillment of the ancestral promise made to Abraham (Rom 9:7, 10;
Gal 4:28), as evidence of Abraham's righteous work (Jas 2:22), and as the
middle term of the formula characterizing God as the "God of Abraham,
Isaac, and Jacob" (Matt 22:32//Mark 12:26//Luke 20:37, Acts 3:13; 7:32;
cf. Matt 8:11//Luke 20:37 where the triad also occurs). Abraham's sacrifice
was not employed typologically by any New Testament writer, though the
writer of Hebrews comes the closest: "By faith Abraham, when put to the
test, offered up Isaac. He who had received the promises was ready to offer
up his only son, of whom he had been told, 'It is through Isaac that descendants shall be named for you'" (Heb 11:17–18). The use of the term
"only son" (*monogenē*) is a favorite expression, especially in the Gospel of
John, to describe the relationship of God to Jesus: Jesus is God's "only"
(*monogenē*) son (cf. John 1:18; 3:16, 18; 1 John 4:9). Possibly some christological echoes may have been heard in the use of the term to describe
Isaac's relationship to Abraham here in Hebrews as well.

From the patristic period on, however, Christian theologians did see
Isaac's experience as a foreshadowing prefiguration of Christ's crucifix-
ion.[92] Ambrose wrote: "Isaac is therefore a type of the suffering of Christ."[93]
Irenaeus, Origen, Tertullian, Melito, Augustine, and many others also saw

in the Isaac story the foreshadowing of various details from Christ's passion.[94] Each was a "beloved son" offered as the consummate sacrifice by his father. Both sacrifices took place upon a hill. The thorns of the bush that trapped the ram were the thorns of Christ's crown. The ram in the bush was Christ on the cross; Isaac was Christ in the Eucharist.

The linkage between the sacrifice of Isaac and the crucifixion was found in early Christian art as well. As Alison Moore Smith has noted: "[A] story regarded as of such importance by the Church had frequent representation in Early Christian art. It is depicted on Early Christian monuments of all classes: frescoes, sarcophagi, mosaics, glasses, gems, and lamps."[95] Smith isolated five different "types" of representation through about the sixth century. From the sixth to the eleventh century, "the sacrifice was seldom reproduced in art," a point Smith explains by noting that "the Crucifixion, which it [the sacrifice of Isaac] had symbolized, began to appear upon monuments at this time."[96] She goes on to note that "during the four centuries [twelfth–sixteenth] following that period it had renewed and widespread popularity in representation, owing no doubt to a revival of interest in its symbolic connotations."[97]

Pontormo's depiction fits what Smith has called the "Hellenistic Type": "Usually he [Abraham] is bearded. Holding the knife in his right hand, with his left he often grasps the head of Isaac who kneels on the ground or stands beside the lighted box-shaped altar with hands shackled as Christ's were in the apocryphal version of the Crucifixion."[98] So even taken on by itself, the sacrifice of Isaac depiction could contain visual elements that echoed the Crucifixion and, in Pontormo, did so.

Often, these links were much more explicit. In chapter twenty-five of the medieval illustrated manuscript the *Biblia Pauperum*, the sacrifice of Isaac was the subject of a visual illustration to the left of the central subject, Christ on the Cross.[99] This sacrifice of Isaac was entitled "the father sacrifices his son, who typifies Christ" and was accompanied by a quote from and interpretation of Gen 22:10: "We read in Gen. xxii, that when Abraham had stretched forth his hand to slay his son, the angel of the Lord from heaven prevented him, saying, 'Stretch not forth thine hand against the child.' Abraham signifies the heavenly Father, who sacrificed His Son, to wit, Christ, for us all, on the Cross, that thus He might show us a sign of His fatherly love."[100]

At some early point, the typological interpretation of Isaac's sacrifice made its way into the liturgy of the Mass, prefiguring the sacrifice of Christ in the Eucharist. As the priest extended his hand over the host, he would pray: "Supra quae propitio ac sereno vultu respicere digneris et accepta habere, sicuti accepta habere dignatus es munera pueri justi Abel et *sacrificium Patriarchae nostri Abrahae.*"[101] Rosemary Woolf has further observed that a number of illuminated medieval sacramentaries have as their second most frequently illustrated subject (next to the Crucifixion), the sacrifice of Isaac.[102] In fact, the sacrifice of Isaac was frequently found as an illumination tucked into the rounded, Carolingian T of the first words of the canon of the mass, *Te igitur*, visually uniting the Tau cross (symbolizing the crucifixion of Christ) with the sacrifice of Isaac in the Mass.[103]

The linkage of the sacrifice of Isaac to the Eucharist prepares the way for connecting the sacrifice of Isaac not just to the sacrifice of Christ on Calvary but to his re-sacrifice in the Mass. As Leah Sinanoglou has demonstrated, the sacrifice in the Mass is that of the Christ Child in the elements of the Eucharist.[104] The link between Isaac and the infant Christ was one especially exploited in the medieval Corpus Christi plays.[105] This connection may explain in part why Isaac is almost always depicted in these plays as a child even though medieval commentators were generally uniform in placing Isaac's age at the time at twenty-five or thirty.[106]

Abraham and Isaac plays were also connected to performances of the *Rappresentazione dell'annunziazione*, and this point brings us closer to Pontormo's depiction. As we noted earlier, John Shearman established that in 1513, Pontormo was working under Andrea di Cosimo Feltrini refurbishing SS. Annunziata for the forthcoming presentation of the *Rappresentazione dell'annunziazione*.[107] Of special interest is the fact that D'Ancona has documented that other *sacre rappresentazioni* were featured as interludes within the *Rappresentazione dell'annunziazione*.[108] Among those often featured was *Abraam e Isaac*.[109] Through his participation in the preparation for this observance of the festival at SS. Annunziata (which as we have already observed coincided also with the arrival of Leo X in Florence), Pontormo may not only have had first-hand exposure to a performance of *Abraam e Isaac* and its christological overtones, but also would have viewed it within the context of the marvelous spectacle of the *Rappresentazione dell'annunziazione*, where the Annunciation was dramatically performed. And just as importantly, Pontormo's audience would have had the same opportunity of viewing Abraham and Isaac within a larger framework of the infancy narrative.

Linking the Sacrifice of Isaac with the Visitation

Already a witness to the connection between the sacrifice of Isaac and the annunciation to Mary, Pontormo (most likely upon the advice of his patrons, the Servites) relocates the link between Isaac and Christ, backward

from the crucifixion (as in the *Biblia Pauperum*) and forward from the Annunciation to the scene of Mary's visitation. Such a connection appears
to be unprecedented in the history of art,[110] and Pontormo secured the
linkage through several different strategies.

First, the central inscription ANVE OPTIME DEUS links the two
scenes together. As Wasserman has noted, "Previous attempts to deal

Figure 21. Copy of Pontormo. *Visitation.* 1834. Photo. From *Pittura a fresco di Andrea del
Sarto e d'altre celebri autori disegnate e incise a contorni da Alessandro Chiari con illustrazioni
del Professore Melchior Missirini,* Florence, unpaginated.

with the inscription have been unsatisfactory."[111] Especially problematic is Kurt Forster's conjecture (widely followed) that the ANVE be read as A[N]VE, echoing the angel's greeting to Mary at the Annunciation (and part of the liturgical Ave Maria), and rendered "Hail, Best God."[112] As Wasserman observes, "making a letter irrelevant is not an option when dealing with Medieval and Renaissance inscriptions."[113]

Wasserman suggests, in light of the fact that words are often abbreviated in Greek and Latin inscriptions, that ANVE is actually missing a letter and should be reconstructed as ADNVE ("look favorably").[114] This word is the second person imperative of *adnuere.* Wasserman bolsters his argument by noting that an 1834 engraved copy of the fresco has an abbreviation sign above it (Figure 21).[115] We accept Wasserman's reconstruction with one slight emendation. In our opinion, the abbreviated word should probably be rendered ANNVE, the favored term for "look favorably" in ecclesiastical Latin.[116] Further, close examination of the engraved copy reveals that the abbreviation siglum is placed above and between the letter N and V, suggesting that it is the second "N" that has been omitted. One might wonder why the artist would omit a letter in this inscription. The best answer may be simply one of symmetry. By reducing the word ANNVE to ANVE, Pontormo is able to balance ANVE on one side with DEVS on the other. This symmetry matches the symmetry of the two flanking inscriptions, each with three rows of three letters each.

We would also slightly modify Wasserman's translation ("Look favorably [upon us], O Best Lord, [for we are of faith]")[117] to something like, "Look favorably, most excellent God," since the vocative, *optime,* is used three times in the Vulgate translation of Luke and Acts to render the honorific Greek term *kratiste* ("most excellent Theophilus," Luke 1:3; "most excellent Felix," Acts 24:3, NIV; "most excellent Festus," Acts 26:25) and is best rendered this way here as well.[118] The inscription's intention seems to be to invoke divine favor upon both Abraham's and Mary's faithfulness.[119]

Inscription	Forster	Wasserman	Hornik & Parsons
ANVE OPTIME DEVS	A[N]VE OPTIME DEVS	ADNVE OPTIME DEVS	ANNVE OPTIME DEVS
	"Hail, Best God!"	"Look favorably [upon us], O Best Lord, [for we are of faith]"	"Look favorably, most excellent God"

Second, the two scenes are united by the cluster of complex gestures of the figures to the right of Mary and Elizabeth. The figure kneeling to the right of Elizabeth is presumably Joseph, who turns to the standing figure of Zechariah. With his right hand, he points to the scene of Elizabeth and

Mary and with his left hand points upward toward the sacrifice of Isaac.[120] Likewise, Zechariah points to the Old Testament scene overhead,[121] and a third female figure behind Joseph directs the viewer's attention toward Zechariah as well. That the viewer is to interpret these scenes in light of each other is made unmistakably clear by these characters in the lower part of the fresco.

Finally, and more tentatively, one may wonder about the identity of the nude child seated on the steps in this light.[122] The figure, when mentioned, is usually treated as a compositional figure and as example of Pontormo's indebtedness to classicism.[123] There is a remarkable similarity in features between this figure and that of Isaac above. Not only are both nude, but both are also ruddy-complexioned and red-headed. If this figure is meant to represent Isaac, then he, seen in tandem with the prophet holding an open book,[124] standing to the right of the nude, may be taken as a visual reminder that the ancestral promise that God made to Abraham first realized in Isaac's birth has now reached its complete fulfillment in the arrival of the Christ Child, a truth to which Mary bears witness.

Role of Mary

Mary also plays an important role in Pontormo's *Visitation*. In addition to standing at the center of the scene and receiving the adoration of Elizabeth, there is a sense in which the inscriptions described above also portray Mary's actions as well. *Numini debet eum* (he owes him to God) refers to Mary as well: she owes him [Christ] to God. As Timothy Verdon has observed: "with a faith equal to Abraham's — she [Mary] acknowledges her debt to God, offering her son (i.e., emotionally accepting the necessity of his self-oblation, attuning her heart to his own willingness to accept the cross)."[125]

Likewise the second flanking inscription applies to Mary as well. NEC IVRAT VANE: "She does not promise in vain." Earlier in Luke's story, Mary had promised to accept what Gabriel proclaimed God had planned for her: "Here am I, the servant of the Lord; let it be with me according to your word" (Luke 1:38). Furthermore, Forster also notes certain verbal links between the Latin text of Gen 22:17 and the earlier annunciation to Mary: *"benedicam tibi et multiplicabo semen tuum"* (I will bless you and multiply your seed; Gen 22:17); "Ave, gratia plena, Dominus tecum, *benedicta tu in mulieribus*" ("Hail, [you who are] full of grace, the Lord is with you, you are blessed among women"; Luke 1:28).[126]

Finally the plea "ANNVE OPTIME DEUS" ("Most excellent God, look favorably") applies also to Mary. Mary's faithfulness in recognizing her debt to God and in promising to be obedient to God is no less deserving of the same divine approval that falls upon Abraham's faithfulness. This emphasis on Mary (a point made also in Luke) is important because it was precisely Pontormo's patrons, the Servites of SS. Annunziata, who in the early sixteenth century, developed to a maximum the theology of Mary as "Mother of Sorrows."[127]

Hermeneutical Reflections

More and more Christian theologians are turning to the rich resources of patristic and medieval interpretation in order to address the vexing questions of modernity and postmodernity.[128] In this light, Jacopo Pontormo's *Visitation* is an unusually rich visual and theological fare. We may reflect briefly on the hermeneutical significance of our painting, especially for heirs of the free church tradition, who face serious challenges from the cultural right and from the cultural left. The intent here is to give a specific, though hopefully not provincial, example of the incorporation of Christian art into the life of contemporary faith communities. In the summer of 2000, the major denominational expression of Baptist thought in America, the Southern Baptist Convention, modified its confession of faith in terms of the role of women in marriage and ministry. Women are to be "graciously submissive" to their husbands and "the office of pastor is limited to men as qualified by Scripture."[129] For those who wish to resist such interpretations on biblical and historical grounds, the visual aspects of the Christian tradition provide relatively unexplored resources. Of course, any hermeneutic dealing with ancient visual texts must reckon with the facts that (1) most of these depictions of women are commissioned, executed, approved, and paid for by men and (2) that *our* interests and concerns were not necessarily those of the original audience.[130]

For Pontormo the message *given* is determined to a large degree by the guidance provided by the three inscriptions. Those inscriptions make clear that in this scene, Mary is not defined only or perhaps even primarily by her role as mother. Rather, she, like her ancestor Abraham, is admired for her confession of faith. Like Abraham, Mary too owes her child to God, and the recognition that this child belongs to God, indeed IS God, is the Epiphany in which both Luke and Pontormo invite their respective audiences to participate. The centrality of Mary is underscored also by the fact that the two male figures, Joseph and Zechariah, are reduced to roles of silent gesturing — roles, ironically, often associated in the biblical tradition with female characters.

But the message *given* is not always exactly the same as the message *received*.[131] Although the inscriptions limit the possible meanings of the

Visitation, and even if, as we hope, we have deciphered their cryptic messages accurately, there remains a delightful ambiguity. Given the Servites' interest in Mary, the historical meaning given probably does have to do, as we have argued, with the parallels between Abraham and Mary, Isaac and Christ. But for example, the meaning received by Renaissance women, no doubt a significant part of the worshiping community at the Annunziata, need not have been limited to those parallels. And, of course, the third-person singular verbs allow for either a male or a female subject. Thus, we imagine that some beholders of the Visitation might have applied the inscriptions also to Elizabeth.[132] In this case, Elizabeth, too, owes her unborn child to God, and God has not promised a child to her and Zechariah in vain. Nor is her twofold confession that Mary is blessed because of her faith (1:45) and that the prenatal Jesus is "her Lord" (1:43) made in vain. And finally Elizabeth, too, is one upon whom God can look favorably. The appeal of Elizabeth to Renaissance women may be in her relatively ordinary existence.[133] Mary, from the beginning to the end of her life, was different from other women. She was from a wealthy family, immaculately conceived, had herself a virginal conception, painless birth, perpetual virginity, and at the end of her life was assumed into heaven. Remember that the story of Elizabeth, on the other hand, was little embellished in the literary sources. Nothing much about her own birth or parentage survives save the name of her mother (which was confused in the tradition). Granted that her advanced age made the conception of John the Baptist an impressive miracle: nonetheless that conception took place in the "old-fashioned" way (even if the emphasis here was on "old"!). And, despite the fact that in one late medieval work the angels Michael and Gabriel dig Elizabeth's grave while the souls of Zacharias and Simeon sing, Elizabeth dies as she lived, in an ordinary manner.[134] Evidently her frequent appearance in visual depictions is dependent almost entirely on someone else — John the Baptist, Zechariah, or in this case, Mary — and the importance of this scene, here placed as it is in a sequence of the Virgin's life, is for Mary's, not Elizabeth's, life. Nonetheless, Elizabeth is the first human character in Luke to recognize the true identity of Jesus, calling him "her Lord," and that before he was even born. She functions as a prophet even though she is not explicitly called one. The point here is that in Elizabeth, the early sixteenth-century community of women had a resource for evoking an emotionally satisfying, spiritually edifying, and politically powerful interpretation that if God could look favorably on the rather ordinary saint Elizabeth because of her faith, God could look favorably also on the now anonymous but faithful lives of women who first experienced this painting. Thus,

the *Visitation* is also a potential resource for those interested in drawing on ancient sources to address contemporary issues — in this case,
the role of women in the faith and practice of contemporary Christian
communities.

On the other hand, Pontormo's *Visitation* provides a resource for ad-
dressing the interpretations of the cultural left. In her recent book,
Abraham on Trial: The Social Legacy of Biblical Myth, Carol Delaney has
argued that the Abraham story is the foundational myth that lies at the
root of much if not all child abuse and violence against women and children in the West.[135] Part of the problem with Delaney's work is that she
does not take into account sufficiently the history of biblical interpretation
that has struggled with precisely the same issues she has raised about this
and other texts. Luke Timothy Johnson has observed: "The function of
such interpretation within both Judaism and Christianity has not been to
reinforce the violent tendencies of the stories, but to mitigate and trans-
mute them. Midrash and allegory represent strategies of reading within
religious traditions that seek to combine loyalty with criticism, that try to
save those aspects of the text that give life while also challenging those
elements that are morally questionable."[136] Pontormo's *Visitation* represents one allegorical reading that emphasizes the life-giving aspect of the
Abraham story, and as such functions as a kind of Christian midrash on
Gen 22 — a midrash that could still well serve contemporary communities
of faith in their theological reflection and liturgical appropriation of these
sacred texts.

Conclusion

Drawing on liturgical, visual, and exegetical sources, Jacopo Pontormo
stands in a long tradition of interpreters who have connected the suffering
of Christ with the sacrifice of Isaac. What is new in Pontormo's work is
the parallel between Abraham and Mary. The Renaissance worshiping
community, prompted to contemplate the epiphany by the minor figures
in the scene, may have thus first experienced Pontormo's and his patrons'
visualization of the visitation text. So also may the modern worshiper add
his or her voice to the petition ascribed to Abraham, Mary, and yes, even
Elizabeth: "Most Excellent God, look favorably" upon us as well, in the
confidence that God "does not promise in vain!"

Notes

1. Giorgio Vasari, *Le Opere di Giorgio Vasari: Le Vite de' più eccellenti pittori, scultori ed architettori scritte da Giorgio Vasari pittore Aretino,* (1568) (ed. Gaetano Milanesi; 9 vols.; Florence: Sansoni, 1885), 6:246.

2. Janet Cox-Rearick, in the *Dictionary of Art* (ed. Jane Turner; 34 vols.; New York: Grove's Dictionaries, 1996), 25:221–24. See also S. J. Freedberg, *Painting in Italy, 1500–1600* (Harmondsworth: Pelican History of Art, 1971, rev. 1983), 102–4, for a detailed synopsis of the artist's life and works.

3. The fresco painting is 13′ x 11′2″.

4. For an example of this subject, see Sandro Boticelli (1444/45–1510), *Madonna of the Magnificat,* 1482, tempera on panel, Uffizi, Florence, as illustrated in Edwin Hall, "*Aureola Super Auream:* Crowns and Related Symbols of Special Distinction for Saints in Late Gothic and Renaissance Iconography," *Art Bulletin* 67 (1985): 567–603.

5. Charles H. Talbert, *Reading Luke: A Literary and Theological Commentary on the Third Gospel* (New York: Crossroad, 1982), 22.

6. Ibid.

7. On this emphasis on Mary, see Mark Coleridge, *The Birth of the Lukan Narrative: Narrative as Christology in Luke 1–2* (Journal for the Study of the New Testament Supplement Series 88; Sheffield: Sheffield Academic Press, 1993), 76.

8. See below, however, on the manuscripts that replace Mary with Elizabeth as the speaker in Luke 1:46.

9. See Coleridge, *Birth of the Lukan Narrative,* 79–80.

10. R. Alan Culpepper, "Luke," in *The New Interpreter's Bible* (vol. 9; Nashville: Abingdon, 1995), 54.

11. Talbert, *Reading Luke,* 22.

12. Coleridge, *Birth of the Lukan Narrative,* 85.

13. Culpepper, "Luke," 54–55.

14. Robert C. Tannehill, *Luke* (Nashville: Abingdon, 1996), 53. Mary's speech also echoes many of the themes found in Hannah's song recorded in 1 Sam 2:1–10.

15. Talbert, *Reading Luke,* 22.

16. Tannehill, *Luke,* 54.

17. Although some Latin manuscripts attribute this speech also to Elizabeth, it is generally agreed that the original text of Luke reads the name "Mary" (or perhaps had no named subject). On the textual problem, see Bruce M. Metzger, *A Textual Commentary on the Greek New Testament* (2d ed.; New York: United Bible Societies, 1994), 109, and on the history of interpretation regarding the identity of the speaker of the Magnificat, see especially Stephen Benko, "The Magnificat: A History of the Controversy," *Journal of Biblical Literature* 86 (1967): 263–75. What concerns us is whether or not the Latin text naming Elizabeth as the speaker might have influenced Pontormo or his patrons. Since Pontormo's *Visitation* seems to depict the introductory part of the episode with Elizabeth's lips parted as if in speech, the extent of Elizabeth's speech (e.g., whether it ends in v. 45 or 55) would affect in part the iconographic interpretation. Because the Vulgate includes the name of Mary, we shall limit the focus of our attention to 39–45, though we shall still pay some attention to the mention of Abraham and his descendants in v. 55.

18. The Greek at this point is difficult, and there is some question about its translation. Some take Abraham in apposition to the fathers: "He remembered mercy, even as

he spoke to our fathers, that is, to Abraham and to his seed forever." Others view 1:55a as parenthetical, rendering the following translation, "Because he remembered mercy for Abraham and his seed forever, even as he spoke to our fathers." On the history of the translation difficulties, see Darrell L. Bock, *Luke, 1:1–9:50* (Grand Rapids: Baker Books, 1994), 159–60. In either case, Mary chooses to end her speech with a reference to the Abrahamic covenant.

19. Abraham is mentioned a total of twenty-two times in Luke and Acts. See Nihls A. Dahl, "The Story of Abraham in Luke-Acts," *Studies in Luke-Acts: Essays Presented in Honor of Paul Schubert* (ed. Leander E. Keck and J. Louis Martyn; Philadelphia: Fortress, 1966), 139–58; Robert L. Brawley, "For Blessing of All Families of the Earth: Covenant Traditions in Luke-Acts," *Currents in Theology and Missions* 22 (1995): 18–26.

20. See Gertrud Schiller, *Iconography of Christian Art* (trans. Janet Seligman; vol. 1; Greenwich, Conn.: New York Graphic Society, 1971), 55.

21. In the *Protevangelium of James* (12:1–2), we are told that Elizabeth (like Mary) was spinning thread for the temple veil when Mary arrived at her home.

22. Cited by Mary Lee Wile, "Elizabeth," *Daughters of Sarah* 22 (1996): 45–59.

23. Jacobus de Voragine, *The Golden Legend: Readings on the Saints* (trans. William Granger Ryan; Princeton, N.J.: Princeton University Press, 1993), 2:150.

24. See the *Life of John according to Serapion*, cited in *New Testament Apocrypha* (ed. Wilhelm Schneemelcher; trans. R. McL. Wilson; vol. 1; Louisville: Westminster/John Knox, 1991), 467–68.

25. Schiller, *Iconography*, 55.

26. Feminist studies and/or studies that focus on the female characters include: Jean-Pierre Ruiz, "Luke 1:39–56: Mary's Visit to Elizabeth as a Biblical Instance of Mentoring," *Apuntes* 17 (1997): 103–5; Loretta Dornisch, "A Woman Reads the Gospel of Luke: Introduction and Luke 1: The Infancy Narratives," *Biblical Research* 42 (1997): 7–22; Turid Karlsen Seim, "Searching for the Silver Coin: A Response to Loretta Dornisch and Barbara Reid," *Biblical Research* 42 (1997): 32–41; Arie Troost, "Elisabeth and Mary — Naomi and Ruth: Gender-Response Criticism in Luke 1–2," in *A Feminist Companion to the Hebrew Bible in the New Testament* (ed. Athalya Brenner; Sheffield: Sheffield Academic Press, 1996), 159–96; Krister Stendahl, "And Why Is This Granted to Me?" *Harvard Divinity Bulletin* 24, no. 2 (1995): 23–24; Ben Witherington III, *Women in the Earliest Churches* (Cambridge: Cambridge University Press, 1994); Tina Pippin, "The Politics of Meeting: Women and Power in the New Testament," in *That They Might Live: Power, Empowerment, and Leadership in the Church* (ed. Michael Downey; New York: Crossroad, 1991), 13–24; Janice Capel Anderson, "Mary's Difference: Gender and Patriarchy in the Birth Narratives," *Journal of Religion* 67 (1987): 183–202.

27. From the perspective of liberation theology, see Ernesto Cardenal, *The Gospel in Solentiname* (trans. Donald D. Walsh; 4 vols., Maryknoll, N.Y.: Orbis, 1982), and the accompanying *The Gospel in Art by the Peasants of Solentiname* (ed. Philip and Sally Scharper; Maryknoll, N.Y.: Orbis, 1984), esp. 8–9 where the Visitation is discussed and depicted; Gustavo Gutiérrez, *A Theology of Liberation: History, Politics and Salvation* (Maryknoll, N.Y.: Orbis, 1973); Gail R. O'Day, "Singing Woman's Song: a Hermeneutic of Liberation [Ex 15:21; 1 Sam 2:1–10; Lk 1:46–55]," *Currents in Theology and Mission* 12 (1985): 203–10; D. Sölle, "Meditation über Lukas 1," in *Die Revolutionäre Geduld* (Berlin: Gedichte, 1974), 26; also the brief treatment of recent interpretations of the

Magnificat in François Bovon, *L'Évangile Selon Saint Luc (1,1–9,50)* (Geneva: Labor et Fides, 1991), 94–95.

28. Major monographs, exhibition catalogs, and collections of essays on the artist and his paintings include Frederick Mortimore Clapp, *Jacopo Carucci da Pontormo: His Life and Work* (New Haven: Yale University Press, 1916); Luciano Berti, *Pontormo* (Florence: Edizione d'Arte il Fiorino, 1966); Kurt W. Forster, *Pontormo: Monographie mit kritischem Katalog* (Munich: Bruckmann, 1966); Luciano Berti, *L'opera completa del Pontormo* (Milan: Rizzoli, 1973); Luciano Berti, *Pontormo e il suo tempo* (Florence: Banca Toscana, 1993), 190; Philippe Costamagna, *Pontormo* (Milan: Electa, 1994); Carlo Falciani, *Il Pontormo e il Rosso. Guida alle opere* (Florence: Giunta regionale toscana, 1994); Anna Forlani Tempesti and Alessandra Giovannetti, *Pontormo* (Florence: Octavo, 1994); Roberto Ciardi and Antonio Natali, *Pontormo e Rosso: atti del convegno di Empoli e Volterra progetto Appiani di Piombino* (Florence: Giunta regionale toscana, 1996).

29. Freedberg (*Painting in Italy*, 102) states Pontormo's apprenticeship as with Albertinelli c. 1508–10 and then continued with Piero di Cosimo.

30. Giorgio Vasari, *Le Opere di Giorgio Vasari: Le Vite de' più eccellenti pittori, scultori ed architettori scritte da Giorgio Vasari pittore Aretino* (1568) (ed. Gaetano Milanesi; 9 vols. Florence: Sansoni, 1885), 7:246. On the relationship between Pontormo and Piero di Cosimo, see Louis Alexander Waldman, "Fact, Fiction, Hearsay: Notes on Vasari's Life of Piero de Cosimo," *Art Bulletin* 82 (2000): 171–79.

31. Scholars agree that Pontormo was about eighteen when he began his association with Andrea.

32. These include a *Faith and Charity*, 1513–14 (Florence, Uffizi), originally surrounding the arms of Pope Leo X over the portico of SS. Annunziata, Florence; *The Hospital of St. Matteo*, c. 1514 (Florence, Accademia); and the *Virgin and Child with Saints*, c. 1514 (Florence, SS. Annunziata) for S. Ruffillo. For a summary of Pontormo's work in Florence, see Eva Darragon, "Pontormo à Florence," *Revue de l'Art* 51 (1981): 51–60.

33. For the relationship between Pontormo and the Medici, see Janet Cox-Rearick, *Dynasty and Destiny in Medici Art: Pontormo, Leo X and the Two Cosimos* (Princeton, N.J.: Princeton University Press, 1984). For the cultural and historical settings in contemporary Florence and its influence on Pontormo, see Paolo Simoncelli, "Pontormo el la cultura fiorentina," *Archivio storico italiano* 153 (1995): 488–527, and J. N. Stephans, *The Fall of the Florentine Republic, 1512–1530* (New York: Oxford University Press, 1983), respectively.

34. Cox-Rearick, *Dictionary*, 222. This commission is discussed below as part of the preparation for the visit of Leo X on November 15, 1515.

35. Panel paintings executed immediately following the Florence *Visitation* include three scenes from the story of Joseph painted for the bridal chamber of Pier Francesco Borgherini, 1515–17 (London, National Gallery), a *Portrait of a Jeweller*, c. 1518 (Paris, Louvre), a *Portrait of a Musician*, c. 1515–16 (Florence, Uffizi), and a *Portrait of Cosimo de'Medici il Vecchio*, 1519 (Florence, Uffizi).

36. For San Michele Visdomini, see David Franklin, "A Document for Pontormo's Michele Visdomini Altarpiece," *Burlington Magazine* 132 (1990): 487–89.

37. For Poggio a Caiano, see J. Kliemann, "Vertumnus und Pomona: Zum Program von Pontormos Fresko in Poggio a Caiano," *Mitteilungen Kunsthistorisches Institut, Florenz* 16 (1972): 293–328, and M. Winner, "Pontormo's Fresko in Poggio a Caiano," *Zeitschrift*

für Kunstgeschichte 35 (1972): 153–97. More recently, see Litta Mari Medri, *Pontormo a Poggio a Caiano* (Florence: Octavo, 1995).

For the Certosa del Galluzzo, see Elizabeth Pilliod, "Pontormo and Bronzino at the Certosa," *Getty Museum Journal* 20 (1992): 77–88.

For the Capponi chapel, see John Shearman, *Pontormo's Altarpiece in S. Felicità: The 51st Charlton Lecture, University Newcastle-upon-Tyne* (Westerham: University of Newcastle-upon-Tyne, 1968); Leo Steinberg, "Pontormo's Capponi Chapel," *Art Bulletin* 56 (1974): 385–99.

38. Comparison and further examination of the two *Visitation* paintings will be the subject of a future study. For recent scholarship on the *Visitation* in Carmignano, see Mariano Apa, *Pontormo. La Visitazione a Carmignano* (Carmignano-Florence: Arti Grafiche Albano, 1994); Rosanna Caterini Proto Pisani, Maria Grazia Trenti Antonelli, and Litta Medri, *Il Pontormo: le opere di Empoli, Carmignano e Poggio a Caiano* (Venice: Marsilio Editori, 1994), 31–50; *Pontormo e Rosso. La "maniera moderna" in Toscana: Empoli and Volterra,* 1994 (Florence: Giunta regionale toscana, 1996); Christoph Bertsch, *Jacopo Pontormo Le Quattro Donne di Carmignano* (Florence: Edizioni Medicea, 1998).

39. See the exhibition catalogs on paintings, *Mostra del Pontormo e del primo manierismo fiorentino* (ed. U. Baldini, Luciano Berti, and Luisa Marcucci; Florence: Palazzo Strozzi, 1956) and on drawings, *Mostra di disegni dei primi manieristi italiani* (ed. U. Baldini, Luciano Berti, and Luisa Marcucci; Florence: Uffizi, 1954) for a discussion of the first mannerists.

For Bronzino, see Robert B. Simon, "Bronzino's Portraits of Cosimo I de'Medici" (Ph.D. diss., Columbia University, 1985).

40. For the frescoes at San Lorenzo, see Charles de Tolnay, "Les Fresques de Pontormo dans le choeur de San Lorenzo à Florence," *Crit A.* 33 (1950): 38–52; Janet Cox-Rearick, "Pontormo, Bronzino, Allori and the lost Deluge at S. Lorenzo," *Burlington Magazine* 134 (1992): 239–48.

41. Pontormo's written letters to Benedetto Varchi requesting that he be permitted to participate in the debate are published by Varchi in *Due lezioni di M. Benedetto Varchi* (Florence, 1549), 132–35.

42. See Jacopo Carucci Pontormo, *Diario: Codice Magliabechiano VIII 1490 della Biblioteca nazionale centrale di Firenze* (Rome: Salerno, 1996), or *Pontormo's Diary* (ed. Rosemary Mayer; New York: London Press, 1979).

43. John Shearman, "Rosso, Pontormo, Bandinelli and Others at SS. Annunziata," *Burlington Magazine* 102 (1960): 152–56. For the life of Andrea di Cosimo Feltrini, see Vasari, *Le Opere di Giorgio Vasari,* 5:204–10.

44. Shearman, "Rosso, Pontormo, Bandinelli and Others at SS. Annunziata," 154. A payment of 3 lire, 15 soldi, dated January 31, 1513, to *"porto Jacopo di bartolomeo dipintore."*

45. Clapp, *Pontormo,* 9.

46. Vasari, *Le Opere di Giorgio Vasari,* 6:248.

47. Shearman, "Rosso, Pontormo, Bandinelli and Others at SS. Annunziata," 154.

48. Ibid.

49. Vasari, *Le Opere di Giorgio Vasari,* 6:248. Shearman ("Rosso, Pontormo, Bandinelli and Others at SS. Annunziata," 154), focusing on archival documentation, calls this story "legendary embroidery," which does not concern his study. For additional commentary on the probability and/or possibility of Vasari's story see Clapp, *Pontormo,* 9n. 15.

50. Clapp, *Pontormo*, 10.

51. Shearman ("Rosso, Pontormo, Bandinelli and Others at SS. Annunziata," 154) clarifies the previous scholarship regarding the documents related to Pontormo's payments for this work.

52. Vasari, *Le Opere di Giorgio Vasari*, 6:250.

53. Clapp (*Pontormo*, 10) cites the following sources as contemporary evidence of the popularity of the putti: Vasari, VI:248; Francesco Bocchi, *Le bellezze della città di Firenze*, 1581 (ed. M. Giovanni Cinelli; Florence: Gugliantini, 1677), 415; Giuseppe Richa, *Notizie istoriche delle chiese fiorentine divise ne'suoi Quartieri* (Florence: P. G. Viviani, 1754–62) V:52.

54. Clapp (*Pontormo*, 12) states that Pontormo also worked with Ridolfo del Ghirlandaio in the papal chapel of S. Maria Novella during the summer of 1515. Pontormo painted a *St. Veronica Holding the Sudario* in fresco in a lunette above the door. In the center of the ceiling, he painted a tondo of God the Father descending. He also painted the four medallions (each with a putto) and squares (the arms of Leo supported by putti) on the ceiling. These are completely repainted.

55. Forlani Tempesti and Giovannetti, *Pontormo*, 110–11.

56. Shearman, "Rosso, Pontormo, Bandinelli and Others at SS. Annunziata," 154–55.

57. The date on the fireplace: A. D. M. D. X. IIII.

58. Forlani Tempesti and Giovannetti, *Pontormo*, 111.

59. Elisabetta Marchetti Letta, *Pontormo. Rosso Fiorentino* (Florence: Scala, 1994), 9.

60. Shearman ("Rosso, Pontormo, Bandinelli and Others at SS. Annunziata," 154) reviewed and updated the accuracy of the documentation: "Here again Milanesi (Vasari, *Le Opere di Giorgio Vasari*, 6:258 n. 1) had spotted some of the payments, but simply stated that between April 1515 and June 1516, Pontormo received on various occasions 73 lire. Clapp (*Pontormo*, 275–76) again published in full a series of payments from December 1514 to June 1516, missing only one." Shearman published the final document to be discovered. Clapp (ibid.) also states that Fra Mariano dal Canto alle Macine commissioned Andrea del Sarto and Franciabigio. Five of the six scenes from the life of San Filippo Benizzi (the *Calling and Ordination* was painted by Cosimo Roselli c. 1476) were commissioned solely to Andrea del Sarto.

61. Berti, *Pontormo e il Suo Tempo*, 190. For more on why the particular scene of the Visitation was chosen for this cycle, see Jack Wasserman, "Jacopo Pontormo's Florentine Visitation," *Artibus et Historiae* 32 (1995): 39–53.

62. James Beck ("The Young Pontormo and Albertinelli," *Burlington Magazine* 122 (1980): 623–24) argued that Clapp misread the documents that enabled him to claim Pontormo entered into Albertinelli's bottega at the age of nine in 1503. Given this evidence, an entrance of the young boy into his first workshop probably occurred between twelve and fourteen years of age.

63. Vasari, *Le Opere di Giorgio Vasari*, 5:67.

64. Clapp (*Pontormo*, 18) discussed several sketches by Pontormo drawn between 1513 and 1518 which have their source in the Michelangelo. Luisa Marcucci, *Quaderni Pontormeschi: Vol. 3. La "Maniera" del Pontormo* (Florence: Tipografia Giuntina, 1956), 9, also finds the Battle of Cascina to be a source for the Pontormo *Visitation*.

65. Letta, *Pontormo. Rosso Fiorentino*, 13.

66. Salvatore S. Nigro, *Pontormo: Paintings and Frescoes* (New York: Harry N. Abrams, 1994), 2:2. See also Irving L. Zupnick, "Pontormo's Early Style," *Art Bulletin* 47 (1965):

345–53, especially 347, 349, and 352, for a discussion of the stylistic influences on the *Visitation*.

67. See Heinrich Wölfflin, *Classic Art: An Introduction to the Italian Renaissance* (trans. Peter and Linda Murray; New York: Phaidon Publishers; distributed by Oxford University Press, 1961), 153–54.

68. Ibid. On the possible iconographic significance of this architectural space, see Wasserman, "Jacopo Pontormo's Florentine *Visitation*," 45, 48–50.

69. See Frederick A. Cooper, "Jacopo Pontormo and Influences from the Renaissance Theater," *Art Bulletin* 55 (1973): 380–92, for a discussion of Pontormo's part in various Florentine *feste* and theatrical decorations.

70. Janet Cox-Rearick ("The Drawings of Pontormo: Addenda," *Master Drawings* 8 [1970]: 363–78) discusses a preparatory drawing of the boy on the steps identified by I. Fenyo, "Sur Quelques Dessins italiens du XVIe siècle," *Bulletin di Musée National Hongrois des Beaux-Arts* 19 (1961): 59–60; fig. 45. See Cox-Rearick, "Drawings of Pontormo," cat. 11–13a, for additional drawings related to the *Visitation*. Drawings are not the focus of our study, but we find it necessary to mention the specific drawings related to the fresco in discussion. Some have identified the figure of Diogenes in Raphael's *School of Athens* as a possible compositional source.

71. Robert W. Gaston, "Attention and Inattention in Religious Painting of the Renaissance: Some Preliminary Observations," *Renaissance Studies in Honor of Craig Hugh Smyth* (Florence: Giunti Barbera, 1985), 253–68. Gaston does refer to Pontormo's work, though his attention is directed toward Pontormo's "other" *Visitation* at Carmignano. The study of figures in religious painting seen in contemplation was the subject of an informative article by Giancarlo Fiorenza on "Dosso Dossi, Garolfalo, and the *Costabili Polyptych*: Imaging Spiritual Authority," *Art Bulletin* 82 (2000): 252–57.

72. Ibid., 264.

73. Ibid.

74. Ibid.

75. Ibid., 263.

76. Ibid.

77. Ibid., 265.

78. Ibid., 263.

79. Gaston also discusses the "chorus effect," which is taken up below under the discussion of the figures of Joseph and Zechariah.

80. Forster (*Pontormo*, 129), for example, considered the flanking inscriptions indecipherable.

81. Quoted by permission from private correspondence with Monsignor Timothy Verdon, Canon of the Florence Cathedral, dated October 17, 1999. Msgr. Verdon is also cited (with no details) for his interpretation of these inscriptions by Tempesti and Giovannetti, *Pontormo*, 111. We are most grateful for Msgr. Verdon's assistance with these inscriptions.

82. See Wasserman, "Jacopo Pontormo's Florentine *Visitation*," 59.

83. Ibid., 42.

84. The inscription was published by William Forsyth, *The Entombment of Christ* (Cambridge: Cambridge University Press, 1970).

85. Wasserman, "Jacopo Pontormo's Florentine *Visitation*," 42. Wasserman goes on to cite "from among innumerable examples" Cosimo Tura's *Enthroned Madonna*.

86. Verdon (in private correspondence) actually offers two alternatives, NUMINI DEBET EVM ("He owes him to God") or NUMINI DEDIT EVM ("He gives him to God"). Either is possible and the difference in meaning only slight; nevertheless, we prefer the former because it appears from Figure 6 that the "B" of the DEB is still faintly visible, and it is also much easier to see how a "B" (rather than a "D") could in this case be mistaken for an "E." Also *dedet* does not occur as an inflected form in the Vulgate.

87. Wasserman, "Jacopo Pontormo's Florentine *Visitation*," 42. Interestingly, at this point, Wasserman (in our opinion rightly) abandons the Domjulien inscription (which read "NE IVRAS VAN" and is rendered as a second-person imperative "nor swear in vain"). The second half of the Domjulien inscription not only reads NE instead of NEC, but it reverses the order of the last two words. Verdon (private correspondence) offers the slightly different reconstruction "NEC VANE IURAVIT" (Nor *did* he swear in vain).

88. See Wasserman, "Jacopo Pontormo's Florentine *Visitation*," 42. Verdon (private correspondence).

89. On the development of this theme of the threats to and fulfillment of the ancestral promise, see Walter Brueggemann, *Genesis* (Atlanta: John Knox Press, 1982).

90. Translation: "that we should be saved from our enemies and from the hand of all who hate us in order to perform the mercy with our fathers and to remember the holy covenant which he promised to Abraham our father."

91. Verdon, private correspondence.

92. On this point, see now Robin Jensen, *Understanding Early Christian Art* (London: Routledge, 1999).

93. Ambrose, *De Cain et Abel*, i.8. Latin: "Isaac ergo Christi passuri est typus."

94. See Irenaeus, *Adversus Haereses*, iv.5; Origen, *In Genesim*, ix; Tertullian, *Liber adv. Judaeos*, x; Melito, *Frag.* ix, x, xi, xv; Augustine, *De Civitate Dei*, xvi, 32. Other references may be found in volume 209 of Migne's *Patrologia Latina* in the Index of Old Testament figures, col. 245. On the history of the christological interpretation of the sacrifice of Isaac, see especially David Lerch, *Isaaks Opferung Christlich Gedeutet: Eine auslegungsgeschichtliche Untersuchung* (Tübingen: J. C. B. Mohr, 1950).

95. Alison Moore Smith, "The Iconography of the Sacrifice of Isaac in Early Christian Art," *American Journal of Archaeology* 26 (1922): 160.

96. Ibid., 168, 169.

97. Ibid., 169.

98. Ibid., 162. Interestingly, Smith (169) claims that "a cursory examination of western monuments down to the fifteenth century seems to show an almost universal adoption of the Asiatic-Hellenistic Isaac on the altar [*the* invariable element] in representations of the scene." While this may be true of monumental art, it does not seem true of Pontormo's fresco.

99. For a facsimile, see *Biblia Pauperum, Faksimileausgabe des vierzigblättrigen Armenbibel: Blockbuches in der Bibliothek der Erzdiözesee Esztergom* (Hanau/Main: Werner Dausien, 1967).

100. Translation from A. N. Didron, *Christian Iconography* (vol. 2; London: Henry G. Bohn, 1891), Appendix III. The Latin text of the quotation reads: "Legitur in Genesi xxii capitulo, cum Abraham gladium extendisset ut filium immolaret angelus domini ipsum de delo prohibuit, dicens ne extendas manum tuam super puerum. Abraham patrem celestem significat qui filium suum scilicet Cristum pro nobis omnibus in cruce

immolavit ut per hoc innueret signum amoris paterni." On the right side of the central subject is the Brazen Serpent and a quotation from Num 21:9. In keeping with the pattern of the *Biblia Pauperum*, quotations from the Old Testament prophets were found in the upper left and right, in this case from Ps 22:16 ("They pierced My hands and My feet.") and Job 41:1 ("Canst thou draw out Leviathan with a hook?").

101. J. Wickham Legge, ed. *The Sarum Missal* (Oxford: Clarendon Press, 1916), 223. Emphasis ours.

102. Rosemary Woolf, "The Effect of Typology on the English Mediaeval Plays of Abraham and Isaac," *Speculum* 32 (1957): 806–7.

103. Ibid.

104. See Leah Sinanoglou, "The Christ Child as Sacrifice: A Medieval Tradition and the Corpus Christi Plays," *Speculum* 48 (1973): 491–509.

105. See Woolf and Sinanoglou. While both Woolf and Sinanoglou focus on the English medieval plays, their ideas can be extended also to those plays whose origins are Italian, see Luigi Grotto, *Lo Isach;* and *La rappresantazione d'Abraam e d'Isaac suo figliuolo;* see A. D'Ancona, *Origini del teatro italiano* (Turin: E. Loescher, 1891).

106. Sinanoglou, "The Christ Child as Sacrifice," 502; Woolf, "The Effect of Typology," 813. Petrus Comestor (b. 1100–10) defends the view that Isaac was a man of twenty-five or thirty years in *Historia Scholastica* and appeals to Josephus as his authority on this point. The minority view among the commentators (that Isaac was a child) is defended by Nicholas of Lyra in *Additio,* ii, and *Replica* for Genesis, xxii, by arguing that had Isaac been an adult his consent would have been required for the sacrifice; cited by Woolf, "The Effect of Typology," 814n44a. Woolf comments, "It is interesting to notice how, although in exegesis the idea of Isaac as a child was associated with a non-allegorical interpretation of the text, in art and literature it particularly served the purposes of typology."

107. Shearman, "Rosso, Pontormo, Bandinelli and Others at SS. Annunziata," 154.

108. A. D'Ancona, *Sacre Rappresentazioni dei secoli XIV, XV, XVI* (Florence: Successori Le Monnier, 1872), 1:43f.

109. On this point, see also Cooper, "Jacopo Pontormo and Influences from the Renaissance Theater," 381.

110. Forster, *Pontormo,* 129, for example, suggests, "Die Parallele von Isaaks Opferung (Bild im Bilde) mit der Heimsuchung ist ikonographisch merkwürdig."

111. Wasserman, "Jacopo Pontormo's Florentine *Visitation,*" 43. We wish to express our thanks to Professor Jeff Fish, Classics Department, Baylor University, who along with Msgr. Timothy Verdon, provided invaluable assistance in working on this inscription.

112. Forster, *Pontormo,* 129, argues further that the greeting AVE "gibt in ihrer vokativen Form Elisabeths Anrede wieder, während sich die bis zur Unentzifferbarkeit abgekürtzen Inschriften in der Kalotte der Deutung enziehen."

113. Wasserman, "Jacopo Pontormo's Florentine *Visitation,*" 44.

114. Ibid., 45.

115. Ibid.

116. Our examination of the Latin Vulgate, for example, showed no occurrences of *adnuere,* while various forms of *annuere* occurred a number of times. In most instances, the word connoted "motion" (waving of the hand, Luke 5:7; Acts 12:17, 21:40, 24:10; winking the eye, Prov 6:13, 10:10), but at least twice the term was used to connote "approval" as in 2 Macc 11:15a: "annuit autem Macchabeus precibus Lysiae in omnibus

utilitati consulens . . . " (cf. 2 Macc 14:20). This same word is, of course, found on the reverse of a dollar bill, *ANNUIT COEPTIS* ("he looked favorably on our beginnings").

117. Wasserman, "Jacopo Pontormo's Florentine *Visitation*," 45.

118. We should note also that the use of the nominative DEVS with the vocative OPTIME avoids the rather awkward construction DEE. This case is similar to the use in Greek of the nominative *theon* where a vocative *thee* is expected.

119. Our interpretation of the inscription in light of the fresco does not agree in detail with that of Wasserman, who spends more time on the role of John the Baptist in the iconography. Still, there are some interesting connections to John the Baptist. Not only has the "most Excellent God" provided a sacrificial lamb to take Isaac's place, at the Visitation, Christ in the womb is himself acknowledged as "the most excellent God" by John the Baptist (1:44) — the first time in Scripture in which Jesus' divinity is explicitly recognized. And this recognition is by John the Baptist, who is the future prophet of his Passion ("Here is the Lamb of God who takes away the sin of the world," John 1:29). The lamb of God's provision, often a detail in visual depictions of the sacrifice of Isaac, is not missing from this scene as some suggest; rather the ultimate provision is to be found in the Lamb of God. Thus, the sacrifice of a father and of the Father are brought into relationship with Christ's forthcoming passion.

120. We are following here the work of Lorenzo Gnocchi, *Il Pontormo e il Rosso* (Marsilio: Comune di Empoli, 1994), 26, who identifies the kneeling figure as Joseph and notes the significance of the gestures. See also Wasserman, "Jacopo Pontormo's Florentine *Visitation*," 39.

121. Such gestures are, of course, especially appropriate for Zechariah since he was earlier struck mute because of his disbelief over the oracle of Elizabeth's pregnancy (Luke 1:20). That curse is not removed until John's birth (see Luke 1:67).

122. For an alternative interpretation, see Wasserman, "Jacopo Pontormo's Florentine *Visitation*," 45.

123. See Wölfflin, *Classic Art*.

124. Wasserman, "Jacopo Pontormo's Florentine *Visitation*," 41, makes the tentative suggestion that the figure may represent St. Luke, since, though lacking the stock iconographical symbols, "he alone among the Evangelists describes the Visitation."

125. Verdon, private correspondence.

126. Forster, *Pontormo*, 129.

127. See William M. McLoughlin, "Our Lady of Sorrows — a Devotion within a Tradition," in *Mary and the Churches* (Dublin: Columbia Press, 1987), 114–21.

128. See, e.g., David Burrell, *Knowing the Unknowable God: Ibn-Sina, Maimonides, Aquinas* (Notre Dame: University of Notre Dame Press, 1986); Ellen T. Charry, *By the Renewing of Your Minds: The Pastoral Function of Christian Doctrine* (New York: Oxford University Press, 1997); Bruce D. Marshall, *Trinity and Truth* (Cambridge: Cambridge University Press, 2000); John Milbank, *The Word Made Strange: Theology, Language, Culture* (Oxford: Blackwell, 1997); Rowan Williams, *Christian Spirituality: A Theological History from the New Testament to Luther and St. John of the Cross* (Atlanta: John Knox, 1980).

129. Relevant news articles, opinion editorials, and various responses to the SBC votes may be found in the archives of the Associated Baptist Press. Their web site is *www.abpnews.com/abpnews*.

130. Margaret R. Miles, *Image as Insight: Visual Understanding in Western Christianity and Secular Culture* (Boston: Beacon Press, 1985), 83.

131. The language of "message given" and "message received" is that of Miles, *Image as Insight*, 30–35, passim.

132. We need not conclude that these female viewers were necessarily literate, since over time, the inscriptions could and most likely were interpreted for those illiterate (both male and female) either formally by priests and other ecclesiastical officials or informally by literate friends and companions.

133. Of course, Elizabeth is not totally obscure, since she is the mother of John the Baptist, patron saint of Florence. Hartt (*History of Italian Renaissance Art*, 556) suggests that the central scene may also be read allegorically. She pays homage to Mary, who, in Hartt's reading, represents Rome. Such a reading is, of course, possible, especially given the political and ecclesiastical struggles between Fra. Girolamo Savonarola of Florence and Pope Alexander VI that culminated in Savonarola's martyrdom on May 28, 1498, just a few years before Pontormo's work for the papal visit of 1516. On this conflict, see Donald Weinstein, *Savonarola and Florence: Prophecy and Patriotism in the Renaissance* (Princeton, N.J.: Princeton University Press, 1970). Savonarola's influence on the art of his day has often been overblown; we have not found any direct connection between Pontormo's *Visitation* and Savonarola's sermons or theology. For a judicious reading of the relationship between Savonarola's preaching and Florentine art, see Ronald M. Steinberg, *Fra Girolamo Savonarola, Florentine Art, and Renaissance Historiography* (Athens, Ohio: Ohio University Press, 1977).

134. Cf. *The Life of John according to Serapion*.

135. Carol Delaney, *Abraham on Trial: The Social Legacy of Biblical Myth* (Princeton, N.J.: Princeton University Press, 1998). Delaney's conclusion is opposite that of Jon Levenson (*Death and Resurrection of the Beloved Son* [New Haven: Yale University Press, 1993]), who argues that the Abraham story works against a pattern of child sacrifice that was sporadically practiced in the ancient Near East, even among some Israelites.

136. Luke Timothy Johnson, "How Not to Read the Bible," *Commonweal* 126 (July 1999): 24.

Figure 22. Domenico Ghirlandaio. *Nativity and Adoration of the Shepherds*. 1483–85. Panel. Sassetti Chapel, S. Trinità, Florence. Photo. With permission from the Ministero dei Beni e le Attività Culturali.

Chapter four

The *Nativity and Adoration of the Shepherds* by Domenico Ghirlandaio

(Luke 2:8–20)

THE STORY OF the shepherds and the angels (Luke 2:8–20) is told immediately after the birth of Jesus. The angels appear in the field and make the announcement that "to you is born this day in the city of David a Savior, who is the Messiah, the Lord" (2:11), which prompts the shepherds to visit the child. The shepherds' adoration of the child is described in Luke 2:16: "So they went with haste and found Mary and Joseph, and the child lying in the manger." As we shall see the scene went largely overlooked in the visual arts for centuries, but eventually this single verse served as inspiration for numerous artists to produce the composition known as the "Adoration of the Shepherds." This subject was very popular in the region of Europe located north of the Alps, and it was hardly less popular in Italy after the late fifteenth century especially. Domenico Ghirlandaio (1449–94), working south of the Alps in the city of Florence, painted a major altarpiece depicting the *Nativity and Adoration of the Shepherds* (Figure 22) for Francesco Sassetti's sepulchral chapel (Figure 23) in Santa Trinità.[1] This painting in some ways typifies the characteristics of the Italian Renaissance (modeling of the figures, local color, anatomical proportion, realistic perspective, use of antiquity), yet it incorporates Northern Renaissance elements in a manner not done before and never repeated again.[2] This point is discussed more fully in the analysis of the painting below.

Overview of the Biblical Text

[8]In that region there were shepherds living in the fields, keeping watch over their flock by night. [9]Then an angel of the Lord stood before them, and the glory of the Lord shone around them, and they were terrified. [10]But the angel said to them, "Do not be afraid; for

93

see — I am bringing you good news of great joy for all the people: [11]to you is born this day in the city of David a Savior, who is the Messiah, the Lord. [12]This will be a sign for you: you will find a child wrapped in bands of cloth and lying in a manger." [13]And suddenly there was with the angel a multitude of the heavenly host, praising God and saying, [14]"Glory to God in the highest heaven, and on earth peace among those whom he favors!"

[15]When the angels had left them and gone into heaven, the shepherds said to one another, "Let us go now to Bethlehem and see this thing that has taken place, which the Lord has made known to us." [16]So they went with haste and found Mary and Joseph, and the child lying in the manger. [17]When they saw this, they made known what had been told them about this child; [18]and all who heard it were amazed at what the shepherds told them. [19]But Mary treasured all these words and pondered them in her heart. [20]The shepherds returned, glorifying and praising God for all they had heard and seen, as it had been told them.

Luke 2:8–20 is part of a unit (2:1–20) that is composed of two parts: the birth of Jesus (2:1–7) and the visitation of the shepherds (2:8–20).[3] It begins with a reference to a census decreed by the Emperor Augustus (2:1). Locating the local events of Judea on the larger world map is typical of Luke in these early chapters (see 1:5; 3:1). The present text raises some historical questions since there is no evidence of a registration of the whole Roman Empire under Augustus.[4] The theological significance, however, is clear. By the time of Luke's Gospel, Augustan propaganda, which praised the peace Augustus had brought to the Roman Empire, was found throughout Roman literature (see Virgil's *Aeneid* and *Fourth Eclogue*) and art (e.g., the *Augustus Primaporta* and *Ara Pacis Augustae,* to say nothing of the Forum of Augustus), and was no doubt familiar to Luke's authorial audience. The Priene inscription boasted: "The birthday of the god [Augustus] marked the beginning of the good news for the world."[5] In Halicarnassus Augustus was called the "savior of the whole world." His birthday was even adopted as the first day of the New Year in parts of Asia Minor.

Luke challenges the conventional wisdom of this propaganda by setting the birth of the Messiah within the context of Augustus's edict. The altar of Christ's peace was a manger; the proclamation of his peace was on the lips of angels: "On earth peace among those whom he favors" (2:14). According to Luke, Jesus' birthday, not Augustus's, divided the epochs of human history. The savior, whose birth meant "news of great joy for all the people," was born "Messiah, the Lord" "in the city of David," not Emperor in Rome. The notice of Jesus' birth is brief (2:6–7), yet the theological and political implications of Jesus' birth for Luke are obvious to his audience.

One of the most important, and often-neglected, details in the report of the birth is the locale where the baby is placed — in a manger, or feeding trough. The term has both inter- and intratextual echoes. The manger recalls the stall or manger of Isa 1:3, and it also evokes the picture of Jesus, lying in a feeding trough, as "food for the world."[6] The theme of food and meals as one of the ways in which Jesus reveals his mission to others runs throughout Luke.[7] A meal in the home of a Pharisee is the context for three important scenes in Luke: Luke 7:36–60, 11:37–54, 14:1–24.[8] The gospel likewise ends with the resurrected Lord sharing a meal with the Emmaus disciples (Luke 24:13–35) and with the eleven (24:36–49).[9]

Figure 23. Domenico Ghirlandaio. View of Sassetti chapel. Fresco. S. Trinità, Florence. Photo. With permission from the Ministero dei Beni e le Attività Culturali.

What modern audience can hear the opening words of the second unit (2:8–20) and resist being swept back into a sentimental stupor recalling Christmas days of past childhood? "Now in this same district there were shepherds out in the fields, keeping watch through the night over their flock." But the authorial audience would most likely have responded to this text in a much different way. Both the setting and the characters would alert the audience that God had chosen to disclose the birth of the Messiah in a dangerous place to a violence-prone group. Sparsely populated countrysides throughout the Roman Empire were havens for vagabonds and thieves, a motif developed fully by Luke (cf., for example, the Good Samaritan in Luke 10).[10]

Admittedly the image of the shepherd has a positive side, rooted in Old Testament imagery (Psalm 23, 68:7; Isa 40:11, 49:10, 56:8; Jer 50:19)[11] and subsequently a dominant image for Jesus and early church leaders (cf. John 10; Mark 14:27/Matt 26:31; 1 Pet 2:25, 5:2–4; Rev 7:17). By the first century C.E. and later, shepherds were despised and often considered thieves in Jewish culture.[12] Additionally, shepherds were often involved in conflict with settled villagers, conflict which usually escalated to violent activities. Josephus reports that a certain Athrongaeus, a shepherd, aspired to Archelaus's throne.

> Now, too, a mere shepherd had the temerity to aspire to the throne. He was called Athrongaeus, and his sole recommendations, to raise such hopes, were vigor of body, a soul contemptuous of death, and four brothers resembling himself. To each of these he entrusted an armed band and employed them as generals and satraps for his raids, while he himself, like a king, handled matters of graver moment. It was now that he donned the diadem, his raiding expeditions continued long afterwards. Their principal object was to kill Romans and royalists, but no Jew, from whom they had anything to gain, escaped, if he fell into their hands....After perpetuating throughout the war many such outrages upon compatriot and foreigner alike, three of them were eventually captured, the eldest by Archelaus, the two next by Gratus and Ptolemy; the fourth made terms with Archelaus and surrendered. Such was the end to which they ultimately came; but at the period of which we are speaking, these men were making the whole of Judaea one scene of guerrilla warfare.[13]

Yet even after he "donned the diadem, his raiding expeditions continued long afterwards. Their principal object was to kill Romans and royalists, but no Jew, from whom they had anything to gain, escaped, if he fell into their hands." Josephus concludes this brief section on Athrongaeus by describing this period in Judea's history as "one scene of guerrilla warfare."

With this reality in mind, the angelic chorus's message, "On earth peace among those whom he favors," delivered to one of the most violent groups in one of the most dangerous places is remarkable! No less shocking is the reaction of these shepherds who, upon hearing this news, decide among themselves to go to Bethlehem to see for themselves "this thing that has taken place, which the Lord has made known to us" (2:15).

The birth of the Messiah, according to Luke, has the power to lift up the lowly, the despised, and the violent (1:52). And these shepherds, whose vocation for the authorial audience at first conjures up an image of a despised and potentially violent group, by their actions — finding the child and "glorifying and praising God" — align themselves with the more positive portrait of the good shepherd, an image already evoked by the mention of the city of *David*, who was, of course, himself a shepherd before becoming king. The very form of the story reinforces the final positive impression of the shepherds. The story is also typical of the Old Testament commissioning story which Luke has already used:

1. *Appearance of an angel:* "Then an angel of the Lord stood before them, and the glory of the Lord shone around them" (2:9a).

2. *Reaction:* "They were terrified" (2:9b).

3. *Angel's message:* "But the angel said to them, 'Do not be afraid; for see — I am bringing you good news of great joy for all the people: to you is born this day in the city of David a Savior, who is the Messiah, the Lord'" (2:10–11).

4. *Giving of a sign:* "This will be a sign for you: you will find a child wrapped in bands of cloth and lying in a manger" (2:12).[14]

Of the elements common to these stories, only the objection to the angel's message is missing. Even though the priest, Zechariah, and the mother-to-be of Jesus, Mary, had (like Moses and Gideon and others) initially resisted the divine message, these lowly shepherds resolve immediately to heed the command implicit in the angelic canticle: "You will find a child wrapped in bands of cloth and lying in a manger" (2:12). Thanks to these shepherds, not only the ox and the donkey recognize the "manger of their lord," God's people, now represented by these shepherds, have begun to know the manger of their Lord also.

A Brief History of the Adoration of the Shepherds in Literature and Art

The story of the Adoration of the Shepherds is, of course, part of the larger Nativity cycle, the story of the birth of Jesus.[15] As such, the shepherds have been overshadowed by other details of the story, especially by the magi (Matt 2). Writers and artists found other ways of creating the bucolic setting, which the shepherds obviously bring to the story. In the gospel of *Pseudo-Matthew* 14 (eighth or ninth century), an ox and ass stand over the infant Jesus' crib. Centuries earlier, this same scene was depicted on a third- or fourth-century sarcophagus that is now located in the Church of St. Ambrose, Milan.[16] Both depict the ox and the ass, recalling Isa 1:3: "The ox knows its owner, and the donkey *its master's crib;* but Israel does not know, my people do not understand." Both omit any reference to the shepherds, yet both nonetheless create a pastoral setting for the scene.

In the church's liturgical calendar, Epiphany emerged in the West by the third or fourth century as an important and distinct feast day on January 6, commemorating the appearance or manifestation of Jesus to the magi, at his baptism, and at his first miracle at Cana.[17] The prominence of the magi in Epiphany secured their importance in the story,[18] ensuring a minor role for the shepherds, especially in art, for centuries.[19]

When the shepherds were treated, it was often to contrast or complement the role of the magi. Playing off the reference in Isa 1:3, cited above, Origen, Augustine, and Gregory of Nyssa all argued that in the story of salvation history, which the Nativity recorded, the shepherds represented the Jews and the magi stood for Gentiles (as the ox symbolized Jews and the ass Gentiles in Isa 1:3).[20] This identification continued through the medieval period as pseudo-Bonaventure's *Meditations on the Life of Christ* attests: " . . . today [Epiphany] the Church is received by Him in the person of the magi, since the Church is assembled from the gentiles, that is, the pagans. On the day of His birth, he appeared to the Jews, as personified by the shepherds. . . ."[21] Additionally, the humility of the shepherds was often highlighted. Bernard of Clairvaux wrote: "To the Shepherds who watched is announced the joy of the light and to them it is told that the Savior is born; to the poor and to those who work hard, not to you who are rich and have your consolations but have abandoned divine joy. . . ."[22] Not surprisingly, this passage was cited approvingly and expanded upon in the Franciscan *Meditations on the Life of Christ.*[23]

Finally, we should note that as at the time of our New Testament text, shepherds in general were viewed with some ambiguity over the next few centuries, especially in art.[24] As we shall see, shepherds in Renaissance Florence likewise had a similarly complex symbolic meaning.

The Artist and the Painting

Domenico Ghirlandaio

Domenico Bigordi[25] was the first of five children born to Antonia and Tommaso Bigordi called Il Ghirlandaio in Florence.[26] He was born the same year as Lorenzo de' Medici, 1449. Domenico was a painter and mosaicist and, according to Vasari, trained as a goldsmith.[27] Vasari also states that Domenico studied with the Florentine painter Alesso Baldovinetti (1425–99).[28] Baldovinetti was open to the new trend of paintings arriving in Florence from the north. By the 1440s every large city south of the Alps was influenced by northern artists through the import of paintings.[29] Works by Hans Memling (1430/40–94), Rogier Van der Weyden (1399/1400–1464), and especially Hugo van der Goes (c. 1440–82) were commissioned by the Portinari and Baroncelli families, agents of the Medici Bank in Bruges.[30] Recent scholarship suggests that Domenico may have also been apprenticed with Fra Filippo Lippi.[31] There are no securely documented frescoes or panel paintings by Domenico prior to 1475, although many have been attributed to him on the basis of style.[32] Influences from Antonio and Piero Pollaiuolo and Verrocchio can be found in these attributed early works.[33] Domenico's early style (c. 1470–80) is marked by clear, rectilinear spatial order; increasingly large and schematized plastic forms occupying ample, fully articulated space; and sculpturesque rendering of light and texture.[34]

The first documented works are the eight lunette frescoes with busts of the church fathers and classical philosophers (1475–76) in the Biblioteca Latina (now Biblioteca Apostolica) in the Vatican Palace, Rome.[35] This was probably Domenico's first trip to Rome, and such a prestigious commission suggests his growing reputation. Domenico returned to Florence by 1476 to work on the fresco of the *Last Supper* (Figure 24) in the refectory of the Badia di Passignano outside of Florence.[36] This painting clearly shows the influence of Andrea del Castagno's fresco of the same subject in 1447 in S. Apollonia, Florence, but also defines the mature work of Domenico Ghirlandaio. Domenico integrated the contours and dimensions of the room into the painted scene. The effect of atmosphere, depth, and viewer's participation in the event became characteristic of the Ghirlandaio workshop.

Domenico built his reputation as an artist of monumental fresco cycles in and around Florence from 1477 to 1480.[37] The success of these works

Figure 24. Domenico Ghirlandaio. *Last Supper.* 1476. Fresco. Badia di Passignano. Photo. With permission from the Vallombrosans, Badia di Passignano.

assisted in his selection, along with Perugino, Botticelli, and Cosimo Rosselli, to paint figures of popes and scenes from the life of Moses and the Life of Christ on the walls of the newly constructed private papal chapel of Sixtus IV della Rovere. Most scholars believe that the iconographic program for the frescoes was not planned by the artists who painted them or even the master who directed the program.[38] Instead, theologians and advisors to Sixtus IV allowed a papal propaganda, a recognizable iconology, and a contemporary style to be painted on the walls of the chapel.[39] During this work in Rome in 1491 and 1492, Ghirlandaio also painted the *Resurrection* altar panel which was replaced by Michelangelo's *Last Judgment* in 1534–41. Ghirlandaio returned from Rome and worked in the Sala dei Gigli of the Palazzo della Signoria between 1482 and 1484.[40] Ridolfo, the first child of Domenico and his first wife, Costanza di Bartolommeo Nucci, was born during this commission in 1483. Ridolfo was the only one of Domenico's nine children who became an artist of any reputation.[41]

Domenico probably received the commission for the funerary chapel of Francesco Sassetti sometime in 1478 or 1479 before leaving for Rome to do the Sistine paintings. Ghirlandaio actually painted the Sassetti frescoes between May 1483 and the chapel's dedication on Christmas 1485.[42] The chapel program, the birth of Christ and the life of St. Francis, are outlined briefly below. Ghirlandaio's final significant fresco cycle, 1486–90, depicts scenes from the life of the Virgin and the life of St. John the Baptist commissioned by Giovanni Tornabuoni for the family chapel in Santa Maria Novella.[43]

The Ghirlandaio *bottega* was one of the most popular workshops in late fifteenth-century and sixteenth-century Florence.[44] Domenico sometimes worked with his brothers, Davide and Benedetto, and his son Ridolfo (1483–1561) inherited the workshop after Domenico's death at the age of forty-four in 1494.[45] The *bottega* continued to prosper under Ridolfo until c. 1550. At that time, the aged Ridolfo turned the workshop over to his adopted son Michele Tosini (1503–77), better known as Michele di Ridolfo del Ghirlandaio, who led that workshop into the elaborate and elegant style of the day, known as *la maniera*.[46]

The Patron and the Commission

Francesco Sassetti (1421–90) was the general manager of the Medici bank, which had branches across Italy and beyond the Alps. His career with the Medici began as a factor in the Geneva branch between 1438 and 1439 and, according to documents, within eight years he became its manager. In 1459, Sassetti married Nera Corsi, the daughter of a recent *gonfaloniere di giustizia* (the highest office a Florentine citizen could hold) and purportedly a descendant of a Roman noble family. Sassetti collected Roman coins and texts and was a promoter of humanistic studies. He had a large personal library from which Lorenzo de' Medici frequently borrowed and eventually became a governing officer of the Studio fiorentino (the fifteenth-century counterpart of a modern university). The Sassetti family had patronized the Church of S. Maria Novella for generations, and Francesco chose to abandon the family plot located in the crypt near the entrance to a room used by the religious confraternity, the Compagnia del Pellegrino.[47] Sassetti had a quarrel with the Dominicans shortly after his donations. The motive for this disagreement remains obscure but was possibly related to his sharing the patronage of the main chapel, installation of a black marble tomb for his properties, or involvement with the endowment of the family altar.[48] In any case, scholars do not believe that the disagreement was based on Francesco's need to have his patron saint painted on the walls of the church's chancel. This is mentioned in a late sixteenth-century document but is dismissed because of the preposterous idea that a Franciscan theme would even be suggested for a Dominican church's patron.[49]

Sometime between 1470 and 1479, Francesco Sassetti acquired rights of patronage and burial in a chapel in the Vallombrosan abbey church of Santa Trinità. Negotiations with the previous chapel owner, which began in early April 1478, were probably delayed by the Pazzi Conspiracy to overthrow the Medici on the 26th of that month.[50] Scholars believe that Ghirlandaio prepared drawings of the *Apparition of St. Francis* for a Franciscan fresco cycle before the spring of 1479.[51] Personal events in the life of the Sassetti family, namely the death in Lyons of their firstborn son, Teodoro, and the birth soon afterward of another boy, Teodoro II, on May 12, 1479, caused Sassetti to instruct Ghirlandaio to change that scene into a lesser-known event from the saint's life, the resuscitation scene.[52] Chroniclers reported that the murals were painted in fulfillment of a vow and that the chapel bore the double dedication to St. Francis and the Nativity.[53] They surmise that the vow may well have been related to this gift of the birth of a son so soon after the death of his firstborn. The placement of the *Nativity,* a favorite theme because of its eucharistic overtones, may also have served as a reminder of and appreciation for the birth of a son to his father and mother. As we shall see, that the actual moment of the narrative depicted the adoration by the shepherds of the Christ Child further emphasizes the spectator/patron's appreciation for the life of the Christ Child and, more specifically, the patron's appreciation for the life of their child and sense of renewal.

The Program of the Chapel Fresco Cycle

Domenico did not have to look far to find sources for a St. Francis cycle. Three can be found in the Franciscan church of Santa Croce in Florence: Giotto's frescoes in the Bardi chapel, Taddeo Gaddi's painted panels for a sacristy cupboard, and Benedetto da Maiano's marble reliefs for the pulpit in the nave carved in the mid-1470s.[54] Ghirlandaio certainly knew all three works. His St. Francis cycle combines places and events which have a personal relevance to the patron's life.[55] This personal significance of the chapel paintings for the patron extends to the subject chosen for the altarpiece of the chapel, the *Nativity and Adoration of the Shepherds.*

The three walls of the chapel are divided into three levels. The upper level of lunette frescoes are in chronological order beginning on the left with *Francis renounces his worldly Patrimony.*[56] Usually Assisi was painted in the background of this scene, but here Ghirlandaio painted a view of Geneva where Sassetti made his fortune.[57] The lunette of the altar wall depicts the *Confirmation of the Franciscan Rule by Pope Honorius III* set in the political center of Florence with the Palazzo della Signoria and Loggia dei Signori visible in the background.[58] The right wall shows the *Trial by Fire.*[59] The second level on the left above the tomb of Nera Corsi Sassetti shows the *Stigmatization of St. Francis* with a view of La Verna, where the event occurred and similar to Benedetto da Maiano's relief at Santa Croce, but Ghirlandaio added buildings from Pisa.[60] The chronological order then

Figure 25. Domenico Ghirlandaio and Assistants. *Four Sibyls.* Fresco. Sassetti Chapel, S. Trinità, Florence. Photo. With permission from the Ministero dei Beni e le Attività Culturali.

jumps to the opposite wall with the *Funeral of St. Francis* placed above the tomb of Francesco Sassetti.[61] The final scene, in chronological order, is on the altar wall above the altarpiece and shows the posthumous miracle of *St. Francis Resuscitating the Roman Notary's Son.*[62] The Church of Santa Trinità, Florence (not San Marco in Rome, where the event is believed to have occurred), is visible on the right, and the bridge across the Arno is in the center background. This scene is believed to have been substituted for the initial subject of the Apparition at Arles that appears in a preparatory drawing made by Ghirlandaio before Sassetti's loss of his son Teodoro I in 1479. Through this scene, and in the altar panel discussed below, appreciation, thanksgiving, and a renewed sense of life may be found in the heart of the patron and the heart of the chapel fresco cycle. This fresco is placed in the center of the altar wall immediately above the scene of the Christ Child.

Four sibyls are frescoed in the ceiling vault by Ghirlandaio (Figure 25).[63] Three of the sibyls hold scrolls, which identify them (counterclockwise from above the altar): the Eiritraean (IN VLTIMA AVTEM ETATE), the Agrippan (INVISIBILE VERBVM PALPABITVR GERMINABIT), and the Cumaean (HEC TESTE VIRGIL MAGNVS). Borsook and Offerhaus suggest that the fourth sibyl with pen poised upon a still unwritten scroll may be the Cimmerian sibyl because she appears bareheaded and

Figure 26. Domenico Ghirlandaio. *Vision of Augustus on the Capitoline Hill.*
Fresco. Sassetti Chapel, S. Trinità, Florence. Photo. With permission from the
Ministero dei Beni e le Attività Culturali.

with open hair in a contemporary print.[64] The monumental scale of Ghirlandaio's sibyls is unprecedented in Italian art. The popularity of sibyls in Tuscany (one of Francesco's five daughters was named Sibilla) can be traced to a Dominican, Filippo Barbieri, who preached in Florence in 1474 and wrote a treatise about them which was published in several illustrated editions in Rome between December 1481 and the end of 1483.[65]

The Cumaean sibyl is positioned closest to the entrance of the chapel and therefore is not directly above a frescoed wall. It is, however, on the opposite side of the entrance wall. This area above the entrance to the chapel is a fresco of the *Vision of Augustus on the Capitoline Hill* (Figure 26) painted by Domenico.[66] According to several legends the emperor learned that the birth of Christ would happen under an era of peace. Although several versions of this story existed, the one probably used by Ghirlandaio derives from Suetonius's account, a copy of which was available in Sassetti's library.[67] The prophet David stands upon a pillar in fresco just to the left of the Augustus painting. The inscription above him translates "to the safety of the fatherland and Christian glory."[68] David, a symbol of Florence and defender of civic liberty, holds a shield with the Sassetti family coat of arms. David is also the prophet of the Savior's birth, and his image often accompanied that of Augustus on painted floats of the Nativity carried throughout the streets of Florence to celebrate the events of January 6.[69] January 6 commemorated the Epiphany to the magi, the baptism of Christ by St. John (the patron saint of the city), and the wedding at Cana.[70]

The placement and relationship of the Augustus fresco, the Cumaean sibyl and the altar panel of the infant Christ need to be discussed in terms of the spectator. As the spectator approaches the chapel, the lunette fresco of Augustus is visible above the entrance. The relationship between the Cumaean sibyl prophecy, as told in Virgil's *Fourth Eclogue,* and Augustus is further emphasized by Ghirlandaio's placement of the two scenes. The Cumaean sibyl is located on the interior chapel ceiling and is the closest of the four sibyls to the entrance arch of the chapel vault. The Augustus fresco is painted on the wall above this entrance arch and external to the chapel. Therefore their proximity should be noted in an iconographic program of the chapel.[71] Christ was, as we have noted, born under the age of peace (as told by the Cumaean sibyl) and during the reign of Augustus.

The portraits of Nera Corsi Sassetti and Francesco Sassetti (Figure 27) are to the left and right, respectively, of the altar panel. Traditionally,

Figure 27. Domenico Ghirlandaio. *Portraits of Nera Corsi Sassetti and Francesco Sassetti.* Fresco. Sassetti Chapel, S. Trinità, Florence. Photo. With permission from the Ministero dei Beni e le Attività Culturali.

Figure 28. Hugo van der Goes. *Adoration of the Shepherds.* 1475. Panel. Galleria degli Uffizi, Florence. Photo. With permission from the Ministero dei Beni e le Attività Culturali.

the male patron was placed on the left side of the altar panel because it was the proper right of the sacred figures in the painting and thus the privileged side reserved for the male. This technique was a usual method for Renaissance artists working in Italy at this time. But in our painting, the positions are reversed. Two plausible reasons may be given for this reversal.[72] The first suggested reason is that as the viewer approaches the chapel from the central nave, only Francesco on the right side of the chapel is immediately visible. Second, this placement also allows Nera, mother of Teodoro I and II, to be placed closest to Mary, mother of Christ. It should also be noted that the date A.D. MCCCCLXXX[V] is written under the figure of Nera and [X]XV DECEMBRIS under Francesco's portrait.[73]

Stylistic and Iconographic Analysis of the Painting

Artistic Sources and Technique

The *Nativity and Adoration of the Shepherds* shows Domenico's skill at incorporating many sources of inspiration, including classical sculpture, the monumental frescoes of the Sistine Chapel, and contemporary Netherlandish painting.[74] Ghirlandaio was greatly influenced by Hugo van der Goes's *Adoration of the Shepherds* (Figure 28), which arrived in Florence in May 1483.[75] Commissioned for Tommaso Portinari, the manager of the Medici bank in Bruges, it was to decorate his family chapel in the Florentine hospital at S. Maria Nuova.[76] The Sassetti altarpiece bears the date MCCCCLXXV, so we can deduce that Ghirlandaio painted it between May 1483 and the chapel dedication on Christmas 1485.[77]

Ghirlandaio's composition finds its source in the Portinari altarpiece, but perhaps more significantly for Florentine painting, Ghirlandaio uses the adoration of the shepherds, which is a rare theme in Tuscany,[78] as the subject of the Sassetti painting.[79] The donors flank the central panel in the Portinari folding triptych. This triptych style never became popular in Florence. The Sassetti altarpiece retains the square *all'antica* frame, and Ghirlandaio places the patrons in frescoed "panels" on either side of it.[80] Another northern compositional source may be the so-called Eyckian plateau composition, influential in Florence since the 1460s, in which the figures are seen on high ground in the front plane, with a landscape vista falling away behind.[81]

Domenico Ghirlandaio painted the 65 ¾-inch square panel using a tempera technique that was quite similar to that used in his frescoes. He worked on prepared panels with a mixture of tempera and oil. He made incisions with a straight edge in the gesso to indicate the general form of the composition. Skin tones and the broad modeling of drapery were laid in over an underdrawing on the gesso. The descriptive details and highlights in the composition were painted more meticulously with the tip of a brush dipped in tempera. This technique was consistent in his panel paintings and therefore seemed to suit his aesthetic desires.[82]

Iconography

Ghirlandaio's *Adoration* has some distinctive, in some cases unique, interpretations of Luke 2. We turn our attention now to a close analysis of his visual exegesis.

The Nativity

In the center of the composition is the *Nativity*. The visual depiction typically shows the Virgin kneeling next to the Christ Child lying before her, and Joseph can be found somewhere in the composition. Joseph here is in the exact center of the painting. The traditional placement of Joseph is off to one side, as in the Portinari panel. The type, an old man with gray hair, remains. Joseph shades his eyes with his hand as he looks upward toward a flying angel.[83]

Of course, the focus of the *Nativity* is on Mary and Christ, not Joseph. This point is made clear from the inscription on the painting's frame:

IPSVM QVEM GENVIT ADORAVIT MARIA[84]
(Mary adored the very one whom she bore)

The double focus on Mary and the Christ Child is indicated by other elements as well.

This "Nativity scene" does not occur in the infancy narratives of either Matthew or Luke but might be loosely interpreted as following Luke 2:7: "And she gave birth to her firstborn son and wrapped him in bands of cloth, and laid him in a manger, because there was no place for them in the inn."[85] The Nativity, or birth, is, both biblically and visually, the story of the unique and special birth of the savior without the clinical details. During the fifteenth century, the literary sources of these details relied on apocryphal writings[86] and visionary experience, especially that of the Swedish mystic, Saint Bridget.[87] Although the theological interpretation continued to stress the eternal, virginal state of Mary, both before and after the parturition, another key aspect of Christ's delivery was that it occurred without any of the usual pains of childbirth.[88]

The Virgin, triangular in form, is given a place of importance in both compositions. Ghirlandaio allowed the traditional Florentine red gown to be seen from beneath the navy mantle which, while retaining the solemnity of the figure, draws the viewer to the beauty of her face. The facial type is most certainly based on a Florentine, rather than a Netherlandish female model. The contours and shadows on her face and neck emit an internal glow and exemplified Ghirlandaio's highly effective use of light and color. He carefully arranged each form and its lighting so that where the edge of the form meets the background it is always placed against the opposite light level to ensure that the outline of the form is not lost, and *rilievo* is achieved.[89] The facial expressions of the Virgin in the two paintings differ as well. The Ghirlandaio Virgin depicts not only a woman who reflects upon the Savior, but a mother who looks at and prays for her child. There is a physical and emotional distance between the Virgin and child in the van der Goes that Ghirlandaio eliminates.

The intimacy and relationship between mother and child is further emphasized in the Ghirlandaio painting by the placement of the infant on the fanned-out mantle of the Virgin. The shape of this drapery extends the beauty of the Virgin to the most sacred area of the composition, the body of Christ. Whereas van der Goes placed the radiant child on bare ground in the center of the composition, Ghirlandaio's drapery provided a soft material for the infant's body and covers the sheaf of wheat, symbol of the Eucharist, under his head.

The Eucharistic themes would not have been missed by the fifteenth-century spectator. While it is not common today to associate the infant Christ with the Eucharist, such identification was common in the medieval and Renaissance periods. In the *Vitae Patrum,* attributed to Gregory of Tours, an Egyptian monk is unable to affirm that the elements of the Sacrament are transformed into the literal body and blood of Christ.[90] Two fellow monks pray for divine revelation and accompany him to Mass. The loaves on the altar appear to all three to take on the form of an infant. As the priest reached to break the bread, an angel from heaven stabbed the child with a knife and caught his blood in a chalice. Before receiving the Sacrament, the unbelieving monk cried out, "Lord, I believe that the bread laid on the altar is Thy Body and the Chalice is Thy Blood." The infant's bleeding flesh then returned to the semblance of bread, and the monks communed. They returned to their cells, praising God for providing such a powerful antidote for doubt.

More relevant for our discussion is the story of the Christmas Mass celebrated in 1223 by St. Francis of Assisi in the village of Greccio and recounted by his disciple Thomas of Celano in his *Vita prima*, shortly after Francis's death in 1228.

> At length the saint of God came, and finding all things prepared, he saw it and was glad. The manger was prepared, the hay had been brought, the ox and ass were led in. There...Greccio was made, as it were, a new Bethlehem....The saint of God stood before the manger, uttering sighs, overcome with love, and filled with a wonderful happiness. The solemnities of the Mass were celebrated over the manger and the priest experienced a new consolation. Frequently too, when he wished to call Christ Jesus, he would call him simply the Child of Bethlehem, aglow with overflowing love for him; and speaking the word Bethlehem, his voice was more like the bleating of a sheep. His mouth was filled more with sweet affection than with words. Besides, when he spoke the name Child of Bethlehem or Jesus, his tongue licked his lips, as it were, relishing and savoring with pleased palate the sweetness of the word.[91]

Afterward, Thomas reports that the hay that had been placed in the manger was kept and proved to be a source of miraculous healing for both animals and women suffering from difficult childbirth. Thomas concludes this story of the "first crib" with these words:

> Later, the place on which the manger had stood was made sacred by a temple of the Lord, and an altar was built in honour of the most blessed father Francis over the manger and a church was built, so that where once the animals had eaten the hay, there in the future men would eat unto health of soul and body the flesh of the lamb without blemish and without spot, our Lord Jesus Christ.[92]

Details of this story spread rapidly in medieval christendom, assisted by Thomas's prompt reporting of the event no more than eight years after its occurrence, and maintained by the subsequent enthusiasm of the Franciscans. The presence of cribs during the Christmas season in the homes of believers became and remained popular in Europe. The shaft of wheat under the Christ Child's head is Ghirlandaio's perhaps more subtle, but no less effective, way of linking the Nativity with the celebration of the Eucharist.

Not so subtle is Ghirlandaio's use of a sarcophagus for the Savior's manger. The motif of the sarcophagus is not derived from any traditional representations of the Nativity, neither written nor contained in the iconographic precedents, and is never followed.[93] In Luke's Gospel, of course, the story of Jesus' birth alludes to his death (see e.g., Luke 2:34–35). More important is the fact that the "Christ Child as Sacrifice" was a ubiquitous theme in late medieval liturgy, sermons, and *Corpus Christi* plays, a point argued persuasively by Leah Sinanoglou.[94] Nor were allusions to Christ's sacrificial death altogether missing from visual depictions of the Nativity. The medicinal imagery in the Portinari altarpiece points to the therapeutic dimension of Christ's sacrificial death, certainly an appropriate emphasis for a painting made for the chapel of Florence's largest hospital, S. Maria Nuova.[95] Slightly later than our painting (1510–15), in Grünewald's Isenheim Altarpiece (also commissioned for a hospital), the tattered swaddling clothes in which the Christ Child is wrapped prefigured the torn loincloth of the crucified Christ.[96] That Ghirlandaio chose to allude to Christ's death with a sarcophagus may take on more poignant dimensions given the personal history of the Sassettis, whose first son, Teodoro (as we noted earlier), died during the execution of this commission.

Ghirlandaio, like van der Goes, used hidden symbolism in seemingly irrelevant details of the Nativity scene. Several of these details provide additional confirmation of the connection between the infant Christ's birth and passion. Ghirlandaio's replacement of a lamb for a hat in the arms of the van der Goes's standing shepherd not only identified the shepherd's occupation but is a well-known symbol of Christ's atoning death (cf. the words of John the Baptist in John 1:29: "Here is the Lamb of God who takes away the sin of the world!"). Ghirlandaio also replaced van der Goes's vase of cut flowers with a goldfinch, again a symbol of Christ's passion.[97]

The Adoration of the Shepherds

The subject of the adoration of the shepherds was rare in fifteenth-century Florence.[98] Christina Knorr has observed, "before the arrival of the Portinari Altarpiece, whenever the Christ Child is adored in an altar-piece in fifteenth-century Florence, it is the magi who are the adorers...."[99] In the case of the Portinari Altarpiece, the choice of shepherds rather than magi may have been part of an anti-Medicean undertone intended by the patron, himself a manager of the Medici bank who may have been severing ties with the Medici at the time of the commission.[100] Knorr concludes that "the manifold allusions contained in this depiction of the Magi would certainly be better attuned to Medicean self-promotion than those associated with the shepherds."[101] Important to note here is Knorr's suggestion that shepherds in fifteenth-century Florence, despite centuries of association with Christian iconography of the "good shepherd," would still be viewed as less magisterial than the foreign dignitaries, the magi who, in Matthew's account, graced the infant Jesus with their presence. The magi are not, of course, entirely absent from Ghirlandaio's depiction. They are to be seen passing under an archway on the left-hand side of the painting, thus collapsing the traditional temporal distance of twelve days between the time of the shepherds' visit (Christmas Day) and that of the magi (Epiphany, January 6).

In this sense, the shepherds' prominence in Ghirlandaio's interpretation reenacts the ambiguity of their significance, an ambiguity that we have seen existed in Luke's own day. This statement seems to be true even if Ghirlandaio sought to make his shepherds a bit more respectable than their prototypes by van der Goes.[102]

References to Classical Antiquity

Classical elements are a common feature in Florentine paintings by 1483. Each artist and patron chooses to incorporate different classical structures in unique ways which are sometimes relevant to them personally or to the community in which they live. Often the patron and/or artist will seek the assistance of a humanist for the iconography. Domenico probably received assistance from Francesco Sassetti's friend, the humanist Bartolomeo Fonzio (1445–1513).[103] The sarcophagus and pilasters (each with a Latin inscription), the triumphal arch above the procession of the magi, and the cityscapes of Jerusalem and Rome all have significance to the patron and spectator and contribute to the meaning of the painting.[104]

The pilasters supporting the sarcophagus and the triumphal arch have inscriptions by Fonzio.[105] Fonzio introduced the theme of the successive reigns of the Hebrews, of the Romans, and of Christ, through the story of the Roman general, Pompey. The inscription upon the triumphal arch through which the magi pass cites the Roman general who conquered Jerusalem:

GN[AEO]. POMPEIO MAGNO HIRCANVS PONT[IUS]. P[OSUIT].
(Hircanus, High Priest, Erected [This] For "General" [Imperator]
Pompey the Great)

This inscription suggests that the Jewish high priest, Hircanus, erected the monument in gratitude to Pompey, who after the conquest of Jerusalem reinstated him in his office.[106] Saxl notes:

> There is no doubt that the historical Hircanus never erected a triumphal arch for Pompey because the practice of erecting such arches had hardly begun in 63 B.C. . . . I do not know of any obvious connection between the history of Pompey and the coming of Christ, and it would therefore seem that Fontius' interest in the famous Roman caused him to invent the two inscriptions which, through the history of Pompey, interconnect the history of the three great religions. This is the purpose of the classical details which form a strange contrast to the figures and the landscape in Ghirlandaio's picture. Only the spectator who understands the meaning of the ruins, the sacred figures and those who surround them, grasps the full content of the miracle of the Nativity as Sassetti and Fontius conceived it.[107]

The pilaster on the left records the date of MCCCCLXXXV. The manger-sarcophagus used for the Savior's crib, together with the ancient pilasters supporting the roof, are the foundations for the new temple succeeding its Hebrew and pagan predecessors.[108] The letters on the sarcophagus read:

ENSE CADENS SOLYMO POMPEI FVLVI[VS]
AVGVR
NVMEN AIT QVAE ME CONTEG[IT]
VRNA DABIT
(Falling at Jerusalem by the sword of Pompeius, the augur Fulvius says,
"The Urn which contains me shall produce a God!")[109]

The first inscription on the arch indicates the triumph of paganism over Judaism; the second signifies the victory of Christianity over the heathen world.[110]

Cityscape

The most distant hill on the right is believed to be Jerusalem with the Dome of the Rock visible. In the center of the background is a view of Rome, which includes the Torre delle Milizie and the mausoleum of Hadrian.[111] Therefore, the two world empires, Hebrew and Roman, are now in the background to the beginning of Christ's new kingdom. This interest in the political dimensions of Christianity's triumph is supported by the larger iconographic program discussed earlier that includes reference to Augustus, as well as an inscription near the prophet David (discussed below) that reads "to the safety of the fatherland and Christian glory."

Additional details support this point: in the foreground of the painting is a stone (a pun on Sassetti's name — "a little stone"), prompting Borsook and Offerhaus to suggest that "even the Sassetti, by means of the family emblem, participate discretely in the scene."[112] Also in the foreground are bricks, metaphors of reconstruction and the triumph of Christianity over paganism.[113] For patron, painter, and viewer, the future of the Florentine Republic was inextricably linked with the success of the Christian Church. What is striking here is that while the political triumph of Rome over the Hebrews is described in military terms (the general Pompey conquers Judea; an apocryphal prophet dying in battle predicts a coming deity), the triumph of Christianity over the Roman empire is depicted in the birth of a child, not with the symbols of warfare. And already the birth of that child points forward to his death.

Concluding Hermeneutical Reflections

Luke, like Ghirlandaio, was also interested in the relationship between things religious and political, though the two seem to have construed that relationship quite differently. Luke alone among the evangelists takes pains to set the story of Jesus' birth against the backdrop of the Roman Empire. He notes that the census prompting Mary and Joseph to sojourn to Bethlehem was the result of "a decree" that "went out from Caesar Augustus." We have already noted that for Luke the "peace" that Christ's coming brings is celebrated by the angelic host before the shepherds. The contrast between Christ's peace and Augustus's Pax Romana was surely clear to Luke's audience. Though scholars disagree about exactly how, almost all agree that in his second volume, the Acts of the Apostles, Luke attempts to legitimate Christianity, then a tiny Jewish messianic sect, within the larger Roman empire, trying to forge a way for the movement to survive while at the same time holding true to its central tenets.[114] By Ghirlandaio's day, of course, hindsight shows that Christianity had triumphed and stood in a succession of "global" empires from the Hebrews to the Romans to the Christians.

A brochure distributed today by the contemporary Vallombrosans in Santa Trinità contains the words, "The Church of Santa Trinità has for nine hundred years been officiated by Vallombrosan Benedictine monks; they invite the visitor to admire the works of art found inside, but above all to perceive the spiritual values of silence, contemplative prayer and interior joy."[115] These words are a reminder that the vast majority of the art produced during the Renaissance and Baroque periods was intended as spiritual aids for the meditation and contemplation of believers on various aspects of the life of Christ and his followers. Ghirlandaio's *Adoration of the Shepherds*, like the Gospel of Luke before it, makes the bold move of placing Christianity on the larger political landscape. And like the Third Gospel before him, Ghirlandaio makes the audacious claim that the transition of world dominance from the Romans to Christianity is to be found, not in Constantine's conversion or his mighty Christian army, but rather in the birth of a child who is first adored by lowly shepherds, not cosmopolitan magi. Further, no sooner has the child been born than the audience is asked to reflect on Christ's death already foreshadowed in the symbols surrounding his birth (a sarcophagus, a goldfinch, a lamb, a wheat sheaf) and to contemplate the social and political implications which an embrace of this child and his good news must surely entail.

Notes

1. Scholarship on the Sassetti Chapel includes: Aby Warburg, *Gesammelte Schriften* (Berlin: Akademie Verlag, 1902; 1932, rept. 1998); Marco Chiarini, *Il Ghirlandaio alla Capella Sassetti in Santa Trinità* (Milan: Silvana Editoriale d'Arte, 1961); Warman Welliver, "Alterations in Ghirlandaio's S. Trinità Frescoes," *Art Quarterly* 32 (1969): 269–81; Artur Rosenauer, "Ein nicht zur Ausführung gelangter Entwurf Domenico Ghirlandajos für die Cappella Sassetti," *Wiener Jahrbuch für Kunstgeschichte* 25 (1972): 187–96; Eve Borsook and Johannes Offerhaus, *Francesco Sassetti and Ghirlandaio at Santa Trinità, Florence* (Doornspijk: Dovaco, 1981); Peter Porçal, "La Cappella Sassetti in S. Trinità a Firenze: osservazioni sull'iconografia," *Antichita Viva* 23 (1984): 26–36; Enrica Cassarino, *La cappella Sassetti nella chiesa di Santa Trinità* (Lucca: Pacini Fazzi, 1996); Ernst H. Gombrich, "The Sassetti Chapel Revisited: Santa Trinità and Lorenzo de' Medici," *I Tatti Studies* 7 (1997): 11–35; Martin Seidel, "Devotion, Repräsentation, Historiographic und/oder Politik? Zur ikonographischen Genese und Anordnung sowie zu Vorbildern von Domenico Ghirlandaios Fresken in der Sassetti-Kapelle," *Wiener Jahruch für Kunstgeschichte* 50 (1997): 159–71.

2. Porçal, "La Cappella Sassetti in S. Trinità a Firenze," 26.

3. Charles H. Talbert, *Reading Luke: A Literary and Theological Commentary on the Third Gospel* (New York: Crossroad, 1982), 31.

4. On these problems, see Raymond E. Brown, *The Birth of the Messiah: A Commentary on the Infancy Narratives in the Gospels of Matthew and Luke* (Garden City, N.Y.: Doubleday, 1977), 547–56 (who rejects the historicity of the reference); and Darrell L. Bock, "Excursus 2: The Census of Quirinius (2:1–2)," in *Luke, 1:1–9:50* (Grand Rapids: Baker Books, 1994), 903–9 (who defends it).

5. For the full translation and discussion of the Priene inscription, see Frederick W. Danker, *Benefactor: Epigraphic Study of a Graeco-Roman and New Testament Field* (St. Louis: Clayton Publishing House, 1982), 215–22.

6. The eucharistic overtones of the Christ Child in the manger were prominent throughout the medieval church. See especially, Leah Sinanoglou, "The Christ Child as Sacrifice: A Medieval Tradition and the Corpus Christi Plays," *Speculum* 48 (1973): 491–509. This point is developed later in connection with Ghirlandaio's painting.

7. On the theme of food in Luke, see Robert J. Karris, *Luke: Artist and Theologian. Luke's Passion Account as Literature* (New York: Paulist, 1985).

8. Robert Tannehill calls these three passages "type-scenes" because they share certain features in common. See Tannehill, *The Narrative Unity of Luke-Acts: A Literary Interpretation* (vol. 1: *The Gospel According to Luke;* Philadelphia: Fortress, 1986), 170–71.

9. For a defense of translating the phrase *enōpion autōn ephagen* (literally, "he ate before them") as "he ate with them," see ibid., 291–92.

10. See Douglas Oakman, "The Countryside in Luke-Acts," in *The Social World of Luke-Acts* (ed. Jerome H. Neyrey; Peabody, Mass.: Hendrickson, 1991), 151–80.

11. But this was not true of the Hebrews' Mesopotamian neighbors, many of whom regarded shepherds almost as outlaws. See Herbert Schneidau, "The Hebrews against the High Cultures: Pastoral Motifs," in *Sacred Discontent: The Bible and Western Tradition* (Baton Rouge: Louisiana State University Press, 1976).

12. Midrash on Psalm 23, for example, claims: "Rabbi Jose bar Hanina taught: In the whole world you find no occupation more despised than the shepherd, who all his days walks about with his staff and his pouch. Yet David presumed to call the Holy One, blessed be he, a Shepherd!" cited by Herbert Schneidau, "Shepherd," in *A Dictionary of Biblical Tradition in English Literature* (ed. David Lyle Jeffrey; Grand Rapids: Eerdmans, 1992), 710.

13. Josephus, *Jewish War,* II.60–65.

14. See Benjamin Hubbard, "Commissioning Stories in Luke-Acts: A Study of Their Antecedents, Form and Content," *Semeia* 8 (1977): 103–26. See also comments in chapter 2.

15. For an exhaustive (1,000+ pages!) history of the interpretation of the birth of Jesus from the early church to the high middle ages, see Hanns Peter Neuheuser, *Zugange zur Sakralkunst: Narratio und institutio des mittelalterlichen Christgeburtsbildes* (Cologne: Bohlau, 2001).

16. Cited by David R. Cartlidge and J. Keith Elliottt, *Art and the Christian Apocrypha* (London: Routledge, 2001), 18.

17. In the East, Christmas and Epiphany were collapsed into one great Feast celebrated on January 6.

18. Jacobus de Voragine, *The Golden Legend: Readings on the Saints* (trans. William Granger Ryan; Princeton, N.J.: Princeton University Press, 1993), 1:41, gives a brief treatment of the shepherds who represented human reason and discernment, while he gives extensive attention to the magi in his discussion of Epiphany (78–84). On the magi, see Richard C. Trexler, *The Journey of the Magi: Meanings in History of a Christian Story* (Princeton, N.J.: Princeton University, 1997); Rab Hatfield, *Botticelli's Uffizi "Adoration": A Study in Pictorial Content* (Princeton, N.J.: Princeton University Press, 1976).

19. For example, Stefano Liberati, *Gloria in Excelsis Deo: Immagini della Nativita nelle Incisioni dei Grandi Maestri dal XV al XX Secolo* (Rome: Fratelli Palombi, 1999), 26, claimed, "L'Adorazione dei pastori e un episodio quasi sconosciuto all'iconografia sacra fino ai XIII e XIV...." For examples of shepherds at the Nativity before the thirteenth century, see Louis Reau, *Iconographie de L'Art Chrétien,* vol. 2, *Iconographie de la Bible,* Part 2, *Nouveau Testament* (Paris: Presses Universitaires de France, 1957), 2/2, 234, and Gertrud Schiller, *Christ's Incarnation — Childhood — Baptism — Temptation — Transfiguration — Works and Miracles* (vol. 1 of *Iconography of Christian Art;* trans. Janet Seligman; Greenwich, Conn.: New York Graphic Society, 1971), 97–98. The earliest noted by Schiller, *Iconography of Christian Art,* I, plate 145, is of a lone shepherd standing nearby the infant Jesus on a sarcophagus in Deckel, dating c. 320–25.

20. See Origen, *Homilies on St. Luke;* Augustine, *Sermons* (Migne, PL 38:1026ff; also 39:2005ff.); Gregory of Nyssa (Migne, PG 45:1138). H. Leclerq, "Mages," *Dictionnaire d'archeologie chrétienne et de liturgie* (Paris, 1931), 10.1.986, also cites Fulgentius (d. 533) as equating the shepherds with the Jews and the magi with gentiles.

21. *Meditations on the Life of Christ: An Illustrated Manuscript of the Fourteenth Century* (ed. Isa Ragusa and Rosalie B. Green; trans. Isa Ragusa; Princeton, N.J.: Princeton University Press, 1961), 46–47.

22. Bernard, *Serm. I in vigilia nativitatis Domini*, Migne, *PL* 183.130.

23. *Meditations*, 36–37.

24. For example, Cartlidge and Elliott (*Art and the Christian Apocrypha*, 55–57) note the gradual disappearance of Good Shepherd in fourth- and fifth-century art. Furthermore, Priscilla Baumann ("A New Interpretation of the Sheep-Bearer Image in Romanesque Capitals in Auvergne," *Revue Mabillon* 66 [1994]: 447–48) argued that the negative rendering of the shepherd motif in twelfth-century Auvergne reflected a polemic against pagan beliefs and the worship of false gods. See also Avital Heyman ("Good or Bad Shepherds in Twelfth-Century Auvergne: Visual Evidence of Social Structures and Tensions," *Gazette des Beaux Arts* 136 [2000]: 57–68), who follows and expands Baumann's argument.

25. The major monographs and collected essays on Ghirlandaio include: Henri Hauvette, *Ghirlandaio* (Paris: Plon-Nourrit, 1907); Gerald S. Davies, *Ghirlandaio* (London: Metheun, 1909); J. Lauts, *Domenico Ghirlandaio* (Vienna: Anto Scholl & Co., 1943); Attilio Sabatini, *Domenico Ghirlandaio* (Florence: Illustrazione Toscana, 1944); Emma Micheletti, *Domenico Ghirlandaio* (Florence: Scala, 1990); Wolfram Prinz and Max Seidel, *Domenico Ghirlandaio: 1449–1494; atti del convegno internazionale, Firenze 16–18 ottobre 1994* (Florence: Centri, 1996); Ronald G. Kecks, *Domenico Ghirlandaio* (Florence: Octavo, 1998).

26. The de'Bigordi and del Ghirlandaio family tree is illustrated in Giorgio Vasari, *Le Opere di Giorgio Vasari: Le Vite de'più eccellenti pittori, scultori ed architettori scritte da Giorgio Vasari pittore Aretino* (1568), (ed. Gaetano Milanesi; 9 vols.; Florence: Sansoni, 1885), 3:282–83.

27. See ibid., 3:253–78, for the life of Domenico Ghirlandaio. Jean K. Cadogan, "Domenico Ghirlandaio," in *Dictionary of Art* (ed. Jane Turner; 34 vols., New York: Grove's Dictionaries, 1996), 12:547–55, states that Domenico was admitted to the confraternity of S. Paolo on May 12, 1470, and according to the matriculation book was either apprenticed to, or practicing as, a goldsmith.

28. This statement is supported by Cadogan (*Dictionary of Art,* 548) who cites archival documentation.

29. Michael Rohlmann, "Flanders and Italy, Flanders and Florence. Early Netherlandish painting in Italy and its particular influence on Florentine art: an overview," in *Italy and the Low Countries — Artistic Relation: The Fifteenth Century* (Florence: Centro Di della Edifirmi srl, 1999), 49–50. See also Michael Rohlmann, *Auftragskunst und Sammlerbild. Altnierderländische Tafelmalerei im Florenz des Quattrocento* (Alfter: VDG, 1994).

30. Micheletti, *Domenico Ghirlandaio,* 4. See also Patricia Ruben, "Domenico Ghirlandaio and the meaning of history in Fifteenth Century Florence," in Wolfram Prinz and Max Seidel, *Domenico Ghirlandaio,* 97–108.

31. See Francis Ames-Lewis, "Drapery 'Pattern' Drawings in Ghirlandaio's Workshop and Ghirlandaio's Early Apprenticeship," *Art Bulletin* 63 (1981): 59. More recently see the following two studies in Wolfram Prinz and Max Seidel, *Domenico Ghirlandaio,* Ronald G. Kecks, "La formazione artistica del Ghirlandaio," 43–60; Artur Rosenaur, "Osservazioni circa lo stile del Ghirlandaio," 61–70.

32. Cadogan, *Dictionary of Art,* 548–49.

33. Ibid. These works include a *Baptism of Christ* in a frescoed lunette and the *Virgin and Child Enthroned with SS. Sebastian and Julian* in S. Andrea a Brozzi, near Florence which reveal the influences of Antonio and Piero Pollaiuolo and Verrocchio. See also Micheletti, *Domenico Ghirlandaio,* 4–5.

34. Cadogan, *Dictionary of Art*, 548–49.

35. Ibid., 549.

36. For a discussion of the *Last Supper* paintings, see Micheletti, 12–19, and more recently, Giorgio Bonsanti, "Il restauro dell'*Ultima Cena* di San Marco," in Wolfram Prinz and Max Seidel, *Domenico Ghirlandaio*, 109–11.

37. The cycle dedicated to St. Fina in the Collegiata Pieve, San Gimignano is painted c. 1477–8. Ghirlandaio painted a *St. Jerome* and a *Last Supper* in the Ognissanti, Florence, c. 1480.

38. Leopold D. Ettlinger, "The Sistine Chapel before Michelangelo," *Religious Imagery and Papal Primacy* (Oxford: Clarendon Press, 1965), 6.

39. For more on the theories of the persons involved in the program of the 1480s frescoes, see ibid., 7–11.

40. Ibid.

41. Micheletti, *Domenico Ghirlandaio*, 4.

42. Chiarini, *Il Ghirlandaio alla Capella Sassetti in Santa Trinità*, 30.

43. Micheletti, *Domenico Ghirlandaio*, 30–61. For recent scholarship on the Tornabuoni fresco cycle, see the following articles in Wolfram Prinz and Max Seidel, *Domenico Ghirlandaio*: Rab Hatfield, "Giovanni Tornabuoni, i fratelli Ghirlandaio e la cappella maggiore si Santa Maria Novella," 112–17; Frank Martin, "Domenico Ghirlandaio *delineavit?* Osservazioni sulle vetrate della Cappella Tornabuoni," 118–40; Cristina Danti, "Osservazioni sulla tecnica degli affreschi della Cappella Tornabuoni," 141–49.

44. Most recently, see Jean K. Cadogan, "Sulla bottega del Ghirlandaio," in Wolfram Prinz and Max Seidel, *Domenico Ghirlandaio*, 89–96.

45. Ridolfo, David and Benedetto Ghirlandaio share a chapter in Vasari, see *Le Opere di Giorgio Vasari*, 6:531–48.

46. For Michele Tosini, see Heidi J. Hornik, "Michele di Ridolfo del Ghirlandaio (1503–1577) and the Reception of Mannerism in Florence" (Ph.D. diss., Pennsylvania State University, 1990); Heidi J. Hornik, "The Testament of Michele Tosini," *Paragone* 543–45 (1995): 156–67; Heidi J. Hornik, "The Strozzi Chapel by Michele Tosini: A Visual Interpretation of Redemptive Epiphany," *Artibus et Historiae* 46 (2002): 98–118. For the relationship between Michele and Ridolfo, see also David Franklin, "Towards a New Chronology for Ridolfo Ghirlandaio and Michele Tosini," *Burlington Magazine* 140 (1998): 445–56.

47. The information in this paragraph is documented by Borsook and Offerhaus, *Francesco Sassetti and Ghirlandaio at Santa Trinità, Florence*, 10–14.

48. Ibid., 13.

49. Ibid.

50. Ibid., 14.

51. Ibid., 18; Kecks, *Domenico Ghirlandaio*, 124.

52. Warburg, *Gesammelte Schriften*, 1:131–32. For a recent discussion of Warburg's study of Ghirlandaio, see Patrizia Castelli, "Aby Warburg e Ghirlandaio: questioni di metodo," in Wolfram Prinz and Max Seidel, *Domenico Ghirlandaio*, 199–212.

53. Borsook and Offerhaus, *Francesco Sassetti and Ghirlandaio at Santa Trinità, Florence*, 18–19. See also Kornelia Anger, *Der Franziskus-Zyklus Domenico Ghirlandaio in der Kirche Santa Trinità zu Florenz unter besonderer Berücksichtigung der Franziskus-Ikonographie vom 13.bis zum 17. Jahrhundert* (Bocchum: dissertation, 1990), and summary in *Das Münster* 44 (1991): 322–23.

54. Borsook and Offerhaus, *Francesco Sassetti and Ghirlandaio at Santa Trinità*, 27.

55. For recent scholarship on Ghirlandaio's ability to blend religious storytelling and family recordkeeping, see Patricia Rubin, "Domenico Ghirlandaio and the Meaning of

History in Fifteenth Century Florence," in Wolfram Prinz and Max Seidel, *Domenico Ghirlandaio,* 97–108.

56. Ibid.; Kecks, *Domenico Ghirlandaio,* 128, 130. Borsook and Offerhaus notice that the same view appears in the portrait of Ghirlandaio of Sassetti and Teodoro I, today located in the Metropolitan Museum, New York.

57. Ibid., 27.

58. Warburg (*Gesammelte Schriften,* 1:26) notes that in Giotto's version for the Bardi chapel, the Roman location of the room in which the pope and his curia are gathered is identified by the clipaeus with St. Peter's bust in the gable. For a summary of the identifications of the figures in the fresco as told in the scholarship, see Kecks, *Domenico Ghirlandaio,* 130.

59. For a discussion of this painting, see Kecks, *Domenico Ghirlandaio,* 136.

60. Ibid., 136–37. Borsook and Offerhaus (*Francesco Sassetti and Ghirlandaio at Santa Trinità, Florence,* 28) suggest that Ghirlandaio probably chose Pisa because it stands at the end of the Arno River which begins near La Verna. We have found no further research into personal association between the Sassetti.

61. Kecks, *Domenico Ghirlandaio,* 140–41.

62. Ibid., 137, 140.

63. Ibid., 124.

64. Borsook and Offerhaus (*Francesco Sassetti and Ghirlandaio at Santa Trinità, Florence,* 29) cite the print illustrated in Arthur M. Hind, *Early Italian Engraving* (New York and London: Pub. for M. Knoedler and Co., by B. Quaritich, 1938), I, 154 ff; II, plate 256. For a discussion of the sibyls, see Kecks, *Domenico Ghirlandaio,* 124.

65. Borsook and Offerhaus, *Francesco Sassetti and Ghirlandaio at Santa Trinità, Florence,* 29–30. See especially nn. 97 and 98 for a discussion of the scholarship on Barbieri.

66. See Charles de Tolnay, "Two Frescoes by Domenico and David Ghirlandaio in Santa Trinità in Florence," *Wallraf-Richartz-Jahrbuch* 23 (1961): 237–50.

67. Borsook and Offerhaus, *Francesco Sassetti and Ghirlandaio at Santa Trinità, Florence,* 30–31.

68. Ibid., 32; Kecks, *Domenico Ghirlandaio,* 124–25.

69. Borsook and Offerhaus, *Francesco Sassetti and Ghirlandaio at Santa Trinità, Florence,* 32–33. Borsook and Offerhaus (ibid., 33) also state David's role as the prophet of Judgment Day and give a passage of the mass of the dead which was sung on the first Sunday of Advent immediately before Luke 21:6. See also de Tolnay ("Two frescoes by Domenico and David Ghirlandaio in Santa Trinità in Florence," 244–50) for a discussion of the figure of David in Italian Renaissance art.

70. See Rab Hatfield, "The Compagnia dei Magi," *Journal of the Warburg and Courtauld Institutes* 33 (1970): 107–61.

71. Kecks, *Domenico Ghirlandaio,* 128.

72. Masaccio's *Trinity with Mary, John the Evangelist and Two Donors,* 1428, Santa Maria Novella, Florence, is but one of several examples which shows the male patron, Lenzi, on the spectator's left, i.e., on the privileged side of the sacred figures in the picture.

73. Milanesi, in Vasari, *Le Opere di Giorgio Vasari,* 3:256n. 1, rightly completed the date, making it 1485, a date which can be found also on the altar panel. He failed to complete the date of December 25. He transcribed it as XV. It is generally agreed that the chapel and altar panel were completed by 1485 and that there is a missing 'V' in the year date and an 'X' from XXV. Chiarini (*Il Ghirlandaio alla Capella Sassetti in Santa Trinità,* 30) gives the A.D. MCCCCLXXXVI / XV DECEMBRIS transcription, which translates as 1486 15 December. Kecks (*Domenico Ghirlandaio,* 122) cites de Tolnay and gives the transcription as [X] XV DECEMBRIS/A [nno] D[omini] MCCCCLXXXX [V]. Kecks's transcription

has one too many X's for the decades and reverses the inscription order, while de Tolnay ("Two frescoes by Domenico and David Ghirlandaio in Santa Trinità in Florence," 237) correctly transcribes A.D. MCCCCLXXX [V]/[X] XV DECEMBRIS, signifying the missing 'V' of 1485 and 'X' of 25. Borsook and Offerhaus (*Francesco Sassetti and Ghirlandaio at Santa Trinità, Florence,* 19) transcribe the inscription as: A.D.M.CCCCLXXX [V] / [XX] V DECEMBRIS. The omission of the second 'X' in 25 is unique in the scholarship.

The space before the date of 'XV' in conjunction with the probable dedication of the chapel on Christmas suggests the XXV DECEMBRIS transcription. The fact that masses were held regularly from January 1486 indicates that the chapel was completed in 1485, rather than 1486.

74. Cadogan, *Dictionary of Art,* 552.

75. Bianca Hatfield Strens, "L'arrivo del trittico Portinari a Firenze," *Commentari* 19 (1968): 314–19; Christian von Holst, *Francesco Granacci* (Munich: Bruckmann, 1974), 20, 46n. 75. For a discussion of the influence of van der Goes's Portinari landscape on Ghirlandaio's Sassetti *Nativity and Adoration,* see Francis Ames-Lewis, "Il paesaggi nell'arte del Ghirlandaio," in Wolfram Prinz and Max Seidel, *Domenico Ghirlandaio,* 85–86.

76. Paula Nuttall ("Domenico Ghirlandaio and Northern Art," *Apollo* 143 [1996]: 19) introduces the question that perhaps there was a competition between these Medici bank managers but does not attempt to answer it. For the careers of Sassetti and Portinari, see Raymond De Roover, *The Rise and Decline of the Medici Bank* (Cambridge: Cambridge University Press, 1963).

77. Borsook and Offerhaus, *Francesco Sassetti and Ghirlandaio at Santa Trinità, Florence,* 34. This period of activity corresponds with new documentation regarding the Sala dei Gigli frescoes in the Palazzo Vecchio. See Melinda Hegarty, "Laurentian Patronage in the Palazzo Vecchio: The Frescoes of the Sala dei Gigli," *Art Bulletin* 78 (1996): 264–85.

78. Rare but not unprecedented, cf. the renditions by Taddeo Gaddi (1332–38, S. Croce, Florence) and Taddeo de Bartolo (1404, Church of S. Maria dei Servi, Sienna), both noted by Schiller, *Iconography of Christian Art,* I.97–98.

79. Nuttall, "Domenico Ghirlandaio and Northern Art," 19. For an insightful discussion of more subtle figural innovations originated by Ghirlandaio in the Sassetti altar panel and subsequently copied by other artists, see Nicoletta Pons, "La fortuna figurativa dell'Adorazione Sassetti di Domenico Ghirlandaio in Santa Trinità," in Wolfram Prinz and Max Seidel, *Domenico Ghirlandaio,* 165–74.

80. Nuttall, "Domenico Ghirlandaio and Northern Art," 20.

81. Ibid., 19. For the plateau composition, see Millard Meiss, "Highlands in the Lowlands: Jan van Eyck, the Master of Flémalle and the Franco-Italian tradition," *Gazette des Beaux-Arts* 57 (1961): 281–309. For its integration into Florentine art, see Paula Nuttall, " 'Fecero al Cardinale di Portogallo una tavola a olio': Netherlandish Influence in Antonio and Piero del Pollaiuolo's San Miniato Altarpiece," *Nederlands Kunsthistorisch Jaarboek,* 44 (1993): 122.

82. This paragraph is based on the brief but informative discussion of Domenico's tempera technique in Cadogan, *Dictionary of Art,* 553–54.

83. Nuttall (" 'Fecero al Cardinale di Portogallo una tavola a olio,' " 19) identifies a source for Joseph's gesture in a German print of the *Nativity* by the Master E.S. (active mid-fifteenth century). She argues that German prints provided novel design sources for the Ghirlandaio workshop.

84. Borsook and Offerhaus (*Francesco Sassetti and Ghirlandaio at Santa Trinità, Florence,* 35) note that the same phrase was used in the earlier Nativity altarpiece painted by Bicci di Lorenzo for the Florentine church of San Giovannini dei Cavalieri and that it has been suggested that the source of the text may be in the writings of Sedulius Scotus.

85. Typically the Christ Child is seen nude in paintings identified as *The Nativity.*

86. See Jacobus de Voragine, *The Golden Legend,* 1:48; *Meditations on the Life of Christ,* 32–33.

87. *The Other Gospels: Non-Canonical Gospel Texts* (ed. R. Cameron; Philadelphia: Fortress, 1982), 117. The *Protevangelium* dates to c. 200; Saint Bridget, *The Liber Celetis of St. Bridget of Sweden* (ed. R. Ellis; Oxford: Oxford University Press, 1987), 485–86.

88. See Julia I. Miller, "Miraculous Childbirth and the Portinari Altarpiece," *Art Bulletin* 77 (1995): 254.

89. Julia DeLancey, "Before Michelangelo: Color Usage in Domenico Ghirlandaio and Filippino Lippi," *Apollo* 145 (1997): 16.

90. The text of Gregory of Tours, *Vitae Patrum,* may be found in *Patrologia Latina,* ed. J. Migne, vol. 73, col. 979.

91. Thomas of Celano, *The Lives of S. Francis of Assisi,* sections 84–86; cited by Sinanoglou, "The Christ Child as Sacrifice," 496.

92. Thomas of Celano, section 87.

93. Porçal, "La Cappella Sassetti in S. Trinità a Firenze," 26.

94. Sinanoglou, "The Christ Child as Sacrifice," 491–92.

95. Miller, "Miraculous Childbirth and the Portinari Altarpiece," 257–58.

96. See Andrée Hayum, *The Isenheim Altarpiece: God's Medicine and the Painter's Vision* (Princeton, N.J.: Princeton University Press, 1989), 514.

97. Nuttall, " 'Fecero al Cardinale di Portogallo una tavola a olio,' " 20. The Portinari altarpiece is itself filled with imagery connecting the Nativity scene with the Eucharist; see especially Jeremy Wood, *The Nativity* (London: Scala Publications, 1992), 24–28. For the symbolism of the goldfinch, see the recent article by Marina Belozerskaya, "An Unrecognized Source for Raphael's *Madonna of the Goldfinch,*" *Source* 21, no. 2 (2002): 17–21.

98. In addition to the Baroncelli chapel already cited, there were scenes of the adoration of the magi, executed by Florentine painters, in which the shepherds are also present, if in a less prominent position; cf. Botticelli.

99. Christina Knorr, "The Coming of the Shepherds: A Response," *Art Bulletin* 78 (1996): 370–71.

100. See the exchange between Knorr, "The Coming of the Shepherds," 371 and Miller, "Response," *Art Bulletin* 78 (1996): 391, in the Letters to the Editor section.

101. Knorr, "The Coming of the Shepherds," 371. Nuttall (" 'Fecero al Cardinale di Portogallo una tavola a olio,' " 19) offers another, not incompatible, reason for Ghirlandaio's shepherds: "Was there perhaps an element of one-upmanship in the decision to paint a Florentine version of the exotic Netherlandish altarpiece whose own patron had by this time fallen into disgrace and bankruptcy?"

102. Nuttall observes (" 'Fecero al Cardinale di Portogallo una tavola a olio,' " 19), "The shepherds, coarse rustics in van der Goes, are more refined types in Ghirlandaio." She goes on to comment: "Most tellingly, Ghirlandaio retains the triangular form of their grouping, but unlike van der Goes, whose triangle teeters dramatically on one of its points, giving momentum to the shepherds' entry, he sets his triangle, with greater stability, on one of its sides."

103. See F. Saxl, "The Classical Inscription in Renaissance Art and Politics," *Journal of the Warburg and Courtauld Institutes* 4 (1940–41): 21, 27–29, for an in-depth discussion of Bartolomaeus Fontius, his relationship with Sassetti, and his participation in the inscriptions of the chapel and altarpiece. See also Borsook and Offerhaus, *Francesco Sassetti and Ghirlandaio at Santa Trinità, Florence,* 12, 34; Cadogan, *Dictionary of Art,* 552; Cassarino, *La cappella Sassetti nella chiesa di Santa Trinità,* 98; Kecks, *Domenico Ghirlandaio,* 141. Despite

variations in the Latin or Italian versions of his name, all scholars cite the same birth and death dates for this Florentine humanist.

104. For a summary of the scholarship related to the iconography, see Kecks, *Domenico Ghirlandaio,* 141–42. Our interpretation incorporates the findings of Saxl with Borsook and Offerhaus. For a discussion of the meticulous and authentic quality of Ghirlandaio's sarcophagus in relation to antique sarcophagi, see Timothy Verdon, " 'Dalla natura fatto per essere pittor': Domenico Ghirlandaio e la scultura," in Wolfram Prinz and Max Seidel, *Domenico Ghirlandaio,* 75–77.

105. Saxl, "The Classical Inscription in Renaissance Art and Politics," 28–29.

106. Ibid., 28. Saxl states that this and other stories are meant to indicate the friendly submission of Judaism to Rome.

107. Ibid., 29.

108. Borsook and Offerhaus, *Francesco Sassetti and Ghirlandaio at Santa Trinità, Florence,* 34.

109. This inscription is an elegiac couplet. We are most grateful to Professor Jeff Fish, Classics Department, Baylor University, for his assistance in translating this inscription, as well as the others in this painting.

110. Saxl, "The Classical Inscription in Renaissance Art and Politics," 28.

111. See Borsook and Offerhaus (*Francesco Sassetti and Ghirlandaio at Santa Trinità, Florence,* 34, 35n. 115) for a comparison between these buildings and their appearance in fifteenth-century archaeological maps.

112. Ibid., 35.

113. Nuttall, " 'Fecero al Cardinale di Portogallo una tavola a olio,' " 20.

114. Hans Conzelmann, *The Theology of St. Luke* (London: Faber and Faber, 1960), argues Luke presents a political apology for Christianity to the Roman Empire. Paul Walaskay in *"And so We Came to Rome." The Political Perspective of St Luke* (Cambridge: Cambridge University Press, 1983) argues conversely that Luke is defending the empire to the Church. Philip Esler, *Community and Gospel in Luke-Acts* (Cambridge: Cambridge University Press, 1987) maintains that Luke seeks to reassure Roman Christians that it is possible to have allegiance both to the empire and to the faith.

115. Archdiocese of Florence brochure on Santa Trinità; obtained summer 1999.

Figure 29. Ambrogio Lorenzetti. *Presentation in the Temple.* c. 1342. Panel. Galleria degli Uffizi, Florence. Photo. With permission from the Ministero dei Beni e le Attività Culturali.

Chapter five

The *Presentation in the Temple* by Ambrogio Lorenzetti

(Luke 2:22–38)

THE STORY OF the Presentation in the Temple (Luke 2:22–38) is important for understanding Luke's theology, containing as it does Simeon's *Nunc Dimittis*, one of the four canticles in the infancy narrative. In the long history of the interpretation of this text, few interpretations have plumbed the depths of Lukan theology more profoundly than Ambrogio Lorenzetti's *Presentation in the Temple*, 1342 (Figure 29). In his visual exegesis of this text, Ambrogio was able to capture the importance of the prophecies by Simeon and Anna not only for Luke but for the contemporary Sienese worshiper. After exploring the rhetorical shape of the text, we turn our attention to Ambrogio's reading of it.

Overview of the Biblical Text

22When the time came for their purification according to the law of Moses, they brought him up to Jerusalem to present him to the Lord 23(as it is written in the law of the Lord, "Every firstborn male shall be designated as holy to the Lord"), 24and they offered a sacrifice according to what is stated in the law of the Lord, "a pair of turtledoves or two young pigeons."

25Now there was a man in Jerusalem whose name was Simeon; this man was righteous and devout, looking forward to the consolation of Israel, and the Holy Spirit rested on him. 26It had been revealed to him by the Holy Spirit that he would not see death before he had seen the Lord's Messiah. 27Guided by the Spirit, Simeon came into the temple; and when the parents brought in the child Jesus, to do for him what was customary under the law, 28Simeon took him in his arms and praised God, saying,

> 29"Master, now you are dismissing your servant in peace,
>   according to your word;

³⁰for my eyes have seen your salvation,

³¹   which you have prepared in the presence of all peoples,

³²a light for revelation to the Gentiles
   and for glory to your people Israel."

³³And the child's father and mother were amazed at what was being said about him. ³⁴Then Simeon blessed them and said to his mother Mary, "This child is destined for the falling and the rising of many in Israel, and to be a sign that will be opposed ³⁵so that the inner thoughts of many will be revealed — and a sword will pierce your own soul too."

³⁶There was also a prophet, Anna the daughter of Phanuel, of the tribe of Asher. She was of a great age, having lived with her husband seven years after their marriage, ³⁷then as a widow to the age of eighty-four. She never left the temple but worshiped there with fasting and prayer night and day. ³⁸At that moment she came, and began to praise God and to speak about the child to all who were looking for the redemption of Jerusalem.

The passage divides into three units: the setting (22–24), the characterization and speech of Simeon (25–35), and Anna's prophecy (36–38).[1] As Charles Talbert has noted, in the setting (22–24) the ritual of the purification of the mother has been interwoven into the ritual dealing with the redemption of the firstborn in an ABB¹A¹ pattern:[2]

A   "When the time came for their purification according to the law of Moses" (22a)[3]

B   "they brought him up to Jerusalem to present him to the Lord" (22b)

B¹ "as it is written in the law of the Lord, 'Every firstborn male shall be designated as holy to the Lord'" (23)

A¹ "and they offered a sacrifice according to what is stated in the law of the Lord, 'a pair of turtledoves or two young pigeons'" (24).

In this arrangement, the two middle terms deal with the dedication of the firstborn child (in a ritual described in Exod 13), and the outer two terms deal with the ritual of the purification of mothers after childbirth (described in Lev 12:1–8). The telescoping of these two events into one is Luke's way of focusing on the religious piety of Jesus' parents. This emphasis on the parents' piety is repeated in 2:27 and forms a transitional summary to the next scene: "When they had finished everything required by the law of the Lord, they returned to Galilee, to their own town of Nazareth" (2:39). The combination of these two rituals into one event does not, however, detract from the view that, for Luke, the presentation of the child in the temple is clearly the main issue.

What is not clear is what the Presentation is intended to convey. Talbert and others have argued that what lies behind the presentation account was the prescription in Jewish law that the firstborn child should be consecrated to the Lord (Exod 13:2, 11–16) and redeemed, or bought back, at a price of five shekels (Num 18:15–16) as a reminder of the Exodus.[4] Like Samuel, who at his birth was dedicated to God's service by his mother, Hannah (1 Sam 1–2), Jesus is dedicated by Mary and Joseph to the Lord's service. The fact that no mention of "ransom" money is made by the narrator is intentional. Jesus is left "unredeemed" in order that he may be fully dedicated to God's service, a point he later seems to understand better than his parents (see Luke 2:41–51).[5]

The second subunit consists of a rather detailed description of Simeon (25–28 — "righteous," "devout," "looking forward to the consolation of Israel," filled with the Holy Spirit) and his speech. The characterization of Simeon as a pious man of God is intended to undergird the authority of the speech. The speech actually consists of two oracles. The first (2:29–32), known in subsequent church tradition as the *Nunc Dimittis,* is the fourth and last of the so-called canticles in the Lukan infancy narrative, the other three being the *Magnificat* (1:46–55), the *Benedictus* (1:67–79); the *Gloria in Excelsis* (2:13–14). This oracle, like the first three canticles, is directed toward God and is introduced with the theme of blessing or praise and, using the language of Isaiah (especially Isa 40:5; 42:6; 46:13; 49:6; 52:9–10), celebrates the salvation God has brought through Jesus, providing a light to the Gentiles and glory to Israel.[6] The second oracle (2:33–35) is directed toward Mary and includes a general prediction that "this child is destined for the falling and the rising of many in Israel"[7] and a specific prophecy that Mary's own soul will be pierced.[8]

The third unit consists of a rather detailed description of Anna, emphasizing, like Simeon, her piety (36–37) and a narrative summary of her speech (unlike Simeon where the speech is actually given). The pairing of male and female figures is common in Luke, and both share a common message regarding this child's role in the consolation/salvation/redemption of Israel.[9]

A Brief History of the Feast Day for the Purification of the Virgin/Presentation in the Temple

Luke's account of the Purification/Presentation grew in significance over time. The early Greek church celebrated the encounter between Simeon

and the infant Christ in a festival known as *Hypapante*.[10] Though the
origins of this festival are obscure, by the sixth century, Justinian had
established February 2 as the feast day, and its observance had spread
across the eastern Roman Empire. In the West, the feast celebrating the
Purification of the Virgin was established by the fifth century. By the
seventh century, the ritual had expanded to include a procession with
candles, the blessing of which was associated with Candlemas.

A major objection to the feast was met early on, namely that the Virgin Mary, being pure, had no need for purification. By the twelfth and
thirteenth centuries, responses to these objections were well worked out.
Thomas Aquinas, for example, wrote in his *Summa Theologica*:

> It would seem that it was unfitting for the Mother of God to go to
> the Temple to be purified. For purification presupposes uncleanness.
> But there was no uncleanness in the Blessed Virgin, as stated above
> (III:27–28). Therefore she should not have gone to the Temple to be
> purified. I answer that, As the fullness of grace flowed from Christ on
> to His Mother, so it was becoming that the mother should be like her
> Son in humility: for "God giveth grace to the humble," as is written
> Jas 4:6. And therefore, just as Christ, though not subject to the Law,
> wished, nevertheless, to submit to circumcision and the other burdens
> of the Law, in order to give an example of humility and obedience;
> and in order to show His approval of the Law; and, again, in order
> to take away from the Jews an excuse for calumniating Him: for the
> same reasons He wished His Mother also to fulfil the prescriptions
> of the Law, to which, nevertheless, she was not subject.[11]

Likewise, *The Golden Legend,* a popular work from the thirteenth century, contains a section on "The Purification of the Blessed Virgin Mary,"
in which several reasons are given for her submission to purification, the
first of which is as an example of humility (bolstered as in the case of
Aquinas with an appeal to the way Jesus also submitted to the law).[12] The
importance of this text and its associated feast day was well established
in the liturgical life of the fourteenth-century church, the period during
which the artist Ambrogio Lorenzetti flourished. We turn our attention
now to the life and work of that artist.

The Artist and the Painting

The Sienese painter Ambrogio Lorenzetti (born c. 1290 — died 1348/49)
worked during the period before the Renaissance known as the Trecento.[13] Although the scholarship is limited on Ambrogio's *Presentation*

in the Temple (Figure 29) — signed and dated 1342[14] and today located in the Uffizi — is considered to be one of his major altarpieces in art historical surveys of the Italian Renaissance and of Sienese altarpieces.[15] George Rowley wrote the first major monograph on Ambrogio and makes several observations about the painting, which are discussed below.[16] Recent scholarship has focused on Ambrogio's masterpiece in fresco, *Il Buon Governo,* in the Palazzo Pubblico, Siena.[17] Hayden B. J. Maginnis, however, has devoted much attention to *The Presentation* since its restoration in 1985–86 and recognizes its importance in the development of panel painting during the 1300s.[18]

Ambrogio Lorenzetti

Ambrogio was a contemporary of the Sienese artists, Simone Martini (active 1315–44) and his brother Pietro Lorenzetti (c. 1290–1348?). Simone, a student of Duccio (active 1278–1318), dominated the Sienese art world until his departure for Avignon late in life.[19] Simone's style incorporated the Byzantine style of Duccio with an elegance inspired by French Gothic sources. The Lorenzetti brothers rarely collaborated but developed individual styles. Pietro Lorenzetti followed more directly the style of Duccio. Pietro may have visited Florence since his work reflects an influence of Giotto (c. 1277–1337) in the proportions of his figures (though he could also have seen works by Giotto and his followers in many other locations throughout Italy). Records indicate that Ambrogio worked in Florence on two occasions from c. 1319–23 and from 1327 to 1333.[20] Unlike Giotto whose sculptural figures find their roots in the world of Roman antiquity, Rowley rightly observes that Ambrogio "achieved breadth and power through the more pictorial Byzantine means of area and his own modeling contours."[21]

Ambrogio's figures are neither monumental nor sculptural, but his manipulation of space within the composition — perspective — indicates his fascination with problems typically associated with the Renaissance of the Quattrocento. Striving for realism was the feature that so impressed Lorenzo Ghiberti (1381?–1455) and Giorgio Vasari (1511–74), who were the first to describe Ambrogio's art.[22] Ghiberti, a fifteenth-century Florentine artist and writer of a set of commentaries, recognized Ambrogio's importance and considered him "il famossissimo e singolarissimo" artist of Siena, "a most perfect master, man of great genius and a most noble designer, very skillful in the theory of painting."[23] Vasari, also an artist in his own right but most famous for *Le vite,* called Ambrogio an excellent painter who gave "attention in his youth to letters," and that "the ways

Figure 30. Duccio. *Madonna and Child Enthroned.* Reconstruction of original front panel of the *Maestà,* 1308–11. Photo. Museo dell'Opera del Duomo, Siena.

of Ambrogio were in all respects worthy of praise, and rather those of a gentleman and a philosopher than a craftsman."[24]

Location, Original Appearance, Payment

Until recently, the precise location of *The Presentation in the Temple* in the Siena Cathedral, the original appearance of the altarpiece, as well as the period in which it was actually painted and paid for, have been either uncertain or inaccurately described in the literature.[25] The panel was originally for the Chapel of St. Crescentius in Siena Cathedral, and as Kavin Frederick has recently demonstrated, was part of a larger program of altarpiece commissions, which took twenty years to complete.[26]

Between 1308 and 1311, Duccio completed the *Maestà,* celebrating the Virgin Mary's role as queen of heaven for the high altar in the Siena Cathedral (Figure 30).[27] The Madonna is enthroned in the center of the panel, surrounded by a celestial court of saints and angels. Among the saints prominently displayed are the four patron saints of Siena: Savinus, Ansanus, Victor, and Crescentius.[28] The four chapels placed at the corners of the crossing, where the nave and the transept of the cathedral meet, contained, starting from the chapel to the left, the Chapel of St. Savinus, and moving clockwise: Pietro Lorenzetti's *Birth of the Virgin*, 1342; Simone Martini's *Annunciation*, 1333, in the Chapel of St. Ansanus; Bartolomeo Bulgarini's *Adoration of the Shepherds*, ca. 1351, in the Chapel of St. Victor;[29] and last, Ambrogio's *Presentation*, completed in the same year as his brother's altarpiece, 1342.[30] Maginnis states that the panel located in the chapel of St. Crescentius at the end of the right transept of the cathedral remained there until sometime between 1601 and 1620.[31] As evidence, he cites a list of cathedral works compiled by Fabio Chigi, later Pope Alexander VII in 1625–26, and an account of the cathedral by Alfonso Landi written in 1655.[32] In 1785, Guglielmo Della Valle locates the panel in the monastery of Monna Agnese, and finally in 1822, Ettore Romagnoli records its transfer to the Uffizi.[33]

The original appearance of the painting is revealed by the Cathedral inventories of 1429 and 1458, preserved in the Archivio dell'Opera del Duomo, Siena.[34] The inventory of 1429 describes a chapel dedicated to St. Crescentius with a painting depicting Christ and St. Simeon flanked by other saints. The 1458 inventory states that an altar panel of the Circumcision of Christ with two side panels depicting St. Crescentius and St. Michael was then located in the chapel of St. Crescentius.[35] Not only do these inventories help identify the panel, its predella, and its original location, but they also reveal the iconographic limitations of the recorder. Here the Presentation is confused with the Circumcision, an iconographic issue discussed below.

The records of payment for the panel reveal that work was begun much earlier than the date of 1342 inscribed on the painting.[36] On June 3, 1337, the documents state that the wood was purchased for the panel.[37] By July 1339 Ambrogio received thirty florins as part of what he was owed and a certain "maestro Pauolo Bindi" was paid for making the predella.[38] Another payment to Ambrogio made in January 1340 clearly suggests that substantial work on the painting occurred between 1337 and 1340.[39] Although the 1342 date inscribed on the painting confirms the date of completion, the documents reveal the duration of the activity on the commission.

Iconographical and Formal Analysis of the Painting

George Rowley points out that the earlier examples of the *Presentation in the Temple* in painting, many of which served as precedents for Ambrogio, used the pseudo-Bonaventuran *Meditations on the Life of Christ*, an

Figure 31. Giotto. *Presentation of Christ in the Temple.* 1305. Fresco. Scrovegni Chapel, Padua. Photo. Copyright Scala /Art Resource, NY.

enormously popular work by a Franciscan monk living in Tuscany during the second half of the thirteenth century, as their textual source.[40] Both Duccio in his *Maestà* (Figure 30) and Giotto in the Arena Chapel (Figure 31) select the moment in which Simeon returns the Christ Child to his mother's arms. These documents inspired meditation in a more emotionally charged mode, while the emphasis of Ambrogio's *Presentation* is clearly on a deeper iconographical level.

The Temple Design and Perspective

The inspiration for the temple design, and specifically for the polygonal dome in the Ambrogio panel, began with his understanding of the Dome of the Rock, often identified as the temple of Solomon. Trecento Sienese painters depicted scenes occurring in or around Jerusalem, with temple-like structures having visible polygonal domes.[41] It is not until Ambrogio that the interest in three-dimensional space causes entire buildings, including the temple of Solomon, to appear in a painting rather than just as decorative borders or fictive façades.[42] A second more practical source for the temple, specifically the piers, columns, and colonettes, is found in the nave of the Siena Cathedral or Duomo.[43]

Figure 32. Giovanni di Paolo. *Presentation in the Temple.* 1447–49.
Panel. Pinacoteca, Siena. Photo. Copyright Scala/Art Resource, NY.

Another Sienese artist, Giovanni di Paolo (1403?–83), copied Ambrogio's design for a *Presentation in the Temple* (Figure 32), painted 1447–49,
today located in the Pinacoteca of Siena. Giovanni di Paolo's painting does
not use space as effectively as does Ambrogio. The adage "less is more" certainly applies to the success of the Ambrogio in terms of the narrowness of
the partially visible side aisles. Giovanni di Paolo paints complete side aisles
and leaves the viewer thinking that the figures are cramped within an inadequate nave. The effect achieved by Ambrogio's side aisles is slender with an
emphasis toward the altar and upward to heaven, much the same as a contemporary Italian Gothic church. Ambrogio's architecture complements
the figures rather than competing with them as in the Giovanni di Paolo.

Ambrogio's painting does not represent the one-point linear perspective scientifically developed by Brunelleschi, Donatello, and Leon Battista Alberti during the first two decades of the fifteenth century. Rather his work reflects a perspectival advancement toward a temple interior that is spacious with believable depth while still continuing the tradition of depicting both the interior and exterior façade of the temple. Rowley notes, "Actually the nave is only as wide as the height of the figures, yet we accept the convention until it is called to our attention."[44] Ambrogio does not compromise the size of the figures or the realistic details of the temple's interior. Instead he places the figures on an almost stagelike area behind the piers of the exterior façade and in front of a central nave flanked by single side aisles, only partially visible as discussed above, each with two bays.

Behind the altar, there are at least four additional bays evident from the visible arcade. The usual Sienese or Florentine interior of the first half of the fourteenth century is one, or at most two, bays deep and the width of the room exceeds its depth. Ambrogio inverted this formula. The result is a recessional depth that creates a single vanishing point for the central area of the floor. The outer orthogonals converge on a second vanishing point, much higher in the picture plane.[45]

The Iconographic Program and a "Visual Exegesis"

In order to understand the iconographic significance of the *Presentation in the Temple*, we must begin by exploring the relationship of this altarpiece to the high altar as well as to the altarpieces of the remaining three chapels. Our interest is in understanding how the artist's audience would have viewed this painting in its original setting. After placing Ambrogio's *Presentation* within its original iconographical program, we attend to the significance of the various inscriptions and figures in an effort to understand the painting's overall meaning.

The program of the Trecento altarpieces for the Siena cathedral has a clear mariological focus, celebrating the life of the Virgin Mary.[46] Moving clockwise from the St. Savino chapel, the altarpieces depict the life of the virgin in chronological order, moving from her birth to the Annunciation to the Nativity and finally to the Purification (our Presentation) in the chapel of St. Crescentius. Such a focus on Mary is not surprising in a city that in 1260 had dedicated itself to the Virgin as the "Civitas Virginis" (city of the Virgin) when its army defeated the attacking Florentines at the battle of Montaperti.[47] Duccio's high altarpiece, of course, had already begun this mariological emphasis and contained depictions of the *Annunciation*, the *Nativity*, the *Adoration*, the *Presentation in the Temple*, the *Flight into Egypt,* and also scenes from the end of the Virgin's life: the *Annunciation of the Virgin's Death and Glorification,* the *Return of the Apostles,* the *Death of the Virgin,* the *Dormition* (when Christ gathered the Virgin's soul), the *Apostles Bearing the Virgin's Body to the Tomb,* and the *Entombment of the Virgin.*[48] Duccio's masterpiece, of course, centered on the image of the Madonna enthroned. The four altarpieces of the surrounding chapels amplified those scenes from the life of the Virgin celebrated as feast days (Birth of the Virgin, Annunciation, Nativity, and Purification).[49]

The Duccio *Maestà* also had an explicit christological focus as well. The scenes above and below the main panel from the life of the Virgin were accompanied on the reverse side by thirty-four scenes from Christ's ministry, passion, and glorification including, among others, the *Gathering of the Apostles,* the *Entry into Jerusalem,* and the *Crucifixion* (the last two being twice the size of the rest).[50]

We also see this double emphasis on Mary and Christ in Ambrogio's St. Crescentius altarpiece. This dual emphasis may account in part for the confusion over the title of the piece in the history of scholarship; it has been variously labeled as the *Purification of the Virgin,* the *Presentation of Christ,* and even the *Circumcision.*[51] A detailed iconographic analysis of the various elements in the painting can assist in determining the focus of the painting.

The Painted Inscriptions and the Statuettes

Three textual inscriptions within the painting serve as primary documentation for its iconographical content. Two Old Testament prophets, Moses and Malachi, hold scrolls at the top and center of the panel. Their names are painted behind their heads. They represent a figural type — a gray-haired, bearded man — and their body positions mirror each other. Moses, on the left, wears a blue gown with pink mantle while Malachi's garments reverse those colors (Figure 33). The most significant difference between the figures is the legible Latin inscriptions on the scrolls. The figure of Moses, whose name is painted behind his head, holds a banner with a quotation from Lev 12:8: "If she cannot afford a sheep, she shall take two turtledoves or two pigeons, one for a burnt offering and the other for a sin offering."[52] The viewer is not surprised to find this Old Testament verse cited, since Luke himself quotes part of the same Leviticus quote: "a pair of turtledoves or two young pigeons." The longer citation in the painted inscription makes explicit what is left implicit in Luke: the substitute of pigeons for a sheep was an effort to accommodate those too poor to purchase the larger sacrifice. The material poverty of Mary and Joseph is given no emphasis in the painting beyond this inscription (since

Figure 33. Ambrogio Lorenzetti. Detail of Moses, *Presentation in the Temple*. Galleria degli Uffizi, Florence. Photo. With permission from the Ministero dei Beni e le Attività Culturali.

the dress of Mary and Joseph, while simple, could hardly be described as derelict). In the *Meditations on the Life of Christ,* however, this sacrifice was also understood as a lesson in humility: "If you desire to learn about humility and poverty, consider in the aforementioned events, the donation, the redemption, and the observation of the law and you can easily perceive them."[53]

This humility, as expressed by their obedience to the law, is emphasized also by the statue positioned on the top of the painted pier, visible in the left foreground. Moses, holding the Ten Commandments, is Ambrogio's way of reasserting Luke's emphasis on Mary and Joseph's obedience to the law, though as we shall see later, there is some question in Lorenzetti's depiction (as in Luke itself) whether or not the ritual of purification was actually fulfilled.

The other painted inscription is found on a banner held by the Old Testament prophet, Malachi (whose name, like Moses, is inscribed behind his head), who stands opposite Moses in the top right portion of the panel. He, too, holds a banner, which contains a quotation from Mal 3:1: "And the Lord whom you seek will suddenly come to his temple. The messenger of the covenant in whom you delight."[54]

This text from Malachi is not mentioned in the story in Luke and might puzzle the modern viewer as to why it is included in Ambrogio's painting. This text is the second half of a perhaps more familiar verse which begins "See, I am sending my messenger to prepare the way before me" (Mal 3:1b). Though scholars are divided in their opinion regarding the identities of this covenant messenger and the Lord,[55] there was little ambiguity in Christian interpretation over the first fourteen centuries. This first half of the verse figured prominently in Christian interpretation of the role of John the Baptist as a forerunner to Jesus (see Mark 1:2; Matt 3:1–3; 11:3, 10; Luke 7:27). But the second half of Malachi would also have been very familiar to the artist's audience who would have recognized it as part of the lectionary readings associated with the feast day of the Presentation of the Lord. Furthermore, this verse from Malachi was also quoted (along with Lev 12:8 and others) in the popular fourteenth-century *Biblia pauperum* (the "Bible of the Poor") in association with the picture depicting the Presentation in the Temple.[56] The page on the Purification of the Virgin was laid out in the *Biblia pauperum* as follows:

Central subject. The Purification.

Left subject. The Presentation of the First Born to the Temple.

Right subject. Dedication of Samuel to the Temple.

Left quote. Lev. 12.6. We read in the book of Leviticus, chapter 12, that every woman giving birth to her firstborn must redeem him with a lamb; the poor who are not able to have a lamb must sacrifice a turtledove or two pigeons for the son, and this for her purification. Which the Glorious Virgin fulfilled, though she did not need to be purified.

Right quote. We read in the first book of Samuel, chapter 1, that Anna, the mother of Samuel, when she had weaned Samuel, offered him to Heli, the priest in the temple of God, which offering prefigured the offering of God in the temple, made to Simeon.

Left upper prophet. David. Ps. 10.5. "The Lord is in His holy temple."

Right upper prophet. Mal. 3.1. "The lord whom you desire shall come to his holy temple."

Left verse. Versus. Here is presented the firstborn that he may be redeemed.

Right verse. Versus. Samuel offered denotes you, O Christ.

Left lower prophet. Zach. 2.10. "Behold I come and I will dwell in the midst of thee."

Right lower prophet. Soph. 3.15. "The King of Israel the Lord is in the midst of thee."

From early on, then, in Christian exegesis, the eschatological moment of Yahweh God entering into his temple to purify it and its priests has occurred within the history, and the Lord who enters the temple is none other than the Messiah, the Lord Jesus Christ. The author of the *Meditations on the Life of Christ* observed about the Presentation: "They bring the Lord of the temple to the temple of the Lord," a comment, or something like it, that may have come to the mind of the original audience viewing Ambrogio's picture.[57]

The "regal" scene evoked by Malachi's inscription is reminiscent again of the *Meditations*, in a story amplified far beyond Luke's account, and may help in the identification of the other painted statues in Ambrogio's *Presentation*. After Simeon returns the child to his mother's arms, the *Meditations* described a procession perhaps related to liturgical practices of the fourteenth-century Tuscan church:

> After that they walked around the altar in a procession that is today performed in the whole world. First there came the two venerable old men, Joseph and Simeon, holding hands, exultant, and singing with great joy . . . (Psalm 109,13) "Faithful is the Lord in all His words"; . . . (Psalm 47,15) "For this is the Lord God of ours in eternity and in the time of times He will rule us forever, that is always"; (Psalm 47,10) "O God, we have received your mercy in the midst of your temple. . . . "[58]

The use of the Psalms (as also in the *Biblia pauperum*) to articulate the feeling of exultation at the appearance of the Christ Child in the temple is significant. The audience would have accepted the traditional attribution of the Psalms to David and thus both the content and the very mention of the Psalms would have evoked a royal, messianic message. Thus, given the messianic context associated with the Presentation in the literary sources roughly contemporary with Ambrogio, it would be natural for the artist's audience to identify the figure of the second statue with David (Figure 34).[59] Thus, the painted statue of Moses emphasizes the obedience of Mary to fulfill the law, while the painted statue of David emphasizes the royal lineage of the Christ Child.[60]

Mary, Joseph, and the Attendants

In an insightful article on Ambrogio's *Presentation*, Maginnis has recently argued that "the features that belong specifically to the Purification are found in the left half of the panel; what I regard his [sic] the primary subject matter in the right.... In order to direct our attention to the essential content of the image, the figures of Anna, Simeon and the Christ Child had to stand more or less alone...."[61] Unfortunately, Maginnis's analysis needlessly bifurcates the painting and does not fit the iconographic

Figure 34. Ambrogio Lorenzetti. Detail of David, *Presentation in the Temple*. Galleria degli Uffizi, Florence. Photo. With permission from the Ministero dei Beni e le Attività Culturali.

history of the presentation scene. As Dorothy Shorr demonstrated long ago, it was commonplace to have Mary, Joseph, and in many cases attendants stand opposite Simeon, Anna, and in some cases a second aged, male figure. The *Presentation* rather "shows the group now assembled at either side of the altar, and the chief variations in the presentation of the scene lie in the ceremonial handling of the Child as he passes from his mother to Simeon (later, the High Priest)."[62] In no way then would Ambrogio's grouping of characters be taken by the Trecento audience as a sign of division between them.

That is not to say that there are not some distinctive features about these figures. From an almost infinite number of possibilities, Ambrogio had to choose which moment to depict. Dorothy Shorr has identified six major variations in the iconography that appear in the art of the eighth through the twelfth centuries in chronological order: (1) Mary holds the child; (2) both Mary and Simeon hold the child; (3) the child stands on the altar supported by Mary and Simeon; (4) Simeon alone holds the child in his arms; (5) Simeon returns the child to Mary after the ceremony is completed; (6) the swaddled child is held by Joseph (extremely rare).[63] Clearly here Ambrogio's depiction fits Type 4; Simeon alone holds the child in his arms. We return to this detail momentarily.

Another interesting variation has to do with the doves. In many depictions, Joseph carries the two doves, though occasionally, Mary is holding two large birds. On rare occasions, Anna is depicted with the birds, and in at least one depiction, the birds are carried by the foremost figure in a group of three unidentified young men.[64] In Ambrogio's *Presentation,* the birds are held by the high priest, and it is to his appearance that we now turn our attention.

The High Priest and His Attendants

According to Shorr, an altar was a central element in the iconographic form of the Presentation since at least the ninth century.[65] Rarely, however, does an altar have as much activity surrounding it as does Ambrogio's *Presentation,* with its depiction of the high priest and his attendants. In fact, the high priest is a relative latecomer to the presentation scene, and Shorr has identified Ambrogio's *Presentation* as the first dated appearance in which the high priest can be identified with certainty.[66] The lettering of his headdress, according to Rowley, shows a curiosity with Greek and Hebrew scripts and continues the tradition of fake inscriptions in those languages.[67] Maginnis calls the inscription pseudocufic, which is intended to be the phrase "holiness to the Lord," required on the crown of the mitre by Exod 39:30.[68] The breastplate is decorated with the jewels of the twelve tribes of Israel.[69] He sits in the middle of the composition with the pigeons, mentioned in the inscription, visible beneath the right hand of the high priest. He holds the sacrificial knife in the other hand. The raised hand of a second figure, a priest or a scribe, to the left of the high priest, however, suggests that the sacrifice is being interrupted by what is occurring on the other side of the panel. Here then is a rich irony in Ambrogio's painting. Both the text and its visual representation go to great lengths to depict Mary and Joseph as pious Jewish believers who faithfully fulfill the religious laws and rituals. Yet, clearly here the ritual has been interrupted and there is no sign that it will ever be completed. Still, Ambrogio suggests, Mary and Joseph keep the commandments even though the purification ritual itself remains unfulfilled.[70] It is the activity on the viewer's right that halts the purification ceremony, and it is those characters to whom we now attend.

Anna

In the biblical text, Anna holds a prominent position at the end of the narrative. Like Mary and Joseph (and Simeon, see below), she is pious: "She never left the temple but worshiped there with fasting and prayer night and day" (2:37). In visual art, however, the figure of Anna is not always depicted, and in fact seldom occurs in northern art. Usually (though not always), Anna is depicted as an elderly woman, picking up on a detail in the text where Luke states that Anna was eighty-four years old. While Ambrogio does not choose the dramatic portrayal of prophetic frenzy sometimes associated with Anna (Figure 35), he does use another symbol characteristic of her figure, the prophetic scroll.[71] On Anna's scroll we find a third inscription that contains the conclusion to the scene and summarizes her prophecy of him "to all who were looking for the redemption of Jerusalem." The banderole presents the message of redemption that Anna had waited so long to proclaim. With that message of redemption held securely in her left hand, she raises her right hand and points to the child who was in fact the fulfillment of that long-anticipated redemption.

Simeon and the Christ Child

The viewer's eyes (along with the eyes of most of the figures) are drawn to the character of Simeon, an older, bearded man, holding the Christ Child in his arms.[72] Here is the climax of the scene. Anna points to them. Mary holds the child's white blanket but her attention is directed to the child. Two women behind her look at Simeon while Joseph seems to stop his hand gesture at this very moment. Likewise, the high priest's sacrificial act is arrested.[73]

Figure 35. Ambrogio Lorenzetti.
Detail of Anna, *Presentation in
the Temple*. Galleria degli Uffizi,
Florence. Photo. With permission
from the Ministero dei Beni e le
Attività Culturali.

Simeon shifts his weight to perhaps accommodate an impatient infant.
The rose gown allows the contours of his left leg, especially thigh and bent
knee, to be understood beneath the drapery while the green mantle shows
deep wrinkles along their edges which define movement of the figure's
arms and upper body. Simeon is certainly the only figure whose clothing
depicts movement, an action that further draws the viewer's attention to
these figures.

The infant-like facial characteristics and body position of Jesus have
been noted by scholars as a step toward realism. Rowley comments: "Amaz-
ing as it may seem, the Christ Child was the first example of the rendering
of a real baby under a year old. Hitherto the Child had been a Byzantine
little old man or a Gothic youngster, three or four years of age."[74] Ambrogio has captured an infant, whose toes curl up and wiggle, and who sucks
on his forefinger while peering upward without a keen ability to focus his
eyes yet. He is swaddled in a red cloth. This confines his arms and legs.

This is not a position of comfort for a baby who is awake — thus the necessity of Simeon's responsive movements to the baby's squirming.

But there is much more here than the "realistic" depiction of an infant, and it is here that Ambrogio penetrates most deeply the theological weave of the Lukan narrative. Just as Luke had combined two separate rituals, the purification and the presentation, into a single momentous event, so Ambrogio telescoped two separate moments in the narrative, Simeon's *Nunc Dimittis* and Anna's prophecy, into a single moment of epiphany. In Luke's account, Simeon's speech is followed by Anna's prophecy. In Ambrogio's visual interpretation, the attentive observer will notice that while Anna is holding her prophetic scroll (which begins with the words "at that moment" *et haec ipsa hora*), Simeon's mouth is open to speak. What is he saying? George Rowley has offered a highly suggestive reading, worth quoting here in full:

> Simeon is speaking and there can be no doubt about the gravity of the words. . . . Ambrogio has chosen the most profound moment. It is not Simeon's blessing of the Child or later of his parents, nor the beginning of the nunc dimittis "now lettest thou thy servant depart in peace," nor the words to Mary, "See, I am sending, this Child is sent for the fall and rising again of many in Israel," nor the prophecy of the Messianic redemption of the Laws. This is the prophecy of salvation through Christ, "for mine eyes have seen Thy salvation, which Thou has prepared before the face of all people; a light to lighten the Gentiles, and the glory of Thy people Israel." Each figure is immobile, filled with an awareness of the sacredness of the moment.[75]

Collapsing these two speeches into one moment underscores the message of both that in this child rests the hope of redemption for both Jew and Gentile.[76] Rowley further notes that subsequent paintings influenced by Ambrogio nonetheless failed to capture the significance of the moment: "Giovanni di Paolo made an exact copy of the iconography but lost the meaning, for his painting might be the break-up of a family christening in which, once again, the persistent narrative note has been inserted — the return of the Child to Mary. Similar misreadings are to be found in versions by Bartolo di Fredi and Sano di Pietro. Ambrogio's prototype was influential for a hundred years but he alone has captured the momentous import of Simeon's prophecy."[77]

For Ambrogio, his patrons, and his audience, this event was not simply a historical moment preserved in time. The soteriological implications of the *Presentation* crossed over the centuries to touch even the worshipers

at the Siena cathedral. Not only is Ambrogio the first to attempt to relate the figures of the *Presentation* to the interior of the temple,[78] Carol
Krinsky has shown that Ambrogio's *Presentation* is an example of how the
symbolic temple of Solomon reflects contemporary church design in Trecento painting.[79] She writes: "The process of enlarging a shallow structure
can be appreciated from the fact that Ambrogio Lorenzetti, in his *Presentation of Christ* (1342), 'added a choir after he had tooled in a lower arch
at the end of the nave,' thus converting a building that had been little
more than a pavilion into a church."[80] The effect is to involve the viewer
in this moment of redemption. The Christ Child is still the source of hope
for all who "were looking for the redemption of Jerusalem" and Siena; the
contemporary worshiper is able to proclaim with Simeon, "mine eyes have
seen your salvation!"

Conclusion

In 1978, Raymond Brown published a small pamphlet entitled *An Adult
Christ at Christmas,* intended as a kind of introduction to *The Birth of
the Messiah,* a full-scale (six hundred pages) commentary on the infancy
narratives in Matthew and Luke. In the first chapter, Brown laments the
fact that "the narratives of Jesus' birth and infancy constitute 'the last
frontier' to be crossed in gaining an appreciation of the implications of a
modern scientific (critical) approach to the New Testament."[81]

While we are not arguing that Ambrogio in any way foreshadows the
"scientific" approach to Scripture about which Brown writes, we do con-
tend that in Ambrogio Lorenzetti's *Presentation in the Temple,* there is a
profoundly "adult" message. Ambrogio, who was the first to depict the
Christ Child as a child, is also one of the first artists to see and to depict
the mature christological message embedded in the Lukan account of the
Presentation in the Temple. He visually underscores this point by placing
directly above the high priest in a clipeus on the tympanum of the nave
a figure of Christ, right hand raised in a gesture of blessing, cloaked in
a red shawl, and supported by winged victories.[82] In his *Presentation in
the Temple,* Ambrogio Lorenzetti has recognized that there is, indeed, an
adult message about the infant Christ, a message of salvation and hope
that demands that we "proclaim that revelation to others that they too
may respond in faith."

Notes

1. See Raymond E. Brown, *The Birth of the Messiah: A Commentary on the Infancy Narratives in the Gospels of Matthew and Luke* (Garden City, N.Y.: Doubleday, 1977), 446. Brown sees 2:39–40 as a fourth and concluding part to this section. Because the verses also function as an introduction to the next section, and more importantly, because Ambrogio seems to end his interpretation of the scene with vv. 36–38, we deal only with Luke 2:22–38. For recent interpretations of this text, see Marion L. Soards, "Luke 2:22–40 [expository article]," *Interpretation* 44 (1990): 400–405; Frederick Strickert, "The Presentation of Jesus: The Gospel of Inclusion (Luke 2:22–40)," *Currents in Theology and Mission* 22 (1995): 33–37.

2. Charles Talbert, *Reading Luke: A Literary and Theological Commentary on the Third Gospel* (New York: Crossroad, 1982), 36.

3. The textual problem of whether the text reads "their purification" or "her purification" did not bother the interpreters of Ambrogio's day, because they accepted without question the (more poorly attested) reading of "her purification" found in the majority text. The text-critical problem has vexed modern interpreters, however. See the discussion in Darrell L. Bock, *Luke, 1:1–9:50* (Grand Rapids: Baker Books, 1994), 235–36.

4. See Talbert, *Reading Luke,* 36; also, Bo Reicke, "Jesus, Simeon, and Anna [Luke 2:21–40]," in *Saved By Hope* (ed. J. I. Cook; Grand Rapids: Eerdmans, 1978), 96–108; Bock, *Luke,* 234. Against this view, see Brown, *Birth,* 447–51; R. Alan Culpepper, "The Gospel of Luke," *The New Interpreter's Bible* (vol. 9; Nashville: Abingdon, 1995), 69. The appearance of the child in the temple is not an explicit element of the ritual described in Exodus or Numbers.

5. Talbert, *Reading Luke,* 36. Culpepper's objection ("The Gospel of Luke," 69) that this interpretation "requires a level of familiarity with Jewish law that could hardly have been assumed among Gentile Christians" comes to grief in light of the later evidence. There is a substantial iconographic tradition of Jesus being "bought back" with the prescribed five shekels (see Dorothy Shorr, "The Iconographic Development of the Presentation in the Temple," *Art Bulletin* 28 [1946]: 30, for examples). This tradition was also well-established in the literature as well; see especially pseudo-Bonaventure, *Meditations on the Life of Christ* (trans. and ed. I. Ragusa and R. B. Greene; Princeton, N.J.: Princeton University Press, 1961), 61: "the infant Jesus on the altar, like any other child, gazing at His mother with mature face, meekly and patiently awaiting what he had to do next. There were priests in the temple, and the Lord of all was bought back like a slave for the price of five shekels, according to the custom of the others." Thus, Christians living centuries after the fact were aware of the "redemption of the firstborn," presumably through the Old Testament references (even though their references to it destroy Luke's intention to present Jesus as "unredeemed" and therefore dedicated solely to God's service). Ergo, it is not impossible to think that Luke and his audience would likewise have been aware of such a ritual, at least on a literary level. More is said about the *Meditations* and its relationship to Ambrogio's *Presentation* later in this chapter.

6. On this text and the Lukan infancy narrative in particular, see Mark Coleridge, *The Birth of the Lukan Narrative: Narrative as Christology in Luke 1–2* (Journal for the Study of the New Testament Supplement Series 88; Sheffield: Sheffield Academic Press, 1993). On the Isaianic background of the *Nunc Dimittis,* see Brown, *Birth,* 458.

7. Robert Tannehill ("Israel in Luke-Acts: A Tragic Story," *Journal of Biblical Literature* 104 [1985]: 69–85) points to this text as a kind of outline for the story of Israel throughout the entirety of Luke and Acts.

8. Brown (*Birth,* 462) lists at least eight different interpretations of the sword piercing Mary's soul. Brown's own interpretation (465) that the sword consists of Mary "recognizing that the claims of Jesus' heavenly Father outrank any human attachments between him

and his mother" is certainly plausible (cf. 2:48–50), but should not rule out pain caused by his death or by the conflict he caused in Israel.

9. See Culpepper, "The Gospel of Luke," 72.

10. On the history of the Purification of the Virgin and Presentation of Christ in church liturgy, see Shorr, "The Iconographic Development of the Presentation in the Temple," 17–19.

11. Aquinas, *Summa Theologiae*, III:37:4.

12. See Jacobus de Voragine, *The Golden Legend: Readings on the Saints* (trans. William Granger Ryan; vol. 1; Princeton, N.J.: Princeton University Press, 1993), 143–51, esp. 144–46. In this section, *The Golden Legend* also has much valuable information about the traditions then associated with the *Hypapante,* Candlemas, and the Purification of the Virgin.

13. See Valerie Wainwright, "The Will of Ambrogio Lorenzetti," *Burlington Magazine* 117 (1975): 543–44, for documentation that confirms that Ambrogio Lorenzetti died during the plague in late 1348 or early 1349. Ambrogio had three children, all female, to whom he left his estate. The will states that the Company of the Virgin Mary should inherit his wealth and property in the event that his children, or their heirs, do not survive him. The children must all have died in the same year, or shortly after, and left no heirs themselves because the documents reflect the inheritance going to the Company of the Virgin Mary. Also of interest is the selling of Ambrogio's home for 275 lire. Wainwright, 543, compares this to the 200-lire valuation of Simone Martini's house in 1344 and suggests that the Lorenzetti family may be slightly more wealthy than the Martinis. They were certainly of a comparable social class and financial stature.

14. The painting is signed AMBROSIVS.LAVRENTII.DE.SENIS.FECIT.HOC OPVS. ANNO DOMINI MCCCXLII in the horizontal band along the bottom edge of the panel. The size of the panel is 8′ 5 ⅛″ x 5′ 6 ⅛″.

15. See Frederick Hartt, *History of Italian Renaissance Art* (4th ed.; revised by David G. Wilkins; New York: Harry N. Abrams, 1994), 125–27, and Henk Van Os, *Sienese Altarpieces 1215–1460: Form, Content, Function, Volume 1: 1215–1344* (Groningen: Bouma's Boekhuis, 1984), 82–85.

16. George Rowley, *Ambrogio Lorenzetti* (2 vols.; Princeton, N.J.: Princeton University Press, 1958), 1:18–25. For a detailed review of this text, see Richard Offner, "Reflections on Ambrogio Lorenzetti," *Gazette des Beaux-Arts* 140 (1960): 235–38. For brief discussions of the painting, see the monograph by Eve Borsook, *Ambrogio Lorenzetti* (Florence: Sadea, 1966), 16–17, and Enzo Carli, *Ambrogio Lorenzetti: Dipinti su tavola* (Milan: Aldo Martello Editore, 1962), tavola XVII.

17. For the Palazzo Pubblico, see Enrico Castelnuovo, *Ambrogio Lorenzetti: Il Buon Governo* (Milan: Electa, 1995); Randolph Starn, *Ambrogio Lorenzetti: The Palazzo Pubblico, Siena* (New York: George Braziller, 1994); and Ernst von Meyenburg, *Ambrogio Lorenzetti: Ein Bietrag zur Geschichte der sienesischen Malerei im vierzehnten Jahrhundert* (Zurich: Buchdruckerei Jean Frey, 1903). Literature specifically on the Sala della Pace includes Max Seidel, "Studien zur Ikonographie der Fresken des Ambrogio Lorenzetti in der 'Sala della Pace,'" 16 (1997): 35–90, and Suzanne Maureen Burke, "Ambrogio Lorenzetti's Sala della Pace: Its Historiography and Its 'Sensus Astrologicus'" (Ann Arbor: University of Michigan Press, 1994).

18. See Hayden B. J. Maginnis, "Ambrogio Lorenzetti's 'Presentation in the Temple,'" *Studi di Storia dell'Arte* 2 (1991): 33–50, for a substantial study of the *Presentation in the Temple*. For useful archival documentation, see Maginnis, "Charimenti documentari: Simone Martini, I Memmi e Ambrogio Lorenzetti," *Rivista d'Arte* 41 (1989): 3–23. See also Maginnis, "The Lost Façade Frescoes of Siena's Ospedale di S. Maria della Scala," *Zeitschrift für Kunstgeschichte* 5 (1988): 180–94, related to Ambrogio's architectonic source

for the *Presentation*. This issue is addressed later in the chapter. Maginnis also wrote the entry for Ambrogio Lorenzetti in the *Dictionary of Art* (ed. Jane Turner; 34 vols.; New York: Grove's Dictionaries, 1996), 19:668–72.

19. For Simone Martini, see Pierluigi Leone De Castris, *Simone Martini* (Madrid: Akal, 1992), and Andrew Martindale, *Simone Martini: Complete Edition* (New York: New York University Press, 1988). For recent literature on Duccio, see Enzo Carli, *Duccio* (Milan: Electa, 1998) and Giovann Ragionieri, *Duccio: catalogo completo dei dipinti* (Florence: Cantini, 1989).

20. Jørgen Petersen, "Ambrogio Lorenzetti and Pictorial Space," *Analecta Romana Instituti Danici* 7 (1977): 124. Specifically, Ambrogio painted a *Madonna* for the Pieve in Vico l'Abate outside Florence in 1319. In 1332–34 he joined the Arte dei Medici e Speziali, possibly in order to work in Florence and fulfill a commission for a polyptych for the Church of San Procolo. Hartt (*History of Italian Renaissance Art*, 125) discusses these sojourns.

21. Rowley, *Ambrogio Lorenzetti*, 3.

22. Van Os, *Sienese Altarpieces*, 84.

23. See *Lorenzo Ghiberti: I commentari* (c. 1457), ed. Julius Ritter von Schlosser, as *Lorenzo Ghiberti Denkwürdigkeiten* (Berlin: J. Bard, 1920).

24. Giorgio Vasari, *Le Opere di Giorgio Vasari: Le Vite de'più eccellenti pittori, scultori ed architettori scritte da Giorgio Vasari pittore Aretino* (1568) (ed. Gaetano Milanesi; 9 vols.; Florence: Sansoni, 1885), 1:521–35.

25. Hartt, *History of Italian Renaissance Art*, 126. It was believed that the Lorenzetti brothers competed for one of the altar panels placed in Siena Cathedral in 1342.

26. Kavin Frederick, "A Program of Altarpieces for the Siena Cathedral," *Rutgers Art Review* 3 (1983): 18–35. Frederick builds and corrects the earlier work by Henk Van Os (*Marias Demut und Verherrlichung in der sienesischen Malerei, 1300–1450* [The Hague: Ministerie van Cultuur, 1969]), who first detected a "deliberate plan" in the Sienese altarpieces.

27. Tempera on panel, 6' 10½", Museo dell'Opera del Duomo, Siena. Maginnis ("Ambrogio,") reports that Duccio's *Maestà* was removed from the high altar in 1506. In addition to the *Madonna*, the *Maestà* has numerous compartments depicting scenes from the lives of Christ and Mary.

28. Savinus was the first bishop of Siena and was martyred by scourging. Crescentius was a Roman martyr whose relics are preserved in the cathedral. Son of a Roman nobleman, Ansanus was martyred near Siena. Victor was a native of Siena who was martyred in Egypt. These last three were beheaded. For details on the legends associated with these four, see George Kaftal, *Iconography of the Saints in Tuscan Painting* (Florence: Sansoni, 1952), nrs. 23, 78, 277, 310.

29. It has recently been discovered that this panel, 170.5 x 123 cm, is located in the Fogg Art Museum, Boston. See Elizabeth H. Beatson, Norman E. Muller, and Judith B. Steinhoff, "The St. Victor Altarpiece in Siena Cathedral: A Reconstruction," *Art Bulletin* 68 (1986): 610–31. The authors argue on the basis of stylistic, iconographic, and technical reasons that the St. Victor's altarpiece is to be identified with the (now much reduced) Fogg *Nativity* and also that the altarpiece was flanked by two saints which they identify as preserved on a pair of panels by the Palazzo Venezia Master (*Saint Victor*, 158 x 50 cm; *Saint Corona*, 155 x 52 cm, both c. 1350 and both in Statens Museum, Copenhagen).

30. Chiara Frugoni, *Pietro and Ambrogio Lorenzetti* (Florence: Scala, 1988, printed 1995), 54–55.

31. Maginnis ("Ambrogio," 34n. 10) confirms the replacement of the panel by 1620 with Bartolomeo Bulgarini's *Nativity*. For a state-of-the-research prior to 1933, see Giulia Sinibaldi, *I Lorenzetti* (Florence: Leo S. Olschki, 1933), 188–89.

32. Maginnis, "Ambrogio," 34, and 39nn. 11 and 12.

33. Ibid., 34 and 39nn. 13 and 14.

34. Ibid., 39n. 15.

35. Ibid.

36. Maginnis, "Charimenti documentari," 13–19.

37. Ibid., 13.

38. Ibid., 18. For new research related to a suggestion that a panel in the Siena Pinacoteca may be the central section of the predella, see Beatson, et al., 621n. 67.

39. Maginnis ("Ambrogio," 35) also notes that the delay between the purchase of the wood in 1337 and Ambrogio's payment in 1339 coincides with his work on the Sala della Pace in Siena's Palazzo Pubblico between February 1338 and May 1339.

40. Rowley, *Ambrogio Lorenzetti*, 18. See *Meditations*, 58.

41. Maginnis, "Ambrogio," 24. See also Duccio's *Entry into Jerusalem* and the *Temptation in the Temple* in his Maestà. Pietro Lorenzetti's *Entry into Jerusalem* in San Francesco, Assisi, also depicts a structure with a polygonal dome.

42. Ibid., 11.

43. Ibid., 37. Maginnis draws comparisons between the Ambrogio painting and other features (the figures of the prophets, angels holding gables, sculpted animals, dentils of the roofline) of the Duomo. Elements of Sienese architecture include the crescent-shaped lunettes, which Maginnis sees first appearing on the façade of the Palazzo Pubblico and in the side portal of the unfinished duomo nuovo.

44. Rowley, *Ambrogio Lorenzetti*, 20.

45. The analysis of the perspective stated in this paragraph is taken from the authority on the subject, John White, *The Birth and Rebirth of Pictorial Space* (London: Faber and Faber, 1957), 99. The significance of the contribution made by Ambrogio in the current understanding of the development of perspective is represented by the attention given to this painting by White. White also notes, as is stated above, that the conception of the interior as a whole is not advanced due to the implementation of the older tradition of including the exterior architecture with the interior scene.

46. Another Lukan theme, as Talbert has shown in his description of the Lukan Mary as the "ideal believer" (see *Reading Luke*, 22–26).

47. See E. B. Garrison, "Toward a New History of the Siena Cathedral Madonnas," *Studies in the History of Medieval Italian Painting* 4, no. 1 (1960–62): 5–22; Helmut Hager, *Die Anfänge des italienischen Altarbildes: Untersuchungen zur Entstehungsgeschichte des toskanischen Hochaltarretabels* (Munich: Schroll, 1962), 104–8, 152–53.

48. See Van Os, *Sienese Altarpieces*, 46.

49. In addition to the Nativity, celebrated at Christmas, these feast days held important places in the Church's calendar and still do today in the Roman Church. The birth of the Virgin is celebrated on September 8; the Annunciation is celebrated on March 25, and the Purification of the Virgin/Presentation of the Lord is observed on February 2.

50. See Van Os, *Sienese Altarpieces*, 51–54; also figures 41–42. Van Os is dependent especially upon the reconstruction of the Maestà altarpiece proposed by John White, *Duccio: Tuscan Art and the Medieval Workshop* (London: Thames and Hudson, 1979).

51. This confusion is centuries old and goes back almost to the composition of the painting. The inventory account of 1429 referred to the painting as "the presentation of Christ" while the inventory account of 1458 identified the painting as "the circumcision of our Lord" (see discussion above); also Maginnis, "Ambrogio," 33; Rowley, *Ambrogio Lorenzetti*, 18.

52. Lev 12:8: SI NON INVENERIT MANVS EI[VS] NEC POTVERIT OFFERRE AGNIVM SVMET DVOS TVRTVRES AVT DVOS PVLLOS CHOLVNBE.

53. See *Meditations,* 56.

54. Mal 3:1: ET STATI VENIET AD TEMPLVM SUUM DOMINATVR QVEM VOS QVAERITIS ET ANGELVS TESTAMENTI QVEM VOS VVLTIS.

55. B. Malchow ("The Messenger of the Covenant in Mal. 3:1," *Journal of Biblical Literature* 103 [1984]: 252–55) thinks that the covenant messenger is a priestly figure, while Beth Glazier-McDonald ("*Mal'ak habberit:* the Messenger of the Covenant in Mal. 3:1," *Hebrew Annual Review* 11 [1987]: 93–104) identifies both the "messenger" and the "Lord" as Yahweh. The standard English commentary on Malachi is David L. Petersen, *Zechariah 9–14 and Malachi,* Old Testament Library (Louisville: Westminster/John Knox, 1995).

56. For a facsimile see *Biblia Pauperum, Faksimileausgabe des vierzigblättrigen Armenbibel: Blockbuches in der Bibliothek der Erzdiözesee Esztergom* (Hanau/Main: Werner Dausien, 1967). The *Biblia pauperum* is typically arranged as follows: each page will have three major pictures, a central one from the New Testament, flanked by two from the Old Testament. At the top right and left will be texts, usually explaining how the flanking pictures are prefigurations of the central picture. At the top and bottom center of the page will be four ancient fathers (usually prophets), with banderoles, taken, again from biblical texts. Finally, there are three "tituli," called "versus," usually rhyming, often leonine, to the three pictures.

57. *Meditations,* 56.

58. Ibid., 58–60.

59. Rowley (*Ambrogio Lorenzetti,* 19), claims that Ambrogio's iconographic details extend to the dualism in the statues of Moses with the tales of the law and Joshua with the sun in his hand, one representing ritual purification and the other the deliverance of the Jews. Maginnis, "Ambrogio," 37, and Maria Prokopp, *Pietro und Ambrogio Lorenzetti* (Berlin: Henschelvorlag, 1985), 27, agree with Rowley. Shorr, "The Iconographic Development of the Presentation in the Temple," 28; Borsook, *Ambrogio Lorenzetti,* 17; and Van Os, *Sienese Altarpieces,* 84, identify the figure as David. Shorr comes the closest to giving what is, in our opinion, an adequate explanation for the presence of David: "David . . . above the figure of the Child, would relate to his royal lineage." Given the rich intertextual allusions of the "messianic" text from Malachi, this conclusion seems inescapable and ought to close debate on the identity of the second statuette.

60. See Charles de Tolnay, "Two frescoes by Domenico and David Ghirlandaio in Santa Trinità in Florence," *Wallraf-Richartz-Jahrbuch* 23 (1961): 237–50. De Tolnay (247) states that the figure of David as the youthful hero, the victor over Goliath, whose head lies beside his right foot, is a type which was introduced in Florence as early as the 1330s by Taddeo Gaddi in S. Croce, Cappella Baroncelli. Gaddi (active c. 1328–c. 1366) was one of Ambrogio's competitors, and Ambrogio certainly would have encountered Gaddi's painting in S. Croce while working in Florence from 1327 to 1333. For additional discussion of the David tradition, see Émile Betraux, *Donatello* (Paris: Plon-Nourrit, 1910), and H. W. Janson, *Donatello* (Princeton, N.J.: Princeton University Press, 1957). See also James Hall, *Dictionary of Subjects and Symbols in Art* (New York: Harper and Row, 1974), revised 1979, 92–93, for a discussion of the iconography of David painted as a warrior figure in the history of art.

61. Maginnis, "Ambrogio," 34.

62. See Shorr, "The Iconographic Development of the Presentation in the Temple," 23. Shorr argued further (27): "Until the middle of the [thirteenth] century, there are usually five protagonists in the scene of the Presentation in the Temple. Mary, the Infant,

and Simeon are of course invariably present, Joseph usually plays a humble part. The prophetess Anna appears in Italian representations, but she is seldom present in Northern pictures. In the latter, the Virgin is often accompanied by a young handmaiden. . . . "

63. Shorr ("The Iconographic Development of the Presentation in the Temple," 23–25, with accompanying figures) cites the following as examples of the various types: (1) seated, facing forward, eighth–ninth century, enameled cross, Rome Sancta Sanctorum; leaning eagerly toward Simeon, eleventh century, Ivory altarfrontal, Salerno, Cathedral Sacristy; (2) Drogo Sacramentary, ninth century, Cod. Lat. 9428, Bibliotheque Nationale; (3) detail of the Royal Portal, twelfth century, Chartres, Cathedral; (4) in the east first seen in the tenth-century wall painting in the Chapel of St. Eustathius, Cappadocia, and in the west, in the Golden Evangelistaries written for Henry III in the late tenth or early eleventh century, e.g., Golden Evangelistary, MS. 1, 19, Gotha, Landesbibliothek and Golden Evangelistary, Codex Vit. 17, Madrid, Escorial; (5) Evangelistary, twelfth century, Brandenburg a.d. Hohe, Domkapitel; (6) Hitda Evangelistary, eleventh century, Cod. 1640, Darmstadt, Landesbibliothek.

64. See ibid., 21–26, passim. Figures with doves. Joseph: fresco from Grotta degli Angeli, Magliana-Pecorareccio, tenth–eleventh century, Rome, Corsini Gallery; Mary: Hitda Evangelistary, eleventh century, Cod. 1640, Darmstadt, Landesbibliothek; Golden Evangelistary, MS. 1, 19, eleventh century, Gotha, Landesbibliothek and Golden Evangelistary, Codex Vit. 17, eleventh century, Madrid, Escorial; Anna: Menologium of Basil II, Cod. Vat. Gr. 1613, tenth century, Rome; young man: eleventh century, Ivory Book Cover, London, Victoria and Albert Museum. Shorr, 21, notes that this last image is unusual in that it depicts Christ as walking to Simeon, who stands at the temple entrance.

65. Ibid., 20, see the Enameled Cross, Sancta Sanctorum, Rome. Shorr goes on to note that, given the persistence of the Eastern tradition of the Hypapante, occasionally in some depictions "the altar is completely lacking; in others, an altar is inconspicuously in the background or at one side of the composition and the emphasis is still on the Meeting with Simeon."

66. Ibid., 27–28. She mentions Nicola Pisano's thirteenth-century *Presentation* on the pulpit in the Baptistery in Pisa as a possible candidate, though neither the date of the painting nor the identity of this second elderly, bearded man is certain (27).

67. Rowley, *Ambrogio Lorenzetti*, 20.

68. Maginnis, "Ambrogio," 34, 39n. 9. Maginnis finds the breastplate and priestly vestment in general to be interpretations of the Old Testament text by the painter.

69. Rowley, *Ambrogio Lorenzetti*, 20.

70. It may also be the case that this is Ambrogio's visual answer to the criticism that the Virgin Mary should not need to submit to purification. Her willingness to be obedient to the legal requirement was what was important, not whether or not she completed the ritual since she was, after all, "pure." See the earlier comments by Aquinas and *The Golden Legend* (cited above) on this problem.

71. Shorr, "The Iconographic Development of the Presentation in the Temple," 26. In two of the images which antedate Ambrogio's *Presentation* (the tenth-century Menologium of Basil II, Cod. Vat. Gr. 1613, and the early fourteenth-century pulpit detail in the Pisa Baptistery by Nicola Pisano), Anna is depicted with her hand raised and her head thrown back in a kind of emotional intensity the viewer might associate with prophetic frenzy. Shorr also notes that in three puzzling instances, a figure with Anna's familiar attributes and position is depicted with a beard!

72. The depiction of Simeon as older and bearded was typical in art of this period; see ibid., 26. That Simeon was an old man is not made explicit in Luke, though it is perhaps suggested by Anna's advanced age and the implication that he had been waiting

a long time for this moment. The tradition of Simeon as an older man is found also in the literature subsequent to the New Testament. A sermon attributed to St. Augustine called Simeon "aged" and "long-lived" (cited by Phillip Rogers, "Nunc Dimittis," in *A Dictionary of Biblical Tradition in English Literature* [ed. David Lyle Jeffrey; Grand Rapids: Eerdmans, 1992], 557). See also *Pseudo-Matthew*, 15, which gives Simeon's age as 112. The gist of *Pseudo-Matthew* was preserved in *The Golden Legend* and would have been available to a fourteenth-century audience. That Simeon was also a priest (a tradition to which Ambrogio does not appeal) was also securely anchored in both the literary and visual traditions (see Rogers, 557; Shorr, 29).

73. The only figure whose attention does not appear to be on Simeon and the child is the third figure immediately positioned behind Simeon. Perhaps he has not yet fully grasped the importance of the situation or he is changing position to better see the situation at hand in front of him.

74. Rowley, *Ambrogio Lorenzetti*, 20.

75. Ibid., 18; followed by Maginnis, "Ambrogio," 33.

76. Van Os (*Sienese Altarpieces*, 85) has understood the importance of this moment for Ambrogio, but by failing to take into account the importance of Simeon's pursed lips, he mistakenly identifies the moment as depicted in Anna's prophecy only. Van Os concluded: "It can be no accident that it was Ambrogio, the 'pictor doctus', who outshone his contemporaries in creating a unity of time and action which later theorists were to prescribe as essential to the success of a painting." In our reading, there is more of a "unity of time and action" than even Van Os allowed for.

77. Rowley, *Ambrogio Lorenzetti*, 18.

78. So Shorr, "The Iconographic Development of the Presentation in the Temple," 28.

79. Carol Herselle Krinsky, "Representations of the Temple of Jerusalem Before 1500," *Journal of the Warburg and Courtauld Institutes* 33 (1970): 1–19.

80. Ibid., 11, quoting also Rowley, *Ambrogio Lorenzetti*, 20.

81. Raymond E. Brown, *An Adult Christ at Christmas: Essays on the Three Biblical Christmas Stories Matthew 2 and Luke 2* (Collegeville, Minn.: Liturgical Press, 1978), 3.

82. See Van Os, *Sienese Altarpieces*, 84. The figure recalls Duccio's *Enthroned Madonna* on the high altar who is also supported with winged victories.

Epilogue

Since the iconoclastic controversies of the eighth and ninth centuries, the visual arts have been the subject of much ecclesiastical discussion and debate. More recently, scholars and clergy have been paying more attention to the potential role of the visual arts in the theology and liturgy of the Christian Church. As a result, numerous programs were begun under a variety of nomenclature — religion and the arts, theology and the arts, and so forth. This book is an attempt to join those efforts to recover the visual aspects of Christianity, especially for those heirs of the Reformation whose tradition has led to the neglect, if not deep suspicion, of the visual expression of Christian faith and practice.

At times, these endeavors have been thwarted by the fact that theologians working in the visual arts often did so without recourse to the work of the art historian. The results were often ahistorical readings of the iconography of a work or misconstruals of the social and religious contexts in which the image was produced. Art historians, on the other hand, have often been reluctant or unprepared to explore the theological dimensions of a work of sacred art, and most (with some notable exceptions) have deliberately avoided exploring the hermeneutical implications for the contemporary faith community.

The title of our work, *Illuminating Luke,* is, of course, an allusion to the practice among medieval scribes of visually illustrating the manuscript being copied. The illuminations, often very detailed and elaborate, provided additional interpretive resources for the reader. We have hoped also to illumine the reader with regard both to the message of Luke's infancy narrative and Luke's subsequent "career" at specific moments in its reception history. To be sure, we have chosen some of the "high" moments in the visual exegesis of Luke's infancy narrative. With deceptive simplicity, Leonardo's *Annunciation* captures forever Gabriel's greeting to Mary, "The Lord is with you!" In a startling juxtaposition, Pontormo connects the *Visitation* with Abraham's near sacrifice of Isaac. In the *Adoration of the Shepherds,* Ghirlandaio makes the unprecedented identification of the manger with a sarcophagus, memorializing his patrons' tragic loss of an infant son, while at the same time investing the work with political commentary on Florence's role in the succession of Hebrew, Roman, and Christian "empires." Finally, in his *Presentation in the Temple,*

Ambrogio provides a theologically profound reading of Lukan soteriology by telescoping Anna's prophecy and Simeon's *Nunc Dimittis* into a single moment.

By understanding how these artists and audiences of Renaissance religious art "translated" Luke's Gospel in culturally and religiously appropriate ways, we have sought to locate each of these images within its particular historical context, to understand its iconographic significance, and briefly to comment on how this visual exegesis might inform the contemporary appropriation of both text and image. Our desire has been that our efforts here not only further clarify the interpretive history of the Lukan infancy narrative at some of its most critical moments, but also assist, as it were, in illuminating Luke.

Selected Bibliography

Bacci, Michele. *Il pennello dell'Evangelista: Storia delle immagini sacre attribuite a san Luca.* Pisa: Gisem, 1998.

Baxandall, Michael. *Painting and Experience in Fifteenth-Century Italy: A Primer in the Social History of Pictorial Style.* 2d ed. Oxford: Oxford University Press, 1988.

Benko, Stephen. "The Magnificat: A History of the Controversy." *Journal of Biblical Literature* 86 (1967): 263–75.

Berdini, Paolo. *The Religious Art of Jacopo Bassano: Painting as Visual Exegesis.* Cambridge: Cambridge University Press, 1997.

Biblia Pauperum, Faksimileausgabe des vierzigblättrigen Armenbibel: Blockbuches in der Bibliothek der Erzdiözese Esztergom. Hanau/Main: Werner Dausien, 1967.

Bock, Darrell L. *Luke, 1:1–9:50.* Grand Rapids: Baker Books, 1994.

Borsook, Eve, and Johannes Offerhaus. *Francesco Sassetti and Ghirlandaio at Santa Trinità, Florence.* Doornspijk: Dovaco, 1981.

Brown, Raymond. *The Birth of the Messiah: A Commentary on the Infancy Narratives in the Gospels of Matthew and Luke.* Garden City, N.Y.: Doubleday, 1977.

Cameron, R., ed. *The Other Gospels: Non-Canonical Gospel Texts.* Philadelphia: Fortress, 1982.

Cartlidge, David R., and J. Keith Elliott. *Art and the Christian Apocrypha.* London: Routledge, 2001.

Caudile, Paul J. "Observations on the Iconography of Leonardo da Vinci's Uffizi 'Annunciation.'" *Studies in Iconography* 7–8 (1981–82).

Clapp, Frederick Mortimore. *Jacopo Carucci da Pontormo: His Life and Work.* New Haven: Yale University Press, 1916.

Coleridge, Mark. *The Birth of the Lukan Narrative: Narrative as Christology in Luke 1–2.* Journal for the Study of the New Testament Supplement Series 88. Sheffield: Sheffield Academic Press, 1993.

Conzelmann, Hans. *The Theology of St. Luke.* London: Faber and Faber, 1960.

Culpepper, R. Alan. "The Gospel of Luke," in *The New Interpreter's Bible* 9. Nashville: Abingdon, 1995.

Drury, John. *Painting the Word: Christian Pictures and Their Meaning.* New Haven: Yale University Press, 1999.

Fitzmyer, Joseph. *The Gospel According to Luke: Introduction, Translation, and Notes.* Anchor Bible 28. Garden City, N.Y.: Doubleday, 1981.

Forster, Kurt W. *Pontormo: Monographie mit kritischem Katalog.* Munich: Bruckmann, 1966.

Frederick, Kavin. "A Program of Altarpieces for the Siena Cathedral." *Rutgers Art Review* 3 (1983): 18–35.

Freedman, Luba. "The 'Blurred' Horizon in Leonardo's Paintings." *Gazette des Beaux Arts* 129 (1997).

Gombrich, Ernst H. "The Sassetti Chapel Revisited: Santa Trinità and Lorenzo de' Medici." *I Tatti Studies* 7 (1997): 11–35.

Gössmann, Maria Elizabeth. *Die Verkündigung an Maria: im Dogmatischen Verständnis des Mittelalters.* Munich: Max Hueber, 1957.

Iser, Wolfgang. *The Act of Reading: A Theory of Aesthetic Response.* Baltimore: Johns Hopkins University Press, 1978.

Jeffrey, David Lyle, ed. *A Dictionary of Biblical Tradition in English Literature.* Grand Rapids: Eerdmans, 1992.

Jensen, Robin M. *Understanding Early Christian Art.* London: Routledge, 1999.

Kaftal, George. *Iconography of the Saints in Tuscan Painting.* Florence: Sansoni, 1952.

Kecks, Ronald G. *Domenico Ghirlandaio.* Florence: Octavo, 1998.

Klein, Dorothee. *St. Lukas als Maler der Maria: Ikonographie der Lukas-Madonna.* Berlin: Oskar Schloss Verlag, 1933.

Kraut, Gisela. *Luka Malt die Madonna: Zeugnisse zum künstlerischen Selbstverständis in der Malerei.* Mainz: Wernersche Verlagsgesellschaft, 1986.

Maginnis, Hayden B. J. "Ambrogio Lorenzetti's 'Presentation in the Temple.'" *Studi di Storia dell'Arte* 2 (1991): 33–50.

Miles, Margaret R. *Image as Insight: Visual Understanding in Western Christianity and Secular Culture.* Boston: Beacon Press, 1985.

Neuheuser, Hanns Peter. *Zugange zur Sakralkunst: Narratio und institution des mittelalterichen Christgeburtsbildes.* Cologne: Bohlau, 2001.

Panofsky, Erwin. "Iconography and Iconology: An Introduction to the Study of Renaissance Art." Pages 26–54 in *Meaning in the Visual Arts.* Chicago: University of Chicago Press, 1955.

Pelikan, Jaraslov. *Jesus Through the Centuries.* New Haven: Yale University Press, 1985.

———. *Mary Through the Centuries.* New Haven: Yale University Press, 1996.

Powell, Mark Allen. *What Are They Saying about Luke?* New York: Paulist Press, 1989.

Prinz, Wolfram, and Max Seidel. *Domenico Ghirlandaio: 1449–1494; atti del convegno internazionale, Firenze 16–18 ottobre 1994.* Florence: Centri, 1996.

Ragusa, Isa, and Rosalie B. Green, eds. *Meditations on the Life of Christ: An Illustrated Manuscript of the Fourteenth Century.* Translated by Isa Ragusa. Princeton, N.J.: Princeton University Press, 1961.

Reau, Louis. *Iconographie de la Bible.* Vol. 2 of *Iconographie de L'Art Chrétien.* Paris: Presses Universitaires de France, 1957.

Reicke, Bo. "Jesus, Simeon, and Anna [Luke 2:21–40]." Pages 96–108 in *Saved by Hope.* Edited by J. I. Cook. Grand Rapids: Eerdmans, 1978.

Robb, David M. "The Iconography of the Annunciation in the Fourteenth and Fifteenth Centuries." *Art Bulletin* 18 (1936): 480–526.

Roberts, Helene E., and Rachel Hall. *Narrative Paintings of the Italian School.* Vol. 1 of *Iconographic Index to New Testament Subjects Represented in Photographs and Slides of Paintings in the Visual Collections, Fine Arts Library, Harvard University.* New York: Garland, 1992.

Rosenau, Helen. "A Study in the Iconography of the Incarnation." *Burlington Magazine* 85 (1944): 176–79.

Rowley, George. *Ambrogio Lorenzetti.* 2 vols. Princeton, N.J.: Princeton University Press, 1958.

Schiller, Gertrud. *Christ's Incarnation — Childhood — Baptism — Temptation — Transfiguration — Works and Miracles.* Vol. 1 of *Iconography of Christian Art.* Translated by Janet Seligman. Greenwich, Conn.: New York Graphic Society, 1971.

Shearman, John. *Only Connect . . . Art and the Spectator in the Italian Renaissance.* Princeton, N.J.: Princeton University Press, 1992.

Sinanoglou, Leah. "The Christ Child as Sacrifice: A Medieval Tradition and the Corpus Christi Plays." *Speculum* 48 (1973): 491–509.

Smith, Alison Moore. "The Iconography of the Sacrifice of Isaac in Early Christian Art." *American Journal of Archaeology* 26 (1922).

Talbert, Charles H. *Literary Patterns, Theological Themes, and the Genre of Luke-Acts.* Philadelphia: Fortress, 1974.

——. *Reading Luke: A Literary and Theological Commentary on the Third Gospel.* New York: Crossroad, 1982.

Tannehill, Robert C. *The Narrative Unity of Luke-Acts: A Literary Interpretation.* 2 vols. Philadelphia: Fortress, 1986.

——. *Luke.* Nashville: Abingdon Press, 1996.

Turner, Jane, ed. *Dictionary of Art.* 34 vols. New York: Grove's Dictionaries, 1996.

Unnik, W. C. van. "*Dominus Vobiscum:* The Background of a Liturgical Formula." Pages 270–305 in *New Testament Essays: Studies in Memory of T. W. Manson.* Edited by Angus Higgins. Manchester, England: Manchester University Press, 1959.

Van Os, Henk. *Marias Demut und Verherrlichung in der sienesischen Malerei, 1300–1450.* The Hague: Ministerie van Cultuur, 1969.

Vasari, Giorgio. *Le Opere di Giorgio Vasari: Le Vite de' più eccellenti pittori, scultori ed architettori scritte da Giorgio Vasari pittore Aretino.* Edited by Gaetano Milanesi. 9 vols. Florence: Sansoni, 1885.

Vinci, Leonardo da. *Treatise on Painting.* Edited by A. P. McMahon. Princeton, N.J.: Princeton University Press, 1956.

Voragine, Jacobus de. *The Golden Legend: Readings on the Saints.* Translated by William Granger Ryan. 2 vols. Princeton, N.J.: Princeton University Press, 1993.

Wasserman, Jack. *Leonardo.* New York: Harry N. Abrams, 1975.

——. "Jacopo Pontormo's Florentine *Visitation.*" *Artibus et Historiae* 32 (1995): 39–53.

Woolf, Rosemary. "The Effect of Typology on the English Mediaeval Plays of Abraham and Isaac." *Speculum* 32 (1957).

Index

Abraham, 30
  Isaac, Visitation and, 61, 68, 71–72, 73, 74, 75, 77, 81 n. 18, 82 n. 19, 151
  Jesus Christ and, 73
  Mary, Visitation and, 78, 79, 81
  women, children, abuse and, 81
Abraham on Trail: The Social Legacy of Biblical Myth (Delaney), 81
Accademia del Disegno, 18
Acts, 13
  Luke authoring Gospel of Luke and, 11–14
Adam, 33
adnuere, 77, 89 n. 116
Adoration of the Shepherds. See Nativity and Adoration of the Shepherds (Ghirlandaio)
Adoration of the Shepherds (Bulgarini), 129
Adoration of the Shepherds (van der Goes), 106, 106f, 108, 110, 111, 120 n. 102
Adult Christ at Christmas, An (Brown), 142
Agrippan sibyl, 103
Alberti, Leon Battista, 40, 132
Albertinelli, Mariotto, 62, 65, 86 n. 62
  Visitation, 65, 65f
Alexander VII (pope), 129
Ambrogio. *See* Lorenzetti, Ambrogio
Ambrose, 73
angel
  angelic colloquy, Annunciation and, 49–50
  annunciation story and, 30–32, 77
  baptism v. Annunciation, 45, 56 n. 66
  flying, 45, 47, 107
  Gabriel, 29–30, 33, 34, 43–45, 56 n. 66, 80, 151
  kneeling, 45
  mysteries of Annunciation, 48–50
  nativity, peace and, 93–94, 97
  New Testament and appearing/commission by, 31, 32, 97
  Old Testament and appearing/commission by, 30–31, 32, 97
  symbolizing Matthew, 3
Angelico, Fra, 38, 50–51
Anna, 62
  Presentation in the Temple and, 137–38, 139, 140f, 147 n. 62
  prophecy of, 123–24, 125, 141, 147 n. 62, 148 n. 71, 152
Annunciation
  angel mysteries of, 48–50
  annual celebrations of, 29, 146 n. 49
  biblical text overview of, 29–33
  commissioning stories of, 30–32, 41
  the Fall (of Eve) compared to, 33–34
  Irenaeus's interpretation of, 33–34

John the Baptist's comparison to Jesus', 32–33
  new start of humanity with, 33
  Old Testament, delivering God's message and, 30–32
  other paintings of, 38, 39f, 45, 48, 54 n. 31, 129
  subsequent history of interpretation of, 33–34
  visitation and, 75–76
Annunciation (Credi), 39f, 54 n. 31
Annunciation (da Vinci), 28f, 29, 52 n. 2
  artist of, 35–36
  artistic sources and techniques of, 37–39, 39f, 54 n. 31, 54 n. 32
  barred v. open window of, 55 n. 49
  Gabriel in, 44–47, 44f, 151
  iconography of, 41–52, 55 n. 49
  landscape of, 42–44, 44f
  the lectern and Bible of, 45–47, 46f, 48f
  light and color of, 40
  Mary in, 45–51
  Mary's book in, 48f
  mysteries of, 48–50
  patron, commission and dating of, 29, 35–36, 41
  perspective of, 40–41
  workshop tradition product for, 39–40
Annunciation (Martini), 129
Annunziata, SS., 18, 59, 63–64, 65, 75
Ansanus, 128, 145 n. 28
anti-Marcionite Prologue, 12–13
Antonio, 99
Apparition at Arles, 103
Apparition of St. Francis (Ghirlandaio), 102
Aquinas, Thomas, 126
Archelaus, 96
art
  discursive strategies of, 6–7
  historical imagination with, 6
  intrinsic meaning, 6
  Luke as founder of Christian, 21
  religious significance of, 1
  synthetic intuition of, 5–6
artist
  as Florentine Guild of Doctors and Pharmacists, 19
  St. Luke's face as, 17–19, 17f, 18f
Assumption of the Virgin (Fiorentino), 65
Athrongaeus, 96–97
Augustine, 73
  four living creatures for, 3, 3t
  Harmony of the Gospels by, 4
  Nativity and, 98

157

Augustus, Emperor, 94, 104–5, 112, 113
Ave Maria, 34

Baldovinetti, Alesso, 38, 50, 64, 99
Baptism of Christ (da Vinci), 37, 38f, 44–45
Baptism of Christ (Verrocchio), 37, 38f, 44–45
Baptists, 79
Barberini, 50
Barbieri, Filippo, 104
Baroncelli family, 99, 120 n. 98
Bartolomeo, Fra, 66
    The Mystical Marriage of St. Catherine, 66,
        67f
Battista, Alberti, 132
Battle of Cascina (Michelangelo), 66, 68f
Baxandall, Michael, 48, 50
Benedictus, 125
Benizzi, St. Filippo, 64
Berdini, Paolo, 6
Bernard of Clairvaux, 98
Biblia Pauperum, 74, 135–36, 147 n. 56
Biblioteca Latina, 99
Bindi, Pauolo, 129
Birth of the Virgin (Lorenzetti, P.), 129
Birth of the Virgin (Sarto), 64–65, 66, 66f
Bonventure, 62
Borgherini, Pier Francesco, 63, 84 n. 35
Borsook & Offerhaus, 103, 113
bottega, 39, 64, 86 n. 62, 101
Botticelli, 38, 51, 100
Bronzino, Agnolo, 63
Brown, Raymond, 142
Brunelleschi, 132
Bulgarini, Bartolomeo, 129, 145 n. 31

calf. See ox/calf
Calvin, John
    Harmony of the Gospels, 4
Carucci, Jacopo. See Pontormo, Jacopo
Casentino, Jacopo del, 43
Castagno, Andrea del, 99
Catholic Church, 62, 113, 121 n. 114, 151. See
        also church
Caudile, Paul, 41, 46–47, 55 n. 49, 55 n. 59,
        57 n. 88
celebrations, 29, 111, 115 n. 17, 146 n. 49
chapel fresco cycle program, 102–6, 103f, 104f,
        105f
chiaroscuro, 39, 54 n. 35
Chigi, Fabio. See Alexander VII (pope)
Childs, Brevard, 7
Chiostrino dei Voti, 64
Christianity. See Catholic Church
Christmas, 111, 115 n. 17
Chrysostom, John, 21
church, early, 1–2
Cimmerian sibyl, 103–5
Cioni, Andrea di Michele. See Verrocchio,
        Andrea del
Circumcision (Lorenzetti, A.), 133
Clapp, Frederick Mortimer, 71

classical antiquity, 111–12
Cogitatio (Reflection), 49, 50
Coleridge, Mark, 60
Commentary on Isaiah (Jerome), 21
Confirmation of the Franciscan Rule by Pope
        Honorius III (Ghirlandaio), 102
Conturbatio (Disquiet), 49, 50, 51
Corpus Christi plays, 75
Cosimo, Piero di, 62
Credi, Lorenzo di, 39f, 54 n. 31
Crescentius, 128, 145 n. 28
Cumaean sibyl, 103

da Vinci, Leonardo, Leonardo. See also
        Annunciation (da Vinci)
    Annunciation, 28f, 29, 34, 37–52, 52 n. 2,
        54 n. 31, 54 n. 32
    background of, 35–36
    Baptism of Christ, 37, 38f, 44–45
    landscape of, 42–44
    Last Supper, 35
    Mona Lisa, 35
    painting methods of, 38–41, 54 n. 31, 54 n. 32,
        54 n. 35
    Pontormo and, 59, 62
    St. John the Baptist, 35
    Study of a Sleeve, 44f
    Treatise on Painting, 35
    Tuscan Landscape, 35
    Virgin of the Rocks, 35
d'Amboise, Charles II (Comte de Chaumont),
        35
David, 3, 29, 33, 104–5, 118 n. 69, 136
    Christ Child royal lineage and, 136–37, 137f,
        147 n. 59
    city of, 94, 97
Delaney, Carol, 81
Demas, 12
de'Rossi, Fra Jacopo, 65
Diatessaron (Tatian), 4
disegno, 63
Dome of the Rock, 130
Domenico, 104
Dominus tecum, 51
Dominus vobiscum, 51–52
Donatello, 38, 40, 132
Drury, John, 7
Duccio, 38, 127, 128, 128f
    Madonna and Child Enthroned (Maestà), 128,
        128f, 130, 133
    mariological emphasis of, 132–33

eagle
    symbolizing Mark, 3
    symbolizing spirit, 3
Ecclesiastical History (Eusebius), 13
Eyckian plateau composition, 107
Eiritraean sibyl, 103
Eissler, K. R., 44
ekphrasis, 22

Elizabeth, 30, 31, 32, 60
  death of, 62
  four oracles of, 60
  Jesus and, 80
  John the Baptist and, 62, 69, 80, 91 n. 133
  Visitation and, 61–62, 69, 77, 80, 83 n. 21
  Visitation speech, Mary and, 82 n. 17
  Visitation staging of, 67–68
Emmaus disciples, 95
Epiphany, 79, 98, 105, 111, 115 n. 17
Esau, 50
Eucharist
  Christ Child, nativity and, 108–9, 114 n. 6,
    120 n. 97
  Isaac's sacrifice and, 75
Eudocia, 14
Eusebius, 13
evangelist
  iconographic symbol for each, 3
  individual contributions of, 5
Eve, 33–34, 44
Exodus
  3, pp. 30–31
  39:30, p. 138

Faith and Charity, 64
Feltrini, Andrea di Cosimo, 64, 75
Fiorentino, Rosso, 64, 65
Fitzmyer, Joseph, 11
Fontius, Bartolomaeus, 112, 120 n. 103
Four Styles (Ghirlandaio), 103, 103f
Francesca, Piero della, 40
Franciabigio, 64
Francis renounces his worldly Patrimony
    (Ghirlandaio), 102
François I, 35
Fredi, Bartolo di, 141
Freedman, Luba, 42
Funeral of St. Francis (Ghirlandaio), 103

Gabriel, 80
  Annunciation story and, 29–30, 33, 34,
    56 n. 69, 151
  as baptism v. Annunciation angel, 45, 56 n. 66
  first moment of, 48, 51, 57 n. 80
  as flying angel, 45, 47
  as kneeling angel, 45
  with lectern and Bible of *Annunciation*, 45–47,
    46f, 48f
  sleeve, 44f, 45
  support in *Annunciation*, 44–45, 44f, 151
Gaddi, Taddeo, 45
Galactotrophousa, 15
Gaston, Robert, 69
Genesis
  12–25, p. 72
  22, pp. 73, 74, 78, 81
Gentiles
  ass/magi symbolizing, 98
Ghiberti, Lorenzo, 38, 40, 127

Ghirlandaio, Benedetto, 101
Ghirlandaio, Davide, 101, 37, 40. *See also*
    Nativity and Adoration of the Shepherds
    (Ghirlandaio)
  Apparition of St. Francis, 102
  background of, 99–101, 116 n. 27
  Confirmation of the Franciscan Rule by Pope
    Honorius III, 102
  Four Styles (of sibyls), 103–4, 103f, 105
  Francis renounces his worldly Patrimony, 102
  Funeral of St. Francis, 103
  Last Supper, 99, 100f
  Nativity and Adoration of the Shepherds, 92f,
    93, 99–113
  Portraits of Nera Corsi Sassetti and Francesco
    Sassetti, 105f
  Resurrection, 100
  Sassetti chapel and, 95f
  St. Francis Resuscitating the Roman Notary's
    Son, 103
  Stigmatization of St. Francis, 102
  Trail by Fire, 102
  Vision of Augustus of the Capitoline Hill, 104,
    104f
Ghirlandaio, Ridolfo del, 86 n. 54, 100, 101
Gideon, 31, 32
Giotto, 38, 43, 102, 127
  Presentation of Christ in the Temple, 130f
Gloria in Excelsius, 125
Glossa Ordinaria, 4
Glykophiloussa, 15
Golden Legend (Voragine), 13, 34, 61, 126,
    148 n. 72
goldfinch, 110
Gospel, The, four-fold, 2–3
Gratus, 96
Gregory of Nyssa, 98
Gregory of Tours, 108–9
Grünewald, 110
Guercino
  St. Luke Displaying a Painting of the Virgin, 10f,
    18–19

Haenchen, Ernst, 21
Hannah, 125
Harmony of the Gospels (Augustine), 4
Harmony of the Gospels (Calvin), 4
Hebrew. *See* Jews
hermeneutic, 7
Herod, 62
High Renaissance, 29, 59, 63
Hismeria, 62
historical imagination, 6
history. *See* reception history
Hodegetria, 14–15
Holy Spirit, 29–30, 60
Howe, Eunice, 14
human, symbolizing Matthew, 3
Humiliatio (Submission), 49–50, 51
Hypapante, 126, 148 n. 65

iconography
    of *Annunciation* (da Vinci), 41–52, 55 n. 49
    four symbols, evangelists and, 3
    intrinsic meaning in, 6
    of John the Baptist, 90 n. 119
    of *Nativity and Adoration of the Shepherds*
        (Ghirlandaio), 107–13
    of *Presentation in the Temple* (Lorenzetti),
        129–42, 130f, 131f, 134f, 137f, 140f
    synthetic meaning in, 5–6
    of *Visitation* (Pontormo), 68–79
    visual exegesis actualization in, 7
"Iconography and Iconology: An Introduction
    to the Study of Renaissance of Art"
    (Panofsky), 5–6
Il Buon Governo (Lorenzetti, A.), 127
Illumination of St. Luke (Lindisfarne Gospels), 2
Illumination of St. Luke (MacDurnan Gospels),
    3–4, 4f
interior, ecclesiastical, 43
Interrogatio (Inquiry), 49, 50
Irenaeus, 73
    Annunciation's interpretation by, 33–34
    four living creatures for, 3, 3t
    individual evangelist contributions and, 5
    Luke and Paul as companions and, 11–12
Isaac, 71
    Eucharist and, 75
    Hellenistic type of, 74, 88 n. 98
    Visitation and sacrifice of, 68, 70, 71, 72–73,
        73–74, 75–78, 76f, 89 n. 106
    Visitation, Christ and, 73–75
Isaiah
    7:11, p. 47
Isenheim Altarpiece, 110
Iser, Wolfgang, 5
Israel, 125

Jacob, 60, 73
Jerome
    four living creatures for, 3–4, 3t
    Luke's language style and, 21
Jesus (Christ)
    Abraham and, 73
    Annunciation of, 29–30, 31
    birth of, 5, 94–95
    as child, 56 n. 70, 102, 103, 136–37, 139–42
    Circumcision of, 129, 133
    David and, 104–5
    David, royal lineage and, 136–37, 137f
    Elizabeth, 80
    Eucharist and manger, 108–9, 114 n. 6
    four iconographic symbols of, 3
    Isaac sacrifice and crucifixion of, 73–75
    John the Baptist comparison to, 32–33
    nativity of, 107–10, 114
    as "only son," 73
    peace on earth from, 94, 105, 113
    as second Adam, 33
    Simeon and, 139–42
    Visitation, Isaac and, 73–75

Jews, 98, 112–13, 125, 143 n. 5, 151
John (evangelist)
    Jesus as "only son" in, 73
    lion symbolizing, 3
John the Baptist, 110. *See also Baptism of Christ*
    (da Vinci)
    annunciation of, 32
    Elizabeth and, 62, 69, 80, 91 n. 133
    iconography and, 90 n. 119
    Jesus comparison to, 32–33, 37
    Malachi and, 135
    Zechariah and birth of, 72, 80
Johnson, Luke Timothy, 81
Joseph, 87 n. 79, 107
    poverty and humility of, 133–35
    Presentation in the Temple and, 137–38, 139,
        147 n. 62
    Zechariah and, 77–78, 79
Joseph in Egypt (Pontormo), 63
Judges
    6, p. 31
Justinian, 126

Kavin, Frederick, 128
Kemp, Martin, 40–41
Klein, Dorothee, 19
Knorr, Christina, 110–11
Krinsky, Carol, 142
Kyriotissa, 15

Lamentation (Pontormo), 63
Landi, Alfonso, 129
landscape
    ecclesiastical interior of, 43, 43 n. 55
    exterior implication of, 43
Last Judgment (Michelangelo), 100
Last Supper (da Vinci), 35
Last Supper (Ghirlandaio), 100f
Le vite (Vasari), 127–28
Lecce, Fra Roberto Caracciolo da, 48, 50–51, 52
Leo X (Pope), 35, 75, 83, 84 n. 32
Leviticus
    12:8, pp. 133, 135
lion
    symbolizing John, 3
    symbolizing royal power, 3, 46
Lippi, Filippo, 50, 99
Lorenzetti, Ambrogio, 38. *See also Presentation*
    in the Temple (Lorenzetti, A.)
    background of, 123, 126–28, 130–32,
        144 n. 13, 146 n. 45
    Il Buon Governo, 127
    Presentation in the Temple, 122f, 123, 126–42
Lorenzetti, Pietro, 38, 127
    Birth of the Virgin, 129
Luke
    Acts and Gospel of Luke authored by, 11–14
    background of, 12–13
    death of, 13
    Illumination of St. Luke, ox, and, 3–4, 4f
    infancy narrative of, 125, 151–52

nativity and, 93–95, 107, 110, 113, 121 n. 114
ox/calf symbolizing, 2f, 3–4, 4f, 19
as patron saint of painters and doctors, 19
as Paul's companion, 11–12
as physician, 11–14, 15, 19, 23, 25 n. 14
as second generation Christian, 11
Luke, as painter, 23
    artist self portrait in, 17–19, 17f, 18f
    early images and, 14–15
    as founder of Christian art, 21
    literary prowess and, 19, 21–23, 26 n. 33,
        26 n. 37
    Virgin May authentic likeness and, 149
Luke, Gospel of
    Annunciation and, 41, 60
    dating of, 11
    (Jesus) infancy narrative of, 1, 5
    Luke authoring Acts and, 11–14
    Nativity and, 94–95, 95
    Presentation in the Temple and, 123–24
    unique passages of, 5, 8 n. 4
    Visitation and, 59–60
    1:26–38, pp. 41, 60
    1:39–56, pp. 59–60
    2:1–7, p. 94
    2:7, p. 107
    2:8–20, pp. 93–94, 95
    2:22, p. 3
    2:22–38, pp. 123–24
    2:34–35, p. 110
    6:20–26, p. 3

MacDurnan Gospels
    Illumination of St. Luke, ox, Luke and, 3–4, 4f
Macine, Fra Mariano dal Canto alle, 64
Madonna and Child Enthroned (Duccio), 128,
    128f, 132–33
"Madonna of the Magnificat, The," 60, 61
Madonna. See Virgin Mary
Maestà (Duccio), 128, 128f, 130, 133
magi, 97, 98, 111
Maginnis, Hayden B. J., 127, 128, 137, 138,
    146 n. 43
Magnificat, 125
Maiano, Benedetto da, 102
Malachi, 133, 135–36, 147 n. 59
manger, 94–95, 108–109, 114 n. 4, 151
maniera, 101
Marcion, 12
Marian cult, 15
Mark, 13
    eagle symbolizing, 3
Marriage of the Virgin (Franciabigio), 64
Martini, Simone, 38, 127
    Annunciation, 129
martyrdom, 145 n. 28
Mary. See also Virgin Mary
    angelic colloquy, Annunciation and, 49–50
    Annunciation and, 29–30, 31, 33
    apocryphal book of Tobit and troubled, 52 n. 5
    Christ Child and, 107

Cognitatio (Reflection) of, 49
Conturbatio (Disquiet) of, 49
Elizabeth's four oracles of, 60
Humiliatio (Submission) of, 49–50
as ideal believer, 60, 78–79, 81
immaculate conception with, 29–30
Interrogatio (Inquiry) of, 49
in landscape of Annunciation, 43–44
with lectern and Bible of Annunciation, 45–47,
    46f, 48f
lengthening of fingers of, 56 n. 78
Meritatio (Merit) of, 50
as "Mother of Sorrows," 79
Nativity and Adoration of the Shepherds and,
    106, 107
obedience to law by, 134–35, 137, 139
poverty and humility of, 133–35
pregnancy of, 48, 50, 59
Presentation in the Temple and, 124, 133–35,
    137–38, 139, 147 n. 62
priestly role of, 46–47
purification of, 125–26
as second (pure) Eve, 33–34, 44
spinning, 47
as "Star of Sea," 47
sword piercing soul of, 125, 143 n. 8
Visitation and role of, 59–60, 68–69, 77–79
Visitation speech, Elizabeth and, 82 n. 17
Visitation staging of, 67–68
Zechariah, nativity and, 97
Matthew, 13, 111
    angel/human symbolizing, 3
    Pseudo, 47, 98
Mayron, Francis, 49
Meaning in the Visual Arts (Panofsky), 5–6
meaning, intrinsic, 6
Medici bank, 101, 102, 106, 110, 119 n. 76
Medici, Giuliano de', 35, 63, 64
Meditations on the Life of Christ (pseudo-
    Bonventure), 34, 47, 62, 98, 129–30, 134,
    136
Melito, 73
Melzi, Francesco, 36
Memling, Hans, 99
Meritatio (Merit), 50
Michelangelo, 63, 86 n. 64
    Battle of Cascina, 66, 68f
    Last Judgment, 100
Milano, Giovanni da, 45
Miles, Margaret, 7
Mona Lisa (da Vinci), 35
Monte Oliveto monastery, 29, 36
Moses
    commission of, 30–31, 32
    Presentation in the Temple and, 133–34, 134f,
        137, 147 n. 59
Muratorian
    Acts, Gospel of Luke and, 12
Mystical Marriage of St. Catherine, The
    (Bartolomeo), 66, 67f

National Gallery (London), 7
Nativity (Bulgarini), 145 n. 31
Nativity and Adoration of the Shepherds
     (Ghirlandaio), 92*f*, 113–14
  adoration of the shepherds in, 110–11
  artist of, 99–101, 100*f*, 116 n. 27
  artistic sources and technique in, 106–7, 106*f*,
     120 n. 102
  biblical text overview of, 93–98
  chapel fresco cycle program and, 102–6, 103*f*,
     104*f*, 105*f*
  cityscape and, 112–13
  classical antiquity reference in, 111–12
  commissioning story of, 97
  Eucharist and, 108–9, 114 n. 6, 120 n. 97
  history of, 98–99
  iconography of, 107–13
  Jesus's death and, 110, 114
  Mary and, 106, 107–8
  nativity of, 107–10
  patron, commission and, 100, 101–2
  Roman, Hebrew and Christian Empires and,
     94, 95, 112–13, 151
  Sassetti's portraits and, 105–6, 105*f*
  Sassetti's son death, manger, sarcophagus and,
     102, 103, 108–9, 151
  shepherd's historical image and, 96–99,
     115 n. 11–12, 115 n. 18, 116 n. 24
  sibyls and, 103–5, 103*f*
Nativity of Christ (Baldovinetti), 64
New Testament
  angels appearing/commission in, 31, 32, 97
  Isaac mentioned in, 73
Nicholas of Lyre, 49, 89 n. 106
Nike, 45
Nucci, Costanza di Bartolommeo, 100
Nunc Dimittis (Simeon), 125, 141, 152

Of San Michele (St. Luke), 19, 20*f*
oil on panel
  oil and tempera v., 38–39, 54 n. 32, 107
Old Testament, 72–74, 78, 81, 96, 133–35, 138
  angels appearing/commission in, 30–31, 32, 97
  annunciation echoed in, 30–32
oracles, 60, 125
Ordine de Servi di Maria. *See* Servites
Origen, 73, 98
ox/calf
  symbolizing Jews, 98
  symbolizing Luke, 2*f*, 3–4, 4*f*, 19
  symbolizing sacrifice, 3

Panofsky, Erwin, 5–6
Paolo, Giovanni di
  Presentation in the Temple, 131, 131*f*, 141
paragone, 63
patron/payment
  of *Annunciation* (da Vinci), 29, 35–36, 41
  of *Nativity and Adoration of the Shepherds*
     (Ghirlandaio), 100, 101–2
  of *Presentation in the Temple* (Lorenzetti), 129

Paul, 73
Pazzi Conspiracy, 101–2
peace on earth, 94, 97, 105, 113
Pelikan, Jaraslov, 7
Perugino, 100
Peter, 12, 61
Pierozzi, Antonino, 43, 47
Pietro, Sano di, 141
plague, 15, 144 n. 13
Plummer, Alfred, 19–20
Pollaiuolo, Piero, 99
Pompey, 111–12
Pontormo, Jacopo. *See also* Visitation (Pontormo)
  background of, 59, 60–61, 65–66, 75,
     86 n. 62, 86 n. 64
  Elizabeth or Mary's speech and, 82 n. 17
  Joseph in Egypt, 63
  Lamentation, 63
  St. Veronica Holding the Sudario, 86 n. 54
  Vertumnus and Pomona, 63
  Virgin and Child with Saints, 63
  Visitation, 58*f*, 59, 62–80, 82 n. 17
Portinari altarpiece, 106, 110
Portinari, Tommaso, 99, 106, 110
Portrait of the Virgin and Child (St. Luke), 14–15
*Portraits of Nera Corsi Sassetti and Francesco
     Sassetti* (Ghirlandaio), 105*f*
Powell, Mark Allen, 21
Presentation in the Temple (Lorenzetti, A.), 122*f*,
     133*f*, 137*f*, 140*f* . *See also Purification of the
     Virgin* (Lorenzetti, A.)
  Anna and, 137–38, 139, 140*f*, 147 n. 62,
     151–52
  artist of, 126–28
  Biblia Pauperum and, 135–36, 147 n. 56
  biblical text overview for, 123–25
  Christ Child variation in positioning in, 138,
     148 n. 63
  David and, 136–37, 137*f*, 147 n. 59
  doves in, 138
  feast day for purification of Virgin and,
     125–26, 146 n. 49
  high priest, attendants and, 138–39
  iconography of, 129–42, 130*f*, 131*f*, 134*f*,
     137*f*, 140*f*
  location, original appearance, payment and,
     128–29, 128*f*
  Malachi and, 133, 135–36, 147 n. 59
  Mary and, 124, 125–26
  Mary and Joseph's humility and obedience in,
     133–35, 137, 139
  Mary, Joseph, attendants and, 137–38, 139,
     147 n. 62
  Moses and, 133–34, 134*f*, 137, 147 n. 59
  other depictions of, 130*f*, 131, 131*f*, 138, 141
  printed inscriptions, statuettes and, 133–37,
     134*f*, 137*f*
  prophetic scroll in, 139
  regal scene of, 135–36

Simeon, Christ Child and, 136–38, 139–42,
148 n. 65, 148 n. 72, 149 n. 73, 149 n. 76,
151–52
temple design, perspective and, 130–32, 131f,
146 n. 43, 146 n. 45
visual exegesis and, 132–42
Presentation in the Temple (Paola), 131, 131f
Presentation of Christ in the Temple (Giotto), 130f
Priene inscription, 94
Primavera (Botticelli), 51
Progymnasmata, 22
Protevangelium of James, 33, 47, 62, 83 n. 21
Psalms
10:5, p. 136
Pseudo-Matthew, 47
Ptolemy, 96
Purification of the Virgin (Lorenzetti, A.), 133,
135, 137

Quattrocento color, 40, 127
Quintilian, 22

Raphael, 66–67
reception history
artist, visual image actualized and, 5–6
visual exegesis and, 7
redaction criticism, 5
Revelation, Book of
four living creatures in, 3
Robb, David, 42–43, 45, 55 n. 59
Roman Empire, 94, 95, 112–13, 126, 151
Romagnoli, Ettore, 129
Rosselli, Cosimo, 100
Rowley, George, 127, 129, 132, 140, 141,
147 n. 59

sacrifice, 3
Isaac of, 68, 70, 71, 72–73, 73–74, 75–78,
76f, 87 n. 79, 89 n. 106
Jesus as lamb, 110
Jesus' crucifixion and Isaac's, 73–75
Salviati, Francesco, 63
Samuel, 125, 135–36
Sarah, 30
Sarto, Andrea del, 62, 64, 65
Birth of the Virgin, 64–65, 66, 66f
Sassetti, Francesco, 93, 95f, 100, 101–2, 103,
105–6, 105f, 107, 112, 119 n. 79
Sassetti, Nera Corsi, 101, 102, 105–6, 105f
Sassetti, Teodoro I and II, 102, 103, 109, 151
Savinus, 128, 145 n. 28
Saxl, F., 112, 120 n. 103
Sedulius Scotus, 119 n. 84
Servites, 63, 65, 75, 79, 80
sfumato, 39, 54 n. 35
shepherds
historical image of, 96–99, 115 n. 11–12,
115 n. 18, 116 n. 24
Jews represented by, 98
Sherman, John, 6, 64, 75
Shorr, Dorothy, 138, 147 n. 59, 148 n. 71

sibyls, 103–5, 103f
Sienese altarpieces, 123, 127, 128–29, 132–33,
142, 145 n. 29, 146 n. 50
sign, giving of, 30–31
Simeon
piety speech, Jesus and, 123–24, 125–26, 130,
141
Presentation in the Temple, Christ Child and,
137–38, 139–42, 147 n. 62, 148 n. 65,
148 n. 72, 149 n. 73, 149 n. 76, 151
Sinanoglou, Leah, 75, 110
Sixtus IV della Rovere, 100
Smith, Alison Moore, 74
Sobe, 62
Solomon, temple of, 130, 142
St. Ambrose, 34
St. Ansanus Chapel, 129
St. Bernard, 34
St. Bridget, 108
St. Crescentius Chapel, 128, 132, 133
St. Francis (of Assisi), 102, 109
St. Francis Resuscitating the Roman Notary's Son
(Ghirlandaio), 103
St. John the Baptist (da Vinci), 35
St. Luke Displaying a Painting of the Virgin
(Guercino), 10f, 18–19
St. Luke Drawing the Virgin and Child (van der
Weyden), 17f
St. Luke Painting the Virgin (Giorgio), 17–18, 18f
St. Savinus Chapel, 129, 132
St. Veronica Holding the Sudario (Pontormo),
86 n. 54
St. Victor Chapel, 129
Steinmetz, David, 7
Stigmatization of St. Francis (Ghirlandaio), 102
Streeter, B. H., 21
Suetonius, 104
Summa Theologica, 43
Summa Theologica (Aquinas), 126
synthetic intuition, 5–6

Talbert, Charles, 124, 125
Tatian, 4
Ten Commandments, 134
Tertullian, 73
Tetraevangelium (four-fold Gospel), 2
Theodosios II, 14
Theon, Aelius, 22–23
Theophilus, 12, 21
Thomas of Celano, 108–9
Tornabuoni, Giovanni, 101
Torre delle Milizie, 112
Tosini, Michael. *See* Ghirlandaio, Michele di
Ridolfo del
Trail by Fire (Ghirlandaio), 102
Treatise on Painting (da Vinci), 35
Trecento, 126, 130, 132, 138
Tuscan Landscape (da Vinci), 35

Uffizi, 1, 129

Valentinus, 12
Valle, Guglielmo Della, 129
van der Goes, Hugo, 99
    Adoration of the Shepherds, 106, 106f, 108,
        110, 111, 120 n. 102
Van Os, 146 n. 50, 149 n. 76
Vasari, Giorgio, 36, 39, 59, 63, 64, 99, 127–
    28
    St. Luke Painting the Virgin, 17–19, 18f
Vecce, Carlo, 38
Verdon, Timothy, 70–71, 78, 88 n. 86
Verrocchio, Andrea del, 35, 37, 99
    Baptism of Christ, 37, 38f, 44–45
Vertummus and Ponoma (Pontormo), 63
Victor, 128, 145 n. 28
Virgin and Child with Saints (Pontormo), 63
Virgin Mary
    Annunciation and, 29–30, 31, 33, 47,
        146 n. 49
    celebrating life of, 132–33
    Galactotrophousa, 15
    Glykophiloussa, 15
    Haghiosoritissa, 15
    Hodegetria, 14–15
    Kyriotissa, 15
    Luke, authentic likeness, and, 149
    purification of, 125–26
Virgin of the Rocks (da Vinci), 35
Vision of Augustus of the Capitoline Hill
    (Ghirlandaio), 104f
Visitation
    biblical text of, 59–60
    Elizabeth's four oracles of, 60
    Madonna of the Magnificat and, 60, 61
    Mary praising of God in, 61, 82 n. 17
    Roman Catholic Church and, 62
Visitation (Albertinelli), 65f
Visitation (Pontormo), 58f, 70f, 72f, 76f
    Abraham and, 61, 68, 71–72, 73, 74, 77, 79,
        81, 81 n. 18, 82 n. 19, 151
    artist of, 62–63
    artistic sources and composition of, 65–68,
        65f, 66f, 67f, 68f
    commission and services of, 63–65, 79,
        86 n. 73

Elizabeth and, 61–62, 69, 77, 79, 83 n. 21
Elizabeth or Mary's speech and, 82 n. 17
flanking inscriptions in, 70–73, 70f, 72f, 77,
    88 n. 86–87
hermeneutical reflections of, 79–81
iconography of, 68–79
inattentive figures in, 69–70
Isaac, Christ and, 73–75
Isaac's sacrifice linked with, 68, 70, 71, 72–73,
    73–74, 75–78, 76f, 89 n. 106
Mary and Elizabeth's staging in, 67–68
Mary's role in, 68–69, 77–79
women and, 79–80
visual exegesis, 6–7, 132–42
visualization, trajectory of, 6
Vita prima (Thomas of Celano), 108–9
Vitae Patrum (Gregory of Tours), 108–9
Voragine, Jacobus de, 13, 15, 21
    Annunciation, the Fall and, 34
Vulgate, 77, 82 n. 17, 89 n. 116

Wasserman, Jack
    Annunciation and, 37, 39, 56 n. 66, 56 n. 78
    Visitation and, 71–72, 76–77, 88 n. 87
Weyden, Rogier Van Der, 17, 99
    St. Luke Drawing the Virgin and Child, 17
"what it means/what it meant," 7
White, John, 146 n. 45
Wölfflin, Heinrich, 67
women
    Abraham, abuse and, 81
    Visitation and, 79–80
Woolf, Rosemary, 75
writing
    clarity and vividness in, 21–22
    Luke's painting and, 19, 21–23, 26 n. 33,
        26 n. 37
    Luke's style of, 21–23

Yahweh God, 136

Zachary
    2:10, p. 136
Zechariah, 30, 32, 33, 61, 72, 80, 87 n. 79, 97
    Joseph and, 77–78, 79